LIBRARY MANAGEMENT

AF798295

LIBRARY MANAGEMENT

VOLUME – 2

C.K. Sharma
Kiran Singh

ATLANTIC®
PUBLISHERS & DISTRIBUTORS

Published by

ATLANTIC®

PUBLISHERS & DISTRIBUTORS

B-2, Vishal Enclave, Opp. Rajouri Garden,
New Delhi-110027
Phones : 25413460, 25429987, 25466842

Sales Office
7/22, Ansari Road, Darya Ganj,
New Delhi-110002
Phones : 23273880, 23275880, 23280451
Fax : 91-11-23285873
web : www.atlanticbooks.com
e-mail : info@atlanticbooks.com

Copyright © Atlantic Publishers & Distributors, 2006

ISBN 81-269-0539-5 (Vol. 1)
ISBN 81-269-0540-9 (Vol. 2)
ISBN 81-269-0541-7 (Set)

All rights reserved. No part of this publication may be reproduced, stored in a retrieval system, transmitted or utilized in any form or by any means, electronic, mechanical, photocopying, recording or otherwise, without the prior permission of the copyright owner. Application for such permission should be addressed to the publisher.

Printed in India
at Nice Printing Press, Delhi

PREFACE

The second Volume of my book *Library Management* is presented before you. There are three important aspects of an organizational structure of a library, be it academic, public or special. These aspects are Financial Management, Personnel Management, and Building Management. No library can flourish without these three aspects. We have gone through a number of books on library science and have found that almost all are written in a conventional manner catering to the minimum requirements of the librarians and the students of the subject. In fact, we never dare to expand the field of its study. This work will prove that the courses needs to be programmed on management concept of learning. In libraries we have managerial structure and hence the library science courses should be framed accordingly. The present Volume deals in detail the varied aspects of managerial structure — Service Management, Operational Management (Behind the Screen), Personnel Management, Financial Management, Building Management, Book-keeping Management (in all departments), Information Technology. It would not be out of place to mention here that the two concepts — Library & Society and Library Management — in our book *Personnel Management*, written about twenty years back, have been already followed by the UGC and course framers.

The present book seeks to create something new in the field of Library & Information Science and leave aside all traditional programmes. Librarians should change their attitude and modernise the libraries as service oriented centres. This will give honour to the librarians and his job. Library is not a place of 'Babus' (Clerks) but a place of academicians and administrators.

Our thanks are due to all our professional colleagues and learners who always encouraged us to write something new.

We acknowledge with thanks to M/s Atlantic Publishers and Distributors for publishing this book.

C.K. SHARMA
KIRAN SINGH

CONTENTS

1

FINANCIAL MANAGEMENT

Finance is a motive power. It is essential to run a library efficiently. A library is a public institution. It is maintained by public funds. Every type of library has its financial resources. It may be a grant, donation, tax etc. Librarian and the library authority should clearly understand the nature of the library.

Fundamental Principles of Library Finance

There are some fundamental principles which are to be followed or applied —

1. Nature of the Library

A library may be different in nature — It may be Academic, public or the special as follows —

(a) It may be academic — University, College, School etc.

(b) It may be public — National, State, Regional, Distt., Block or Village.

(c) It may be special — commercial, technical, business or other specialised area.

Every above library has its own characteristic and special features and require funds.

(d) Government libraries.

2. Static or Expending or Growing Libraries

Government libraries are static or rigid in nature. These are not growing libraries. These are for limited purposes and used by limited readers and in limited time. Such libraries need less finance.

On the other hand, library is a growing organism. Library is a trinity of documents, readers and staff. Every item grows and resulted to the growth of the library. It require finance for growing number of reading number of reading material, readers and the staff. Moreover finance is also required for building, furniture, fittings and maintenance.

3. Nature of Finance

There are two types of finance —

(a) Finance is needed for development aspect of the library.

(b) Finance is needed for regular requirements of the library.

Such finance is called —

1. Recurring grant/funds
2. Non-recurring grant/funds

Libraries are not always growing. But while established it require permanent/recurring funds for its maintenance of staff, books and building for its minimum requirements regularly. The expenditure which is accrued every year is to be met by recurring grant, *i.e.* permanent grant/regular grant for every year.

But on the other hand all such expenditure which are required for opening new services, equipments, new staff, building extension etc. are met by Non-recurring or development grant. These funds are provided for a particular period or year for a particular purpose. Such funds cannot be utilised for other purpose, for which they are not given such grant/funds are called Non-recurring grant.

Evaluation Financial Estimation

There are three methods of finding out the amount of finance required for providing satisfactory library service.

1. Per-Capita Method

In this method, a minimum amount per head of population is fixed which is considered essential for providing standard library service.

The minimum is fixed on the basis of —

(a) figures on the basis of cost accounting

(b) cultural development of a community

(c) future needs/programmes

There are other factors which can determine the estimation —

(a) Minimum need of books
(b) Minimum need of journals
(c) Minimum need of staff salary
(d) Minimum need of maintenance
(e) Minimum need of services to the community, the library services.

Naturally the expenditure per capita rises in this case. A backward community atleast in the initial stages of its development, may do well with lesser number of advanced treaties.

The per capita estimate can be based either on the number of literate persons or adults. There are opinions that the tax should be levied on the literates as they avail library facilities. But tax should be levied on illiterates also so that they may be encouraged to utilise the library facilities and take incentive to become literate. They may be provided library facilities through social education, adult education and Audio-visual programmes. Tax should not be levied on children since they have less capacity to pay.

This means that per capita income would include all living persons whether they are, adults, aged or otherwise.

Formula

Population — 100000

Total finance @ Re. 1 per head population = Rs. 100000

This is an *ad hoc* method.

Population can be divided as under —

Children up to	12 years	25% = 25000
Adolescents	13 years to 20 years	25% = 25000
Adults	21 years to 40 years	25% = 25000
Old persons	41 years to 60 years	25% = 25000

Suppose we apply the criterion of literate which is about 35 per cent only in India. This clipping will effect 65 per cent.

The best method is to collect levy on all citizens and to

collect per capita rate on regional basis. The financial share of the various state should be —

Local	—	50%
State	—	37%
Central	—	13%

Local population is to be loaded maximum as they utilise the library services and directly related.

The per capita expenditure on public libraries was less than a naya paisa (5/6 paise) at the end of March 1954 and Rs. 2.5 per head in 1990.

INDIA	-	1954	5/6 paise
		1963-64	3 paise
		1990-91	Rs. 2.5
		USA/UK	Rs. 12.47

Student expenditure —

India	-	1950-51	Rs. 11.00
		1961-62	Rs. 19.00
		1965-66	Rs. 24.00
		1995-96	Rs. 39.00
USA	-	1959-60	Rs. 120.00
		1964-65	Rs. 160.00
		1995-96	Rs. 270.00
UK	-	1960-61	Rs. 105.00
		1965-66	Rs. 150.00
		1995-96	Rs. 256.00

Recommendations

Ranganathan — 50 paise per capita expenditure

ALA Standard — $ 4.47 (Rs. 33.50) — 1964

But it an old statistics which is not applicable.

Robert Committee (London) recommended certain standards but not on the basis of per capita expenditure.

University & College Libraries

UGC Committee (India) (1956)	Rs. 15.00	per student
	Rs. 200.00	per teacher
Kothari Edu. Commission (1964-65)	Rs. 25.00	per student
	Rs. 300.00	per teacher

Ranganathan		Rs. 20.00	per student
		Rs. 300.00	per teacher
	OR	Rs. 50.00	per student Overall

UK Parry Committee (1967)

If library has 50000 Vols.
If library has 3000 Undergraduates
1000 Research Scholars
500 Teachers

Library Expenses = ____ 100000 a year = Rs. 35,00,000

2. Proportional Method

Library authorities provide library funds out of its regular funds. Generally a particular minimum limit is fixed. The basis may be the:

(a) Total budget of the authority

(b) Education budget of the authority

In India various standards have been fixed —

Ranganathan — 1 per cent of the total budget

OR — 6 per cent of the Education budget of Federal, State, Local Govternment

Working Group on Libraries

1½ per cent of the total annual exp. on education.

1963-64 Indian states spent Rs. 6.40 per capita on education

1978-79 Indian states spent Rs. 9.50 per capita on education

It was .0089 per cent of the total budget.

USA	1977-78	Rs. 8804.00	per capita exp. on edu.
	But	Rs. 712.47	spent on public libraries
U.K.	1977-78	Rs. 675.00	(4.31%) Rs. 12 per capita exp.

Academic Library

India. University Edu. Commission (1948-49)	- 6.5% of university budget
Kothari Edu. Commission	- 6.5% of university budget
XVII All India Lib. Conference	- 6 to 10% of the total budget

Detailed Account

The method of detailed account means the estimate on the basis of actual expenditures occurred and the future expenditure in detail. It implies that all items of expenditure are accounted for while preparing financial estimate for a library. The items are —

(a) Salaries/wages

(b) Reading material — Book journals and newspapers

(c) Non-book material

(d) Maintenance — Building & repairing of reading material

(e) Heating, cooling, lighting, rent and interests

(f) Posts, telegraphs, telephones

(g) Stationery and reprographic material

(h) Computer or other machine material and its maintenance expenditure

(i) Miscellaneous

All above expenditure come under recurring expenditure.

Similarly, Non-recurring amount is estimated on the basis of the following items —

(a) Building, its extension.

(b) Fitting and furniture to be added.

(c) Equipment and machines to be installed.

(d) Mobile van to be used.

(e) Other accessories to be installed.

Such expenditures are once purchased and come under Non-recurring grant which is also known as development expenditures.

Infrastructure

Internal organization consists many components like divisions or departments and individual jobs to the employees working there. Their activities or jobs and their appointment, the various systems and equipment, furniture and the big structure, all involve finance management. All services whether administrative, technical maintenance are energetic by finance *i.e.* the budget of the library.

"The governing body/authority of the university is responsible for providing adequate library funds". The main financing authorities are the State Government, the U.G.C., the University and College Management and the trusts or other organizations.

There are mainly four sources of finance; U.G.C. and the State Government, income from various fees and the donations. University libraries depend on the financial support of U.G.C. and the library claims to be a exception of it. "No great university library depend on the financial support as a corner stone of its success..." the high standard in work of this kind cannot possibly be achieved when funds for maintaining on competent staff, occupied by a study flow of work, are provided by jerkey fits and starts. Public libraries are supported by the legislation, state government, the charity organizations or other organization.

There are countries where libraries are financed by the private organizations and no fee is required. On the other hand there are countries where library finances are met partly by library fee. Few States University Grant Commission, has stressed the importance of finance in its report. Throughout this report, on the one hand, that adequate provision for libraries is of Central importance to the universities and indeed to the national system of higher education and to the intellectual standing of the nation on the other hand. The library costs are rising steeply, and no end to this rise can be foreseen. Nationally it will always depend on the skilful use of financial resources which lag behind the demands made on them.

After fixing the responsibilities of finance on the shoulders of the finance-authorities the sole responsibility goes on a qualified librarian. It is easy to collect finance but difficult to utilize it economically and in a better way for maximum use. "From the viewpoint of financial administration, librarian will be concerned with establishing and maintaining satisfactory relations with the officials responsible for academic, financial and business affairs; the sources of library funds, preparation, presentation, and administration of budget; and the business procedures in general. Librarian plays an important role in making a plan of development of library and estimating the budget on the basis of the growth rate". It is the librarian alone who can plan the optimum development of the library.... The librarian knows the capacity of his present library service and can match against the demands likely to be made on it by the further growth of the institute in term of accommodation, finance and the staff.

Financial administration in university or research library, simplicity, foresightness, intensive use, flexibility contingency, anticipation and economy are important among them. Capital structure should be free from complications and suspicion arising statements and should be easily to understand even to a layman. The scope of administration is to be kept in mind. Financial adjustments becomes necessary. "In simple words, the canon of foresight means that besides the need of today, the need of tomorrow should also be kept in view. All precautions should be taken to avoid unnecessary expenditure and wasteful use. Funds actually required should be procured and aimed to make the best use of them. A wasteful use of capital is almost as bad as inadequate capital. Contingency covers the risk of internal financing and hence has to be estimated on the future mini expenditures.

1.1 Internal Sources

In academic institutions there are several standards which form the budget planning like, purchases of permanent nature, library programme, clear accounting procedures and the year to year expenditure, library service implications in educational planning, encouragement of all departments to study, and the preparation of budget by the skilled librarian.

There are internal sources of finance, such as *library discount* allowed on books, library fee, library fines and interest on certain money deposits. Library discount is received in two ways; on the purchases of books on a general rate of discount and other special discount allowed by the book dealer for the particular time of payments. Most of the libraries follow the norms of Good Office Committee in India in which U.G.C. is one of the member. In public libraries library discount is fixed by the Director or local authority empowered.

Library fine is second source of income. Fines are imposed with the intention of punishment not as an income. Such fines collected by the library are turned over to general office.

In some universities fines are collected by the university office. Whatever or not the library is credited with or reimbursed for the fines collected, varies among the libraries. There are only few universities or other libraries where such incomes are credited to the library account and are available for expenditure. Generally it has been the practice to deposit the fine with the general account and spent for organizational maintenance or development. Another source is *library fee* (membership fee). This fee is credited to library account and utilized for library purpose. "The university provides library service free of charge, just as it provides lecture rooms, laboratories and other facilities." Moreover, the income from fee can only meet a very small part of the total operating costs of the library. According to a survey of A.L.A. "Special library fee was relatively an important source of income in most of the libraries...a fee was apparently to provide for all library services." In India library fee has been given less importance and levied at nominal rates. But in European countries library fee is charged at higher rates in the name of subscription fee.

1.1.1 *Revenue Sources*

Every library needs finance which is —

(1) Provided by private agencies like private trusts, donations, gifts etc.

(2) Provided by Government agencies like Central Govt., State Govt., Local governments and departments.

(3) Library efforts which are made by library itself, *i.e.*

- (a) Subscription from members
- (b) Library membership fee
- (c) Library fines
- (d) Library discount
- (e) Wear and tear charges.

(4) Library cess/tax which is levied —

- (a) Through library legislation
- (b) Through Government departments.

Libraries collect their revenue by various sources —

1. Subscription rates: There are subscription rates in European countries. Libraries meet their financial requirements by levying subscription fee which may be quarterly, half-yearly and annually. These charges or fee is non-refundable. The rates may be changed as per policy of the library. Such libraries are not in practice in India. Public libraries adopt this type of sources of revenue. But such type of subscription libraries are being started in India also as it is self-financing system and there is no financial burden on any government or organization. In European Countries 95 per cent public libraries and private libraries as well as functioning by arranging their revenue through subscription.

2. Library membership fee: Membership fee is an important source of revenue. It is applied in public and academic libraries both. When a member is involved in a library, he has to pay a library membership fee which is non-refundable. This type of fee is included in the library budget as library income. However, it is not sufficient to meet the whole requirement of the library by membership fee. But it has been proved to be an important source of revenue.

3. Library fine or overdue charges: Every library makes efforts to get the books returned from the members in time. But there are few members which are habitual not to return the books in time or on due date. This habit create indiscipline in the library and increase dissatisfaction among the readers who failed to receive their desired books. Libraries have framed necessary rules to prevent this decrease and levied overdue charges or fine for the period of overdue. It is also a source of revenue but it is insufficient to meet the financial requirement. It hardly help in even maintaining the minimum requirements of the library.

4. Library discount: It is a tradition in Indian libraries to charge library discount on the cost of books. Library discount in academic libraries is based on the recommendations of Good Office Committee. But few academic libraries call quotations for library discount. However, there are different options about library discount. Few libraries think that good and latest books of reputed and leading publishers cannot be obtained on high rates of library discount as publisher allow marginal discount to booksellers or agencies. But on the other hand, general books can be obtained on higher rate of library discount. However, library discount may or may not be considered as revenue of a library.

Library Budget

The recommendations of Education Commission (1964-65) may be regretted as they did not seem to consider the library problems seriously. The commission suggested Rs. 25/- per student and Rs. 30/- per teacher. This ratio was just half of the ratio suggested by the Radhakrishnan Commission. These recommendations of Commission (1964-65) are taken as the unrealistic approach. The grant need revision from time to time and with the increase in the price of books and journals. In 1970 there was a rapid growth in the prices of books and journals from 75.76 per cent to 93.3 per cent and the prices again shot up recently. It is a continuing process and library should consider the changes every two years.

The problems of library budget has been a controversial one. On one hand Radhakrishnan Commission recommended about 6.5 per cent of the educational budget, while Gelfand has suggested 5 per cent as the minimum standard for a college and small university libraries. All such standards need revisions now. A growing and the new library will require more funds.

1.1.2 *Public Library*

The budget is important factor in the organization of any set up. It is a financial image of an institution and also a library. The budget is a financial statement of the estimated revenue and expenditure of an institution for a definite period of time. It represents all logical, comprehension and forward looking financial programme for the coordination of the activities of the various fundamental division. Each library has its own budget based on various problems and development programmes. Library budget has two parts. The income and the expenditure. Income (revenue) part consists of all sources of income.

(a) State Grant;

(b) U.G.C. Grant;

(c) Library fee; and

(d) Library fine.

The budget should also make the necessary provision for necessary items of expenditure in current library operation:

(a) Staff salary;

(b) Books;

(c) Journals;

(d) Building;

(e) Equipments;

(f) Printing and Stationery;

(g) Travel;

(h) Postage; and

(i) Contingency.

Ordinarily, the budget may be considered from several points of view, *i.e.* "The total amount of revenue take expended and the distribution of funds within the total budget." So far as the preparation of budget is concerned, these factors are responsible for estimating:

1. Librarian;
2. Readers.

Library plays an important role in making an assessment of the budget. Librarian is generally aware of the requirement of the funds and also of the expenditure in different departments of the library. He makes necessary estimates of the budget on the basis of past expenditure, future developments and standard norms. "The librarian who expects to secure funds to budget must be able to produce proof that funds are needed.... But the necessary figures cannot be gathered in a hostile efforts to write a good budget just before the estimate is due." Faculty members also cooperate in the preparation of the budget making as they give numbers of books purchased and journals subscribed. Such information is obtained either by written circulation or personal consultation. The budget should have the provision for meeting the expenditure for the new courses introduced and the new members of teaching staff joined.

The budget estimate should be discussed with the authority.

The main purpose of discussion is to know the view of the Head of the Institution. The librarian should be given an opportunity to discuss the tentative budget with the Head of Institute. This preliminary discussion may be only explanatory, but it should be possible for the head to indicate his attitude towards the budget and there may be also an opportunity, for the librarian to discuss long-term prospects. In spite of the fact, the cooperation of library staff cannot be overlooked. Library staff maintain the budget file and binding files etc. "In the presentation of the budget librarian's interpretation of the budget by the numerous studies and investigations of the staff in connection with their specific duties in reference, circulation, cataloguing and other phases of library work."

Allocation of library budget: Because of the many variables involved in library operation, it is very difficult to pay out a permanent plan of the budget. No arbitrary standards will exactly fit in a particular library, the nature of the studies, library holdings, research programmes, physical layout and availability of funds. Library fund may be divided into three categories:

1. Books and periodicals;
2. Staff salary;
3. Maintenance.

Organizations have not made any clear-cut division of the budget in three major items. A very large part of the library budget was spent on books and journals and leaving the other two items a little provide. It effected the library service as sufficient manpower was not there to organize and maintain the book resources. In Great Britain a medium size library provides the following budget allocations:

(i)	Books	53%
(ii)	Journals	22%
(iii)	Buildings	15%
(iv)	Salaries	10%

H.F. Dammers has presented a tentative statistics relating to the actual current operations of the British University libraries:

(i)	Salaries	50%
(ii)	Books	25%

(iii)	Periodicals	13%
(iv)	Building	6%
(v)	Sundries	6%

Capital expenditures are kept separate. Building and maintenance costs are usually set up as a separate budget items. The books are included under capital outlay. SCONUL in his financial report has suggested a firm ratio of 100 : 60 between acquisition cost and staffing cost. The ratio may show considerable variations according to the size and service of the library. It is further explained that due to the increase in library services the cost of staffing will inevitably be higher than at present and may ever be greater than the cost of acquisitions. In its supplementary report, the ratio has been revised between book grant and the salaries to 50 : 50 per cent. The ratio and expenditure adopted between the acquisition and staff is not fixed and purely depend on the size of the library and the service rendered by the library. Service comes first and material afterward. One can achieve the target of reading facilities with 5 staff members on a total collection of 40000 against a total collection of 20000 with 10 staff members, if skilled and highly qualified persons are engaged. In view of the experts: "Service of high order demanded of a library profession. The expenditure on staff will need a higher percentage of book grants, more than 50 per cent."

1.1.3 *Book Fund*

Administration of book fund is one of the important responsibility of library. "It would be useful to evolve certain normative principles on the basis of which the allocation of the book funds among different subjects could be made in an objective manner." Book fund includes the budget allocation of periodicals and their continuation, binding and rebinding in addition to books. The book fund is centralized when no separate allocation is made for departments. The book fund can be divided in two parts:

1. General library, and
2. Departmental funds.

Donald Coney and *Ralph E. Ellsworth* made some studies on 'Book fund'. *Coney* worked out six facts to classify book fund:

(i) Registration;
(ii) Course offered;
(iii) Strength of departmental personnel;
(iv) Strength of post-graduate and research students;
(v) Cost of material;
(vi) Library resources, teaching methods, new courses and new appointments, publication and frequency of publication in department.

Ellsworth has evaluated book fund on the basis of weight of responsibility, as classified under:

(i) Library relativity with each course;
(ii) Educational level of course;
(iii) Dissertations of post-graduate level;
(iv) Doctoral dissertations.

Book budget should be flexible and any rigidity be removed. A general reserve book-budget could be kept with the librarian at his discretion to meet the unexpected demands relating to reference books, printed catalogue, bibliographies and special help to any department for some special collection. Central library has fixed book budget called recurring grant which includes subscriptions of periodicals, serial publications, encyclopaedia sets, postage, transportation charges, binding, printing, catalogue cards etc. The modern tradition is different and the book fund is utilized for books and periodicals only. Book funds are divided according to the needs of readers, population, the faculty members, student and the nature of the library. Some libraries give more preference and utilize the larger portion of book fund for reference books and bibliographies, while the other prefer to spend the large portion on serials. "A good proportion to place in the general funds is 30 to 45 per cent of the total book fund."

Carl M. White has recommended some heads for allocating books funds: "General works, reference books, standing subscription, special material for research; back files, expensive sets; and other special purchases; and subject funds for each recognized department." Departmentalization of book funds is advantageous in many ways as it provides safeguard against unreasonable demands of some faculty members, stimulate faculty members to be more active in book selection, safeguard the librarian blamed for unjust funds to any department, avoids clash among personality and exercise the maximum degree of discretionary powers to the librarian.

Faculty participation in book budget may be avoided if the funds are not even sufficient for central library. Librarian is given full powers to handle the book funds. It will be helpful in two ways:

(a) If funds are limited, the unnecessary demands of readers may be denied, and

(b) Limited funds are hardly be divisionized.

Librarian may consider the urgent needs of the faculties while allocating the limited funds. The faculty members of the "department could count with reasonable assurances upon a sum of money for book purchases, would result in more interest in planning the development of department needs."

Multiple copies of books: In academic libraries by the students for the prescribed syllabus. A large number of funds are required for this purpose. Textbooks are purchased in multiple copies. These books may be out of use after a certain period. Textbooks may be classified as (i) Textbooks needed in multiple copies; and (ii) Textbooks needed in single copy. The extent of multiplying each textbook is a matter of judgment which can be exercised only by each university from year to year, in the light of the curriculum and student enrolment in each subject.

Department or Branch library grant: Libraries are provided with separate development grants for construction of library buildings and furniture and equipments. This grant is coordinated by the State Government and the U.G.C. grant.

1.2 Library Book-keeping

Libraries keep their financial records separately to show the income and expenditure and evaluate the actual need of the library. Separate allotment provision may be made under various heads, *i.e.* library staff; furniture and equipment; books and journals; maintenance; stationery; binding etc. The purpose of the library book-keeping is to control and supervise the library funds, and to ensure and aid in the preparation of budget and see that no funds are misused and withdrawn, to give exact position of the library to the authorities, to provide necessary information regarding the financial position and structure to library agencies.

The following important forms and files are maintained:

1. Invoice bill file;
2. Duplicator order-record file;
3. Bill register;
4. Imprest account register;
5. Caution money register;
6. Stock register;
7. Allocation register.

Financial records are maintained by the officials of the library. It is an internal arrangement. Library accountant is given this responsibility of preparing the library budget and maintaining all files and forms relating to finance. Ranganathan says "A fair amount of book-keeping is done by the accounts section of the libraries also. It is desirable that the library should furnish to the central executive the rough basis figures for the balance sheet, which can be obtained from the account maintained in the library."

1.2.1 *Invoice and Bill File*

Libraries maintain some record of the bills sent to the office for payment. It frequently happens that dealer sends the bill in duplicate or triplicate copies. First the bill is checked with order-copy and it is ascertained that the books are as per order. Books are verified by putting a (✓) tick against each item. Verification and the other formalities relating to payment of bills make it necessary to maintain a convenient and accurate record for reference and verification. A file is maintained to arrange a duplicate or triplicate copy of the bill in university library record. Duplicate bills of the suppliers are arranged in an alphabetical arrangement in each financial year. Monthly record of approved account payable is also maintained. *Lyle* has suggested the following form of monthly record:

ANNUAL RECORD OF THE COST OF SUPPLY AND EQUIPMENT ITEMS

Months	Source						Cost Brought fund		
	Cat.	Cirs.	Order	Per.	R.R.	Res.	Total	Recd.	Balance
July									
Aug.									
Sept.									
Oct.									
Nov.									
Dec.									
Jan.									
Feb.									
Mar.									
April									
May									
June									
Total									

1.2.2 *Duplicate Order Record File*

This file consist of carbon copies of the orders placed. The file should be numbered and each duplicate order copy should be kept in the sequence of the order placed. It will be better if order copies are kept subject-wise and each subject is allotted one file to maintain order record separately in order to work out the current position of the library. As soon as books are received, the invoice or the bill of the books is verified from the order and any discrepancy in supply is detected, is noted on the bill. The items supplied are marked (✓) on the order copy. This avoids duplication of orders for the same book.

The other method is a Order Card method. Order cards are arranged in a tray in classed-alphabetical order. According to this system cards are arranged according to author's name in each subject. On receiving the books, the relevant cards are drawn out of the tray and transferred to shelf list catalogue. Order cards are checked with the invoice and each item like name of the author, title, publishers, edition, price, and format is verified. Card system is a modern system and very much helpful for order-process. It also helps in making payments of the bill. Card system has defects, if it is not honestly followed. It requires sincere and faithful routine at every stage of order-card system. At every stage of order-card system to shelf list tray, the bill number and the dates, and the stock register number is noted on the order-card.

1.2.3 *Bill Register*

It is generally maintained by every library. Bill register is prepared to enter all bills received from dealers. It contains the detail of the bill and the date of sending the bill to university office along with signatures of the receiver. As soon as the books are received in library they are entered in bill register and sent to the section concerned for verification. The section incharge verify the name of the book, author, title, price, condition of supply and certify its genuineness for payment. The serial number of the bill register is entered on the bill called voucher number. The bill register contain the following columns:

1. Serial number;
2. Name of the dealer;
3. Nature of the material purchased;
4. Bill No. and date;
5. Account;
6. Stock register entry number;
7. Date of the bill received;
8. Date of the bill passed for payment;
9. The date of receiving the bill by the library.

1.2.4 *Imprest Account Register*

In each library imprest account is maintained. It is maintained in two ways:

(i) by converting the library income; fines and replacement, in to petty cash or imprest money;

(ii) by establishing a permanent establishment of petty cash or imprest account, the income from fines and replacement is credited to maintenance account. Library maintains separate imprest account or petty cash register in which expenditure are shown and recouped. It will be more easy if petty cash book register is prepared weekly;

(iii) writing out the petty cash account book. This may be called Petty Cash Account Writing;

(iv) closing the week's account in the petty cash book. This is called Petty Cash Account Closing.

1.2.5 *Caution Money Register*

Library collects library caution money from readers against borrowing books from the library. Caution money covers the list of lost or damaged books. In order to obtain the complete knowledge of caution money, a caution money register is maintained on the basis of the cash receipt. This register helps librarian to pass necessary payment order for the refund of the caution money. It is a reserve fund which is refundable to the students.

1.2.6 *Fines and Overdue Register*

Fines and overdue accounts are maintained in library and a separate register is kept with the details of serial number, borrower number, cost of books if lost, overcharge on the price of book, overdue fines and other punishment. This account is kept month-wise and monthly report is sent to finance section. The register is prepared on the basis on cash receipts submitted by the borrowers.

1.2.7 *Stock Register*

Stock register is kept with the aim to keep a record of the purchase of the library other than books and periodicals. It contains the record of furniture and equipment, accessories, stationery, etc. Whatever is purchased out of these items, it is to be entered in stock register in a traditional sequence. Stock register is generally maintained in store section and every item received in store is entered in stock register.

1.2.8 *Allocation Register*

While allocating the book budget among the branches/ departments or the faculties, it becomes difficult to utilize the budget fully without keeping any account. Allocation register solves this problem. It contains the subject-wise pages and the total allotment is written on the top of the storing page of the faculty/branch account.

1.3 Institutional Budget

In its simplest form a budget may consist of three or four lines which summarize categories of expenditure, and this kind of summary is the one used for transmittal of budget information. It is in a sense a coded statement, the key to which is shared by all financial and budget officers because of their knowledge of the process implicit in the bald statement. The use of that key expands it to a complex planning document as each element is broken down into individual expenditures. Even a long and involved budget, including numerous funds or couched in terms of programmes, is merely a representation of which will be done with the allocated sums of money. It is only by the carrying out of the transactions implicit in the accounts. In this way a budget is both object and process, and this dual nature calls forth a variety of responses, depending on the role that an individual plays in relation to that budget. This is to be expected since budgets, like all policy documents, mean different things to different people. An understanding of these different views is essential for effective budget making.

To the library staff the budget represents a kind of control system, something which sets the limits of the resources with which they must seek to achieve their goals. The individual staff member seldom thinks to the budget as a whole, may not indeed think of it at all, except on those occasions when lack of money frustrates a particular need. Activity such as selection may bring further involvement, but in most cases there is little direct responsibility for expenditures.

The chief librarian, however, is concerned to synthesize the budgetary needs to each unit in order to quantify what must be asked for by grouping like expenditures. A similar process is carried out at each successive stage, where the value of each budget proposal in relationship to the whole is reassessed while more and wider priorities are incorporated into the process of political judgment.

INSTITUTIONAL BUDGET

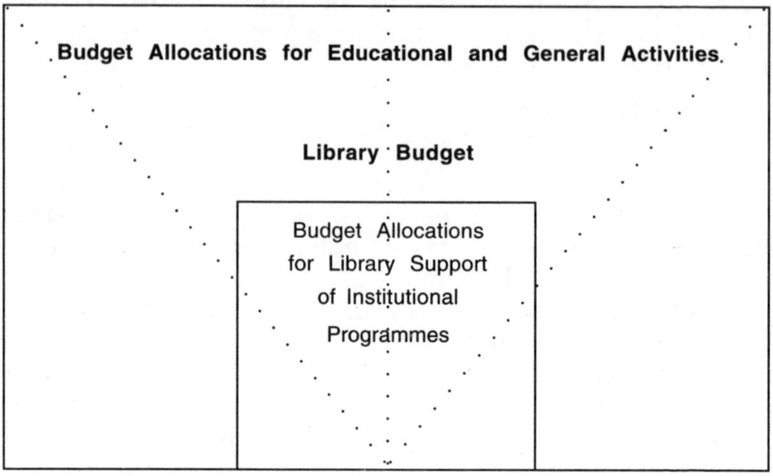

A budget has therefore three aspects: planning, management and control. All three are needed and all will be exercised in some degree by each staff member. Planning is closely associated with the action of budget preparation, but reflects the continuous process whereby the objectives of any organization are assessed, changed and restated. Management is the process by which the necessary resources are obtained and used in order to achieve the objectives of the institution. Control is the process by which adherence to policy is ensured. The major planning effort, for example, usually precedes the beginning of the fiscal year, while the audit side of control will begin after its close. In consequence, those who are involved in one kind of activity rather than another will tend to be more visible when that activity is most important. This fact, though it may seem minor, plays an important part in governing intra-institutional relationships and must be kept in mind by any administrator.

Similarly, the budget itself assumes different forms. The request, which is usually presented in gross terms (such as total salaries, total book expenditures), is transformed in action into multitudes of individual transactions.

The budget itself and the system of control used must provide for such a situation. The chance to acquire a special book or collection may come but once and must be seized.

Similar events may occur in almost any area. The goal of any control system should be to minimize the perturbation by channeling the effects properly. Rigidity of control tends to magnify the effects out of proportion. Flexibility, sensibly applied, will contain them without too much distortion of the original plan of expenditure.

Indeed, budget is a vehicle for the implementation of institutional plans and goals, rather than being, as in the past, simply a technique and the more likely it is to allow the library to function smoothly. For this reason, it is very important (1) to enter the year with close estimates of likely activities and their costs, and (2) to maintain close watch on how actual expenditures tally with those proposed at the beginning of the year.

A moment's contemplation of all changes which may affect the budget suggests that the library administrator must take on the role of Argus. No one person could, however, maintain such vigilance. The librarian must therefore rely on others for much of this information. Most institutions maintain a central office with responsibility for budget and planning, although this responsibility may be assigned to someone with other duties as well. It is vital for the health of the library to maintain good relations with the people responsible for the fiscal administration of the institution. There is a tendency among academics to disregard such mundane matters as "accounting" though at the same time they complain if their needs are not met.

Institutions are subject to the controls imposed by those who provide the money. The hope is that they will understand the goals of the institution and set up controls which help to achieve those goals. Such controls carry with the need for the institution itself to set up policies and procedures for the apportionment and control of the budget. It is necessary for the librarian to know these policies and procedures and to be able to apply them to the library. Exceptions will frequently be needed, and it is more satisfactory to all if requests for such exceptions can be discussed within a common framework. Once again, such a process is smoothed by the establishment of good working relations at all levels, whether with a Vice-Chancellor/Principal/Finance Officer or with the head of accounting. As an example, libraries need to be sure that renewal payments for subscriptions are processed promptly.

The difference between decisions on policy and decisions on money is frequently misunderstood. In general the budget reflects policy decisions by attempting to ensure that the amounts and the distribution of the available money will match the needs of the various programmes which result from decisions on policy. It is true that, occasionally, money or, rather, the lack of it, will be a determinant in whether a particular programme can be undertaken. Further, in a time of financial stress, it may be necessary to reduce expenditures and on such an occasion the details of the budget will assist in making decisions.

Policy decisions are those that determine what services will be given, what resources will be acquired and what changes will be made. They result from a careful consideration of all the relevant facts, including financial ones. Once made, if the decision is to be implemented, provision must be made for its cost. This does not always mean new money, but may also include transfers from one programme or one category of expenditure to another. The latter kinds of adjustments are not always taken into account when decisions are made. Such an omission may well result in failure of the new programme or in a series of *ad hoc* adjustments which damage other programmes. It is highly desirable to require, before making major policy decisions, that a forward estimate of costs be prepared for, say, a five-year period. Such a projection will reveal where and when monetary support is needed and whether all factors have been taken into account. That is to say, policy decisions must be fiscally responsible, but, except in unusual circumstances, financial matters are not the only factor to be considered when making a decision on policy.

The question of priorities becomes of critical importance, particularly since so many library operations are interdependent. With a steady budget, a reduced one, or even an increasing one which cannot cover the effects of inflation, it is clear that a library cannot continue as before. It therefore becomes a question of determining what must still be done, what that will cost and, in a sense, what will be left over for everything else.

In such a situation the allocation of the budget clearly takes on political overtones, and it is essential that the administrator be able to separate fact from emotional reaction. Some expectations will have to be deferred, some programmes modified, either at once or during the course of the fiscal year; but, if the right decisions have been made, the general goals of the library will be maintained.

The making of these choices is, no doubt, an unwelcome added burden; but, if the library staff concerned is financially ingenious, much can be done in the course of the year to redirect and manipulate funds to sustain the decisions made and to lessen their side effects. This is a large part of the meaning of budgetary control, which, as well as having a role in ensuring fiscal responsibility, is concerned with the directing of funds toward the achievement of the library's goals.

1.3.1 *Budgetary Control*

Library budgets reflect the budgetary style of the parent institution. It may be helpful, therefore, to summarize briefly the basic kinds of budgetary systems in use by academic institutions. Five such types may be identified, although there will also be subtypes of each. These are:

1. The object classification budget, which has been the traditional approach and which is based primarily on kinds of expenditure.
2. The programme budget, which is based largely on the measurement of programmes with consequently less emphasis on the objects purchased, and their relationship to organizational units.
3. The performance budget, which is based primarily on the establishment of relationship between the investment of resources and the production of service.
4. The Planning, Programming, Budget System, which combines both the preceding methods, adding cost-analysis and management by objective.
5. The formula budget, which is based on the use of standards and quantitative modes in the allocation of funds.

In fact, the time for budget preparation is now frequently so far advanced that those who must prepare it often cannot estimate accurately the degree of success or failure of budget plans for the current year and must extrapolate from the previous year instead. Such a situation naturally complicates planning and usually means that the budgets arrived at in this manner can be conceived only in gross terms. Nevertheless, even to arrive at such generalized statements, a great amount of detail is required. Those who suffer through such preparatory work frequently wonder at its utility, since the guidelines may change drastically before the actual budget is fixed and allocated. The preparation does, however, require the analysis of needs and expectations and provides a better framework within which to allocate what is eventually received.

A library is concerned with a very wide range of services, whose volume it is unable to control (perhaps even to predict) and with a very substantial purchasing programme for materials. The interactions of the several portions of a library budget are complex and sometimes unpredictable, requiring a greater degree of flexibility than most other administrative areas. Relationships between student enrolment and library use cannot be reduced to a formula. More students probably mean more library use, but it will be distributed unevenly among the various units of the library. The acquisition of materials is affected more by programme changes than by enrolment. In particular, a drop in enrolment does not mean that fewer materials can be bought, unless in discrete areas such as reserves. The effects of inflation play a large role in determining the volume of acquisition, and fluctuations in this kind of programme cannot easily be matched by fluctuations in processing costs, which are principally for personnel. In such cases it is necessary to recognize that at some times there will be excess labour available or to accept a state where there is an almost permanent backlog of some kind. The choice made will depend on the condition which corresponds most closely to the goals of the library.

The request for budget submissions is prepared by the chief librarian and is based on reasonable expectations for the year ahead. The request usually consists of three parts:

(1) policy instructions;

(2) procedural instructions;

(3) financial statements.

The policy instructions set out the guidelines to be used in preparing the budgetary requests and state limits on expansion, or requirements for reduction. These may provide for adding or subtracting personnel in relationship to programmes whether by formula or according to priorities. An amount or a percentage may be provided for inflation, or requests may have to include such a factor. Provision may be made for new programmes and will usually include instructions relating to the necessary justification.

Most budgets have two divisions, one for personnel-related expenses and the other for goods and services purchased. Because libraries purchase a great quantity of one particular things, namely "books", there may be a separate division for books. The names for these budgetary divisions are as varied as the institutions responsible. For consistency's sake, the terms "personnel-related expenses" and "goods and services" will be used for the two major kinds of expenditure, and the term "library materials" will be used to cover books, periodicals, binding and other similar purchases.

The purpose of a budget analysis is to see whether the intended distribution of expenditures is matched by actual expenditures, and what the differences, if any, are. Most budget statements contain a cover sheet which sets out broad categories, followed by detail sheets, most of which are given over to a listing of personnel.

This library, created for the exercise of the imaginative talents of both author and reader, is that of a moderately large academic library, possessed of most features common to such libraries — branches, several departments and the usual budgetary problems.

The budget of the State University Libraries

The State University

University Libraries

Budget Number 550/50

Budget Code 1000

Personal expenses
  Full time positions
  Wages
Allotment
  Goods and services
  Library materials
Reserve
  Total expenditure
  Total Income

The detail provided will vary with the institution, but it is customary to separate the various classes of employees. The following classes of employees will be represented:

(a) *Professional*: These positions may be academic, faculty or non-academic professional. A separate listing may be shown for administrators. If the positions are academic, listings may be by rank. It may be arranged by department, but this is unusual.

(b) *Staff*: These positions may include non-academic professionals, but more usually will be paraprofessionals and any category of employee within the non-exempt classification of the Department of Library.

(c) *Clerical*: These positions generally include all classified positions other than those included under "Staff". Frequently such a grouping is defined by a union contract. Possibly it may be further subdivided to cover non-clerical employees, such as janitors or book lifter, in which case more than one union contract may be involved.

(d) *Part-time Employees*: These positions are more permanent than those paid from wage budgets, but may require annual re-negotiation and may not have available the same fringe benefits as permanent, full-time positions.

(e) *Wages/Salaries*: This portion of the budget is intended to cover all hourly employees.

The most important action in analyzing personnel-related expenses is to allocate them to the various library programmes. A true programme analysis requires that each position be divided according to activity, since this is the only way to discover the exact cost of each activity within the library.

The analysis will indicate full and part-time positions and salaries in each administrative area and should indicate also existing vacancies.

This distribution indicates the personnel-related cost to the library of its major units of activity. The information should be shared with all library administrators, including division heads; although in cases where the institution requires that personal salaries be confidential, any figures that reveal individual salaries should be omitted in statements released widely. Information of this kind assists division heads in budget planning, because it enables them to see their own division in a general context. Without such a background it is difficult, if not impossible, to develop proposals for change.

It is important also to determine whether the vacancy has caused problems; and, if so, problems of what kind. If not, the position may well be a suitable candidate for transfer to another activity. Many vacancies, however, are of a transitory nature. Where, however, a longstanding vacancy results either from difficulty in finding a suitable replacement or from uncertainty over the need for the activity involved, such a vacancy should be considered for transfer, or perhaps for collapsing. The budget or planning officer should, metaphorically and perhaps literally, red circle such positions for further consideration during the process of budget formulation.

PERSONNEL-RELATED EXPENSES

Department	Professional		Semi-Professional		Clerical		Salary	Total
	No.	Cost	No.	Cost	No.	Cost	Cost	Cost
Administration								
Acquisitions								
Cataloguing								
Serials								
General Services								
Lending Services								
Reference Services								
Reserve Services								
Special Collections								
Science								
Engineering								
Life Sciences								

The most likely area of variation is, however, in wage budget expenditure, since this may be affected by use of work-study students (payments for whom do not show up in the library budget) or by the diversion of temporary funds to cover a problem situation. Since it is almost impossible to predict accurately salary expenditure by division, some will be ahead and some behind the proportionate amount of their allocation. If all expenditures were incurred evenly throughout the year, cumulative expenditure would be represented by the diagonal line (e). Although such a distribution is unlikely ever to be the case, mainly because academic institutions do not operate on a uniform basis throughout the year, it forms a useful base against which to compare actual or projected expenditures. Line (a) represents actual expenditure for the period of the fiscal year to date. Line (a^1) represents a projection of this expenditure pattern to the end of the year and line (a^2) represents the initial planned or expected pattern of expenditure. Comparison of the lines will also reveal substantial over-expenditure which, if continued, would lead to an actual budget deficit. While it is presumed that steps would be taken to correct such a situation, either by reducing expenditure or by adding money to the salary budget, the purpose of this analysis would be to determine the cause of the deviation from the original forecast of expenditure. It may, on the other hand, represent the library's response to unexpected long-term vacancies, or a special project which had to be completed in a short time. In such instances the over expenditure will correct itself. All investigations would, of course, seek to relate the deviation in expenditure to programmes or divisions in order to ascertain what specific response is required.

1.3.2 *Collection and Services*

In the sample budget statement, many institutions divide this category into subcategories on the budget statement itself. If this is the case, it may be necessary to obtain approval of any variations. Such line control can be extremely vexatious, since the majority of exception requests would be for small amounts. But the more important effect is the complete loss of flexibility, which makes it impossible to respond quickly either to emergencies or to a necessary shift of priorities. In addition, it may be required either to obtain external approval for all purchases over a stated amount, or even to forward all purchase requests to some agency for approval and processing.

It is assumed here that responsibility for allocation and control is internal to the library. Even where this is not the case, the analysis of expenditures is a fundamental part of budget preparation.

Most institutions have standardized classes of expenditure, for which the nomenclature may differ, and these classes are generally coded to enable the institutions to derive total expenditure figures. Occasionally the coding may be inappropriate for a library.

It is not a common practice to charge heat, light, janitorial services and the like to each administrative unit, although records of such expenditures may be kept centrally. Raffel and Shisko demonstrate the importance of these and other indirect costs when carrying out a cost-benefit analysis, and for true programme budget-planning accurate knowledge of such costs is essential. For the most part, however, librarians do not have to concern themselves with overhead costs of this kind. An exception may arise if or when an institution is faced with a planned reduction in fuel costs or if a true cost is needed for the recovery of a prorated portion from a customer seeking shared cataloguing, computer services or contractual reference services.

Most of these expenditures are "fixed" by the library's programmes. It is possible, but not essential, to prorata all expenditures to units within the library. An example of this approach is sketched by Rogers and Weber. Such a detailed assignment of costs would be necessary in a library where each unit had a high level of autonomy, or in support of a programme budget.

Collection and Services

Object Class	*Type of Expenditure*
	Supplies
	Communications
	Maintenance
	Repairs and Renovations
	Rentals

Computer Services
Miscellaneous
Travel and Research Support
Equipment

Not all budgets include funds for equipment, since this may be regarded as a capital expenditure. Nevertheless, most libraries purchase some equipment each year, and certain kinds of expenditures are predicted by ongoing library activity. An example of such predicted expenditure is the need for catalogue cabinets. If cards are being produced, they have to be stored, and at a certain stage, usually predictable within rough time-limits, catalogue cabinets will have to be purchased. The same is true of cabinets for the storage of microfilm and other equipment directly related to quantities of material purchased. The continuing need for such purchases is sometimes obscured by the effects of building and equipping new library buildings or extension of old ones. On the whole, however, there is a continuing need for new equipment and for replacement of wornout items. Computer services do not always vary with the quantity of activity undertaken, and the nature of the programmes is usually such that the cost will continue roughly the same.

Most budgets include items for miscellaneous expenditure, though this is usually further subdivided by the library. Irregular expenditures for publications (*e.g.*, Union List of Serials), or payment of library memberships will be included. By its nature such a class of expenditure is unpredictable, even though elements within it may be known. Support for travel and research is also unpredictable in detail. Although such expenditure cannot be classed as essential — the library would still survive — it is highly desirable staff investment and one which has become an integral part of the goals of most libraries.

Each individual library can identify without too much difficulty such continuing expenditures. In the sample budget, the proportion of essential expenditures is on the order of 80 per cent. Even that division presumes that travel and research is not essential and that repairs can be postponed indefinitely.

There are three general classes of expenditure: books,

subscriptions and binding. Each class may be defined differently by different libraries. For the purposes of this consideration, books are considered as including all purchases, monographic or otherwise, other than continuing subscriptions. Subscriptions cover periodicals, serials, series, newspapers and long-term microform subscriptions. Binding includes the cost of binding individual monographs, but most of the cost will be for the binding of periodical volumes. The general distribution of library materials costs in the sample budget.

Library Material Costs

Books and other non-subscription costs
Periodical and other subscriptions
Binding
TOTAL

1.3.3 *Income*

Most libraries have some income from sources such as fines, photo duplication charges, sale of materials, or from the sale of the library's own publications. Internally the library may balance these against the costs incurred in obtaining the income; but, unless a project is set up and funded separately as an enterprise, it is usual for income to be set off against projected expenditure. This distinction is important, since librarians not informed concerning budgetary processes may be under the misapprehension that recorded income is over and above the printed budget. In such a situation the proposal may be made, for example, to discontinue fines, without making provision for appropriate, balancing reductions in expenditure.

The procedures in handling income will differ widely. In some institutions all receipts of income are channeled directly to a central fund; and, in such a case, the individual unit may or may not benefit from higher income than anticipated. A further complication, frequently encountered on the disposition of materials, may be the allocation of that income to a surplus and deficiency account for the year in which the original expenditure was made; which means, in effect, that the library does not receive any of the money, except by application to the responsible administrative officer for a special grant. The nature of the process of acquisition and de-acquisition will usually place the library in such a situation, and the librarian should therefore negotiate, if possible, a special status for the library.

A final influence on the statistics that are required is the framework within which the institutional budget is conceived. It may for example, require the use of book/student ratios or comparison of holdings to an ideal table of volume equivalents, or the use of a staff/student ratio in the determination of Public-service staff numbers. All such requirements have a rigidity which may require of the administrator that they insist on exceptions to provide for the unique situation. Such formulae (more correctly their mechanistic application) simplify the judgmental activities of the assessor, but may easily wreak havoc in a library caught in a downward financial spiral, because they are unable to take into account such factors as inertia, inequitable distribution of inflation or the need for different economic responses from different units. All these and more must be the concern of the administrator as he seeks to describe and to justify the library and its activities.

The concept of inertia is an important one for libraries. In physics, inertia is that property of matter by which it continues in a state of rest or of uniform motion unless that state is changed by external force. Its application to libraries is obvious. When an item is purchased, if it is to be made available for use, various kinds of processes have to be carried out before it can end up on the shelf. Equally ineluctably material purchased will have to be housed. Unless some major policy change is initiated this process will continue, since it is one of the basic purposes of a library. Its existence will therefore have major effects on any budgetary proposals. The time and the cost consumed by the application of the necessary force may be exemplified by the changes effected in a library by the adoption of the Ohio College Library Center as a source of cataloguing. Because most of the changes made — collapsing positions, buying equipment, transfer of card-stock purchase money from supplies to services — are irreversible, a new inertial force is set up in the library which will widen its effects as the new programme expands and depends.

1.3.4 *Variables*

(a) *Volumes added*: Number of monographs, serials, microforms, maps, documents, etc., added to the collection. *Factors included*: Number of orders received, number of orders placed, number of volumes received, number of periodical parts received, number of volumes bound, and number of replacements ordered.

(b) *Collection usage*: Total number of volumes issued to readers, including closed reserve volumes and periodicals issued, and resulting activities, plus total use measured by materials resolved in the stacks. *Other factors*: Number of personal reserves made, number of overdues sent out/fine notices, and number of items transferred to reserve.

(c) *Catalogue maintenance*: Number of cards filed in public and other catalogues, number of cards withdrawn. *Factors included*: Number of new cards filed, number of old cards withdrawn, catalogues/shelf-lists/authority files/serials etc.

(d) *Facilities usage*: Count of all patrons leaving the library.

(e) *Reference services*: Number of questions, number of bibliographies and booklists prepared, number of orientational and instructional services given.

(f) *Interlibrary loans*: Number of interlibrary loans and other questions handled.

(g) *Weighted Library SVC units*: Overall calculated workload indicator, to be calculated from above indicators.

A second class of information concerns the institution itself. Information in usually available concerning student enrolments, credit-hours and number of faculty. Not all administrators recognize how important such information is to libraries. The library administrator should make it his goal to have all information of this kind available.

Care must be taken, however, to avoid the pitfalls of some formula budgets in which the size of the budget is related directly to enrolment. While this may be true for such programmes as reserve books, it must be stressed that a more important determinant for libraries is the number of academic programmes at the institution. Information should therefore be collected concerning new academic programmes or changes in existing ones. Ideally the library should be involved in all academic planning, and library needs should be taken into consideration. Unfortunately, this is seldom the case. Whether or not the library has had an opportunity to participate in planning, it is essential to keep a record of new courses and new programmes or changes in either. Information on academic programmes, student enrolments, research projects and number of faculty should be drawn together into an academic profile of the institution.

The procedures used in preparing a budget request will vary according to the priorities and the instructions contained in the budget instructions. At some time in the process, however, the unit heads, who were requested to present a statement of their needs and expectations, should be given a chance to defend that request, or, at the least, be informed of decisions. It is necessary to identify the parts of the budget appropriate to each unit head so that it is clear what resources will be purchased and to demonstrate how those purchases will be used to produce the desired service products, the whole articulated in such a way as to make it clear that consideration has been given both to individual and to collective goals. This exercise is made much easier if individual unit heads have earlier been involved in the budgetary process.

Two situations based on the sample library may help render this concept more understandable. For the past two years the circulation figures have shown an 8 per cent rate of increase. Last year the increase was absorbed by the existing staff, but the lending service librarian now advises the library administration that the staff is having difficulty in ensuring rapid filing of cards and reshelving of books, while still attempting to keep track of overdues and personal reserves. An activity audit is under way in the hope of simplifying some routines, but this is not expected materially to improve the staff/workload ratio beyond the point where they can cope better with the present load. The librarian is requesting two extra clerks and an addition to the wage payroll to handle end-of-term loads. The reported statistics appear to substantiate the claim and the personnel officer confirms the lowered state of morale. In the circumstances the request appears self-justifying. The budget distribution, however, shows the following staff:

2 professional
3 semiprofessional
14 clericals
8 Class IV employees.

Of this number, three are assigned full-time to interlibrary loan and two to photo duplication, while three spend most of their time at the exit desk where they check outgoing materials. In fact, therefore, eight of the staff of nineteen are not engaged in circulation activities *per se.* The lion's share of these activities is borne by authority concerned.

It is not likely that a circulation clerk, the head of reference, the Librarians of the library, the Vice-Chancellor of the university and finally the finance officer will have the same view of a library budget, although they are all involved in it in different ways. To one it may affect the entire context of daily life while to another it is a remote portion of a part of the whole which must be considered. It is partly a matter of the expectations each has of the budget itself and partly a matter of how each one views the budget process.

All budgets are premised on "certain activities — using certain resources, which result in some intended impact on society". The perspective, however, makes a considerable difference to the amount, kind and ordering of information required and to the manner in which it is received. The administrator at a higher level is well aware of the many unpredictable factors that may distort and change a budget either in the course of the approval process or during the time of its implementation, but to dwell on these is to reinforce the view that no one expects adherence to any rules or limitations. Equally, of course, to insist too strongly on known limitations or likely constraints is to suggest in advance that no attempt will be made to overcome or modify the effects of such limitations. Steering a course between these extremes requires all the skill available to any administrator.

The presentation should answer three questions:

(1) What activities are to be carried out?

(2) What resources are required to carry out these activities?

(3) What will the results be and how will they be measured?

As stated by Morris Gelfand, "the budget is conceived of as a planning and control document and an important vehicle of communication and persuasion". If it is to achieve the last stated goals, it must do more than state certain facts — it must convince the reader that they are desirable and attainable. It is necessary, also, to be aware of the fact that the budget presented will, as it passes further on, lose its identity. Gelfand properly stresses that "before undertaking the preparation of a budget, it is essential to identify priorities in the light of what is known about the needs, interests and nature of the community".

Library programmes are eminently difficult to place a value on; and, though librarians seldom admit it, they are also eminently absurd when described in detail, which increases the difficulty in achieving both understanding and appreciation of the need for those programmes. They remember presenting a detailed defense of a request for increased cataloguing support and watching amazement and disbelief vie for supremacy in the face of the most senior administrator present. It may have been his kind heart rather than his head that persuaded him to endorse the request, but it was more likely to have been the agreement of the analysis whose investigations made it clear that it was not a phony request.

Libraries too, have little choice in whether or not they are to provide reference and information services. If they did not, a primary reason for their existence would vanish and a warehouse or storehouse could be substituted. The range, style and variety of services can, however, be controlled, even if only to a limited extent. This may be a matter of necessity (*e.g.*, lack of staff) or a policy (*e.g.*, not providing bibliographic help which students should perform for themselves, or insisting that certain procedures be carried out by the user before calling on the library for further service). Other kinds of limitations arise from the number of users and the intensity of use. It is, for example, less necessary for special collections to be accessible on a round-the-clock basis than it is for reserve books just before an examination period. This information can then be used as evidence to support the choices made and demonstrate that they were made on some rational basis. Such a presentation makes it possible for those evaluating a budget proposal to choose between alternatives according to the values adopted by the institution.

It is perhaps useful first to distinguish between two kinds of need, basic and augmentational. Basic needs can be seen as covering the minimal acquisitions required to keep the collections alive and responsive. They will relate almost exclusively to current output and will include all formats, both unitary and periodical. It may, of course, happen that there is not sufficient money to meet this need. Unless more money is forthcoming, the librarian will be forced to choose between areas; and in such an instance, patron use may very well be the critical measurement. Augmentation is a process concerned with additions aimed at quality, at strengthening that which is and with incremental programmes which respond to changes and improvements in the institution and may also be designed to compensate for great differentials in costs between areas.

Factors to be considered may be grouped under two broad headings, institution-related and library-related. The institutional factors refer to the willingness of the institution (and society) to invest in given educational programmes. This investment is represented by the number of faculty, the research being undertaken (if any), the extent and range of the courses offered, the number of credit-hours, the number of majors and the number of graduate students. It must be admitted at once that some of these statistics may represent either residual investment, as in the case of tenured faculty in a discipline where enrolment has dropped, or substitutional investments such as in a department which carries a very heavy remedial load or provides basic low-level service courses. In most institutions some system of weighing is used to represent the more costly upper division and graduate courses. This might prove useful for the library, and would have the advantage of uniformity; but like most measures, it would be artificial to apply it across the board. Graduate work in the humanities, for example, is much more library-oriented, than, say, in physics, where a major part of the institutional investment consists of laboratories and equipment.

Book buying will be curtailed and the moratorium on new periodical subscriptions will be continued (new subscriptions cannot be placed unless a periodical of equal monetary value is cancelled).

It is essential to remember that the development of the annual allocation of funds for *library materials* concerns the distribution of actual funds, not of an ideal amount. It is therefore requisite that funds be set aside to meet commitments, but that these commitments always be examined in the light of their long-term budgetary effects. Where funds are insufficient to meet all desires, choices must be made between programmes and between kinds of expenditure.

The next consideration in establishing the library materials budget is that of augmentation. Augmentation of resources is a response to demonstrated need, but it carries qualitative rather than quantitative overtones. Work with standard bibliographies may reveal gaps in existing collections. An academic programme in a field new to the library will require substantial investment in older resources, and occasionally the institution from its own funds or from a special grant may provide or earmark funds for establishment purposes. In such instances it is important to remember that this is additional money and should not be seen as substituting for regular support. Other special programmes which would qualify could be a plan to overhaul and update the library's reference and bibliography collections or to embark on a plan for microform enrichment by the purchase over a period of major collections.

Certain other kinds of expenditure are essential, such as the replacement of lost, stolen or mutilated resources or the setting aside of money for an exchange programme that provides materials unobtainable in any other way.

Funding Sources

In all libraries there are funds, large or small, which are predicated. That is, by wish of the donor, or an instruction from the funding sources, they are to be spent in a particular manner or within a specified subject field. It is impossible here to cover the whole area of gifts and endowments. Suffice it to say that libraries should discourage gifts which are so specific that it may be impossible to meet the conditions over a period of years, or which would contribute to an undesirable imbalance. The onerous conditions might be that certain persons should approve all purchases or that the purchases must be placed in a certain library, regardless of whether that library's mission is appropriate or not. A one-time gift on such a basis may be no more than a nuisance, but an endowment that produces annual income may more nearly resemble a dead-weight than an encouragement to the library.

Whether the sets of accounts are simple or complex, a library requires the authority, information and control that is represented by those accounts. Authority to charge expenditures against specific accounts carries with it the responsibility for seeing that those expenditure are properly so charged. There is often a feeling that budgetary control is something carried out by some central office. This is not so: "budget control starts with those responsible for each budgetary unit". This does not necessarily mean only those who are formally responsible for budgets according to the institution's coded distribution, but anyone who is given the task of supervising expenditure on time and things. With this responsibility goes accountability for the results. Without information as to what has already been spent or encumbered, no one is in a position to decide on further purchases. Without the control that is represented by the allocation of specific sums for specific purposes, there would be no way of ensuring that the library fulfils its goals for the year. The monitoring of its progress toward these ends requires the assistance and cooperation of many people within the library.

The longer the period of uncertainty, however, the more difficult it will become to carry out successfully the plans for the year. This is particularly true in the purchasing of equipment items, where there are usually more complex preorder procedures and also long delivery schedules. It is, however, true as well of books and other materials, where the diversities both of source and method of purchase are great, and where the average unit price is low, thus making it essential to maintain a fairly regular distribution of activity throughout the year. If this cannot be done and money is released late in the year, not only does this cause bunching that will be reflected later in other departments, but it militates against careful choice and encourages wasteful purchasing of available expensive items.

As soon as either temporary or permanent budget distribution has been determined, its contents must be passed on to those who will be responsible for handling the various funds. Who these will be is determined by the organization of the library. Some libraries are decentralized to the extent that almost all funds are subdivided by department or branch. Some retain control within the central library administration. Two areas, where responsibility for the handling of funds is usually widespread, are wages and library materials. This is so because in both these areas the funds can be better utilized in furtherance of programme goals by decentralization than by close central control. Responsibility for the actual payment of all salaries is usually centralized and decentralized control over budgets for full-time employees would at best be nugatory — a matter of information rather than power.

Unless there are substantial endowments or a major gift-giving programme, a very high proportion of any library's income is determined at the beginning of the year. Moreover, libraries are not usually income-producing units. There are, however, some standard sources of income, such as fines, photo duplication charges and sale of publications. In the absence of major programme changes, the amount of income from these sources should remain fairly stable. It must be recognized, of course, that the income is offset by expenditures incurred in its production. Generally speaking, this will balance the income, since the library's motive in charging fines, for example, is not profit.

In some situations, however, the relationship of income and expenditure is not so clear. A library may decide, perhaps in order to reduce administrative costs, to farm out certain activities. A contract for the provision of photo duplication services via the use of coin-operated machines will transfer from the library's own photo duplication office a volume of routine activity, allowing the office to concentrate on more specialized activities and on the library's own internal needs. In such a contract provision may well be made for payment of rent, either as fixed payments or as a percentage of total income. The first would be constant, though open to renegotiations each year, but the second would be variable and subject to adjustment during the year, while in each case consideration would have to be given to effects on the library's own operations.

A second kind of variable concerns the sale of library materials or equipment or the reimbursement of the library by another unit for services rendered. The disposition of materials owned by an institution may be governed by quite rigorous procedures but the instrumentalities set up to carry out these procedures are generally inadequate to meet the needs of a library in disposing of library materials, whether withdrawn, duplicates or received by gift. In some instances the control exercised is so extreme that the only means available for disposition are destruction and exchange for value. Where, however, the library is permitted to dispose of surplus materials, the income derived may not even then be solely at the disposition of the library.

1.4 Financial Records

"Budgetary statistics generally depend on the source of income and expenditure of the library." Library budget may be divided in two parts:

(i) Income, and

(ii) Expenditure.

Income record contains the following details:

Income	Recurring	Non-Recurring
(1) Source of Income:		
(a) UGC/ICHR/ ICSSR/CSIR		
(b) State Govt.		
(c) Organization/ Institution		
(2) Gifts and donations		

(*Contd.*)

Income	Recurring	Non-Recurring
(3) Membership fee		
(4) Fines		
(5) Sale of publications		
(6) Sale of waste paper		
(7) Other sources		
Total:		

Budget statement is prepared every year. It is shown in three columns:

(i) Actuals of the previous year;

(ii) Estimate for the current year-uptodate, revised;

(iii) Estimate for the next year; and

(iv) Remarks.

In view of the above, it is clear that "a budget is a financial statement of the estimated revenues and expenditures of an institute for a definite period of time. It represents a logical, comprehensive and forward looking financial programme for the coordination of the activities of the various functional divisions. Budget statement or record is a financial definite record which speaks the back history, present position and future development of the library. It is also a statement for comparing the positions and the trend of development between the past, present and the future." It is indispensable means of obtaining a definite financial aid, as a forecast of means of carrying the plan in to effect; a current guide, a cost summary of operations, and a historical record and basis for the formulation of future policy, in the hands of the administrator.

1.4.1 *Factors*

(i) Comparison with past expenditure;

(ii) Budgeting in accordance with the work programme; and

(iii) By using arbitratory stands and norms.

The expenditure side of budget consists of the following:

(i) Salaries: (a) Basic salary

(b) D.A.
(c) P.F.

(ii) Contingency:
(a) Stationery
(b) Printing
(c) Binding
(d) Telephone
(e) Postage
(f) Electricity

(iii) Furniture

(iv) Binding

(v) Books and periodicals:
(a) New books
(b) Back sets of books
(c) Manuscripts
(d) Periodicals and other serials:
(i) Annual Subscription;
(ii) Back volumes of periodicals.

(vi) Maintenance

(vii) Miscellaneous expenses:
(a) Overtime allowance
(b) Insurance premium.

The budget estimate can also be prepared under four categories. The staff, the library rate, special services and equipment. The number of staff depends on the ratio between the students and the staff. Library budget covers books, periodicals, bindings, sundries, and rise in prices. Special services includes photographic and binding departments which require special staff, furniture and additional finance. Equipments like shelving, tables and chairs, office furniture are also estimated on the basis of requirement and in the increase of the number of books, staff and readers.

According to *Wheeler and Goldhot* "a library budget should be on every item, as well as its general arrangement and presentation. A more detailed list of budget items is given as under:

Receipts	Expenditure
1. Balance on hand	1. Salaries — Professional staff
2. Local tax appropriation	2. Salaries — Clerks
3. Country or state appropriation	3. Salaries — Binding staff
4. Schools board or federal funds	4. Books
5. Gift and endowment income	5. Periodicals
6. Fines and petty cash	6. Binding and mending
7. Other	7. Audio-visual
	8. Rent
	9. Heat, light, telephone
	10. Stationery, printing
	11. Insurance
	12. Other operating expenses
	13. Capital outlay
Total:	

1.4.2 *Financial Reports*

A monthly financial report is as essential for the efficient management of the library. It indicates the expenses and balances during a given time. The monthly report should be sent to authority concern. The monthly report serve as reminder to the branches to enable them to use the allotted funds in time. Disbursements are shown for each major items in the budget with a broken figures for each category. The reports are prepared on loose sheets or single sheets and prepared on each month and the duplicate copy of the same is kept for library record. Library may also keep a permanent register of monthly reports.

Financial report includes the regular staff salary and the contingency staff salaries both.

A model report has been suggested by *Lyle* as under:

MONTHLY FINANCIAL REPORT. Month............

Budget Categories	Budget	Encum-bered	Expen-ded	Total	Fee balance
BOOKS					
I. Departments					
Art					
Biological Science					
Education					
History					
Physical Sciences					
Social Sciences					
Commerce/Management					
Fine Arts					
II. General					
General					
Reference					
Recreational					
Replacement					
Transportation					
Library of Congress card					
Total of I and II					
Periodical					
Binding					
Supplies					
Equipment					
Salaries:					
1. Staff					
2. Statement					
TOTAL					

1.5 Finance

Internal organization consists in recognizing and defining the component elements or divisions of the operation as a whole, then of its smaller parts — departments, and individual jobs, and putting together in simple relationship the component elements. First is to design an organizational plan or structure by (a) identifying the particular activities carried out, (b) arranging the functions in departments; (c) defining precisely responsibilities and duties of each unit; (d) defining the lines of authority and the relationships that exist within and among the units or departments. Administrative duties may be performed on different levels. The Chief Librarian is concerned with the operation of the library as a whole. Policy making, planning and reporting concern also specific activities, and may be performed by members of the staff who are in-charge of these activities.

In almost all types of libraries the principal activities and services, based on traditional function can be categorized as (a) Administrative services; (b) Technical services; (c) Reader's services and (d) Special services.

1.5.1 *Administrative Services*

Administrative activities include:

(1) Preparing and administering the budget;

(2) Selecting, training and supervising the staff;

(3) Creating and planning policies and regulations;

(4) Developing and supervising book collecting policies and procedures;

(5) Preparing reports and memoranda;

(6) Conducting surveys and analysis of services;

(7) Maintaining personal records;

(8) Organizations and participating conferences and professional associations.

(9) Maintaining financial records when required.

Administrative services is concerned with library financing, budgeting and accounting in relation to existing structure, development plants for new facilities and services, alternation of existing services. Library is a growing organism and is essentially a service institution and not a revenue-fetching one.

Public Library: The main sources of revenue are: (1) library rates levied by local authorities; (2) library taxes, levied by state or central authorities. The taxes may either be a surcharge on existing taxes or a fresh levy or library cess particularly on property tax; (3) Government grants. The government grants are necessary for making up financial deficiency in backward areas; (4) Gifts from people; and (5) Fees and fines.

University Library: Sources of income are: (1) funds allocated from the main budget of the institute; (2) endowment income; (3) gifts; (4) fees; (5) fines; (6) the sale of publication; (7) photographic work; and (8) charges for lending rental services.

1.5.2 *Preparing and Administering the Budget*

Planning and preparing the budget involve careful and continuous analysis of sources of revenue, expected expenditure and the need and cost of increased services. The general accounting procedures are, however, laid down by the authority and the chief librarian determines policies and solves administrative problems on the basis of additional data supplied to him for his guidance.

In a larger library book-keeping and accountancy work, or the work may be controlled from the central financial office of the institution.

1.5.2.1 *Budgeting*

"Budget" may be defined as "a statement of the financial position of a sovereign body for a definite period of time based on estimates of expenditures during the period and proposals for financing them" — (*Webster's Seventh New Collegiate Dictionary*). Budget may also mean "a plan for the co-ordination of resource and expenditures".

Budget is different from the Annual Financial Report, which is a factual statement for the previous year.

1.5.2.2 *Procedure for the Preparation of Budget*

Library Budget: Library budget represents a logical, comprehensive and forward-looking financial programme for the co-ordination of the activities of the various functional divisions of the library. A definite financial plan is a forecast of the means for carrying the plan into effect. The budget is the cost summary of operations and is a historical record considering the future policy.

There are three ways in which the librarian can prepare budgetary estimates:

(1) By viewing the past expenditure;

(2) By chalking out the work programme and

(3) By using standards and norms.

1. Viewing the past expenditure: The librarian by his past experience is generally aware of the relative value and thus he can propose a budget which takes into consideration last year's expenditures, the appropriation for the current year, and the estimated expenditures for the next year. All inadequacies, comparisons with the support of other departments, sections or units in the library may be made with other libraries of the same type.

2. Chalking out the work programme: The objectives of the library to taken into consideration in formulating the budget on the basis of the library's needs in terms of service to be offered and work to be accomplished.

The work programme covers fixed charges, modified fixed charges or service station charges, and unit-cost estimate.

Fixed charges include (a) maintenance of the librarian's office, manuscript reading room; (b) maintenance of catalogues and other records; (c) costs of binding supplies, telephone, postage, freight, building maintenance and insurance against fire, theft and pests (white ants) etc.

Unit cost estimates are concerned with the readers, the size of the reserve and general circulation, the demands for bibliographical services, and the books and other materials which will probably be acquired, catalogued and bound during the year.

1.5.3 *Standards and Norms*

Norms or standards are regularly followed. A measure of standardization thus characterizes normal development. The ratio of library expenditures to total institutional expenditure per user or expenditure per library staff member are considered by a library to set up arbitrary standards.

Book-keeping Records

The essential book-keeping records are as under:

1. A ledger showing income with following items (i) appropriation, (ii) transfers from other accounts or additional appropriations, (iii) transfers from the account, (iv) credits. For expenditure should consist (i) encumbrances, (ii) clearance of encumbrances and (iii) expenditures. Lastly, the current balance.
2. An invoice file.
3. A duplicate order record.

Administration of finances in the library has both immediate and long-time objectives. The immediate objectives are financial economy, adequate support, and wise expenditure of funds; the ultimate objective is more particularly a library programme planned, supported, and adapted to changing educational needs. Successful administration and financial planning require an understanding of the sources of income of the library, budgetary procedure, and the keeping of accurate financial records.

1.5.4 *Sources of Income*

There are four main sources of financial support for the libraries. The one is the appropriation or allocation from the current operating funds. In addition, the libraries obtain income from endowments, gifts, and bequests, and fines and fees. If the income from one of them is diminished, the required amount for effective library service must be made up by increased income from one of the other three, or else expenditures must be reduced.

Many libraries in organizations are attempting services which are not justified by their incomes. The temptation for the administrator to add to the functions of his library without providing for a commensurate increase in its expenditures seems a common one; and the librarian, who belongs to an obliging craft, is too prone to accept the added duties and to struggle through somehow.

Income from Endowment

Endowment funds have two elements: (1) principal, and (2) income. It is important that the principal be kept intact since only in this way can the object of endowment be permanently carried out. It is equally important that the income be kept as large as possible in order that the benefits of the fund may be made more extensive. Library income from endowment is comparatively small, but the total budgets of those libraries which do have substantial endowments are well above the average for the libraries generally.

Income from Gifts

Practically all libraries receive gifts of books. Most book gifts come from members of the faculty, alumni, and friends and public. Current expendable gifts are both restricted and unrestricted — gifts for library service in general, for the purchase of books and periodicals in a special field, for library equipments, or for the development of some special type of library service such as microphotography. It may be necessary for the library to submerge its independent programme of gift building into the gift programme of the organization, but the library needs for service should be made known continuously through personal contacts and printed material. Among libraries in endowed private institutions — if not in other types of educational institutions — the Friends of the Library movement has proved a workable programme and has produced some excellent results. Many libraries have Friends groups, sometimes without any formal organization, which assist the library directly by making donations or indirectly by influencing others to give gifts.

If libraries are to secure and to derive the most benefit from gifts, it is necessary to have a definite policy.

1. Any programme for gifts and bequests should be formulated carefully and with long-term objectives which should be kept constantly in the public mind.
2. Memorials in the form of funds for library purposes have a strong appeal to many people because they present the opportunity to carry on the life interest of an individual or a group and can continue a beneficent service through the years.
3. The development of trust funds presents a field for constructive work on the part of library boards and recommends to such boards, or to others responsible

for the administration of libraries, that the possibilities and opportunities presented by such funds be called to the attention of their constituencies.

4. Libraries should look the interest of a large number of people in writing bequests into their wills.
5. Insurance policies, including annuities, offer a form of gifts to libraries, be suggested as the beneficiaries of such policies.

Again, if a special collection is offered be kept as a separate unit, the decision to accept it should be weighted very carefully. Such collections are difficult to administer and costly to maintain. Furthermore, their usefulness is often decreased by the necessity for keeping the books away from the library's own material. When a miscellaneous collection of books is offered as a gift to the library, it is desirable to request the donor to submit a list of the titles for checking against the library's holdings. In this way the librarian has a chance to select what is needed and has not the difficult and time-consuming task of later disposing of unnecessary duplicates.

Gifts should be properly acknowledged and reported in the library report and in the librarian's report. Printed form card or letter may be used to acknowledge gifts. A letter from the librarian adds a more personal touch and creates a warm feeling between the library and the benefactor. Exact and complete records of all gifts should be kept.

Fees, Fines, and Miscellaneous Sources

The special library fee is a relatively unimportant source of income for most of the libraries. But some of the libraries did not levy a special library fee. In favour of the special library fee, it may be said that it has been the sole means of income for a few libraries, that it has helped to build some fine collections in special fields.

The library is a necessary and integral part of the educational and research work of the whole institution. It should serve every instructional and every research department. As the necessary part of the educational work of an institution, the library should be recognized as entitled to a certain proportion of the funds appropriated by the State for Educational purposes.

Most libraries receive a certain amount of money from charges on overdue books, or damaged and lost books, or the sale of duplicates or library publications, but the practice in handling this money varies. In a large proportion the income from such sources is credited directly to the library budget.

The actual money received from the sale of library publications amounts to little or nothing because few libraries have such publications. Those that do are likely to distribute them on an exchange basis. This means that one library receives publications comparable in value to what it sends to another library, but the transaction involves no money except to pay for transportation costs. Librarians have not recorded such transactions in their regular budget reports.

The Budget

Budget should provide a complete financial programme for the year or biennial which it covers. Every library has its own peculiar budgetary problems. Such variables as the size and location of the library, the type of organization which it serves, the period covered by the budget, the physical arrangement of the library, and the organization of library services — all these affect budgetary practices.

1.5.5 ***Principles of Budget-making***

The most important principle is that the budget should make ample provision for necessary items of expenditure in current library operation — for staff salaries, student services, books, periodicals, binding and rebinding, supplies, equipment, printing, travel, postage and express, and other miscellaneous expenditures. Capital outlay for new buildings, additions or alterations to existing buildings, and major items of equipment such as steel stack shelving or carrel equipment will not ordinarily be estimated in the current library budget request. These "capital expenses" are generally provided for in a special request drawn up in consultation with the president for the consideration of the official body of control. Building and maintenance costs are usually set up as a separate budget item.

The final goal of the budget is a thoroughly objective financial estimate of library needs built around the educational services of the library to the organization and to its community. A budget based upon the educational programme must be necessity utilize the complete resources of the organization. The assistance of the clientele will ordinarily be confined to suggestions and advice regarding the book and periodical needs for the period of the budget. This information may be obtained through personal consultation. A new programme or the addition of a new member will undoubtedly affect library expenditures and should be taken into consideration in preparing the budget estimates.

Self-recommendations are important in making decisions on salary increases and the employment of additional personnel for supporting existing services or undertaking new work. Every user of supplies and materials should be represented in the estimate of needs for these materials. The budget estimate for maintaining periodical files, binding, and many other items will also depend upon the assistance and cooperation of the staff. The librarian's interpretation may be reinforced by the numerous studies and investigations of the staff in connection with their specific duties in reference, circulation, cataloguing, and other phases of library work.

A current expense is an expenditure which is "used up" during the current period, that is, it does not result in the acquisition of a fixed asset. Salaries, wages, office supplies, and heat and fuel are common examples. On the other hand, capital outlay results in the addition of fixed assets. Buildings, books, and equipment represent the largest capital outlays of a public library.

Budget Classifications

Some type of budget classification of current operating needs is typical of all library budgets, although there is no universally accepted classification. However, since libraries are requested each year to fill out the expenditures record, it simplifies accounting later to base the budget classification on this form. The two main categories in this form are operating expenditures and capital outlay. Under operating expenditures, there eight main headings: salaries, library staff; wages (student services); books; periodicals; binding and rebinding; audio-visual materials; other operating expenditures (supplies, postage, express, printing, telephone, etc.); and building, operation and maintenance. Books are not included under capital outlay.

LIBRARY EXPENDITURES OF CENTRAL LIBRARY

1.	Salaries: Library staff	Rs. ____________
2.	Wages: Student service	Rs. ____________
3.	Books	Rs. ____________
4.	Periodicals	Rs. ____________
5.	Binding	Rs. ____________
6.	Audio-visual materials (films, recordings, etc.)	Rs. ____________
7.	Other operating expenditures	Rs. ____________
8.	Total operating expenditures (Item 1 to 2)	Rs. ____________
9.	Capital outlay (sites, new building, equipments)	Rs. ____________
10.	Grand total expenditures	Rs. ____________
11.	Total additions during year to endowment for library purposes	Rs. ____________
12.	Total endowment, trust, and invested funds for library purposes (excluding building funds)	Rs. ____________
13.	Total expenditure of institution for educational and general purposes	Rs. ____________

There should be a uniform plan of budget classification. Variations in practice are to be found in the classification of such items as binding, printing, printed cards, and transportation charges. For example, postage and express may be charged to "books" and estimated under this category, or they may be set up as a separate fund. The budget estimate for "equipment" may have to be supported by a complete listing of the equipment items needed for the coming year. The important thing is not so much where a certain item is budgeted and charged in the library accounts as it is that all the items of expenditure be properly specified in the detailed breakdown of the budget.

The budget should represent actual needs estimated as honestly and as accurately as possible, and justified in terms of the educational value of library service to instruction and to the college community. Comparative data, especially comparisons with the finances of other libraries, should be used sparingly and with extreme caution. Unless the libraries are of like size, are situated in the same geographical area, serve organizations having the same type of programme and economic status and having similar problems, the comparison may be meaningless or harmful. A careful study of the library's own activities and work programme provides the soundest basis for making budget estimates. The librarian should be aggressive and convincing in his statement of library needs.

1.5.5.1 *Preparation of the Budget Statement*

When the information needed for making the estimates for the library budget has been assembled, the next step is the preparation of the budget estimate itself. In some institutions, forms and work sheets are provided by the office on which the various branches and departments make their estimates for such items as salaries and supplies.

The form and method of presenting this material in the written report is important. No set rules can be laid down as a matter of necessity for each library to follow. The following suggestion will clarify the position —

1. The statement should show the total amount of money needed and the separate amounts for each major classification and subdivision of the budget.
2. Opening pages of the budget statement may well contain a summary table showing the total amount needed, comparative data on expenditures of the library for at least two years previous to the current budget; and a comparison of the proposed expenditures with those of the current budget year based on expenditures at the time the new budget is being prepared. They should be shown in sufficient detail to reveal the various subdivisions of the budget.
3. The statement should contain a brief analysis of the proposed expenditures, justifying the amounts requested for each item in the budget.

4. The statement should contain tables and figures if these help to support the interpretation of the budget, and it should be neat and attractive in appearance.

1.5.5.2 *Basis of the Budget Estimate*

The librarian's estimate for personnel, books, supplies, and other items in the budget may be based simply on the sum required in the preceding year with a certain percentage added to take care of increases. Such a budget is not likely to be closely related to need and would be exceedingly difficult to defend.

(a) Fixed and variable charges: A second approach to estimating the financial need of the library is to consider the various items of the budget from the point of view of fixed and variable charges. Fixed charges are those which are relatively stable in amount from year to year or which may be estimated with reasonable accuracy from the records Libraries keep in the normal course. The personnel employed in building and processing the book collection or in supplying the services at the loan desks constitute the most important of the variable charges. In recent years, there has been an increased demand by certain administrators and librarians for a more exact determination of the cost of variable charges, based on unit cost studies, in the expectation. Unit cost studies, are intended to show the actual cost of specific tasks done or services rendered. Their application to library accounting has been made chiefly in the technical processes. The cost of library services and operations can be computed; they are not intended to establish standards of cost for measuring performance even though in some quarters they have been employed for this purpose. Until a large number of unit cost studies have been made in libraries of similar type, function, and size, they cannot be used for comparative purposes and are therefore limited in their present usefulness for budget estimating. Until libraries are more adequately staffed, however, and until the techniques of unit cost studies are simplified and refined, it is unlikely that they will be extensively used in the preparation of the budget.

(b) Standards are also important approach widely accepted. In general, the standards set forth these financial criteria as being most closely related to the educational efficiency of the library *i.e.* the percentage of the total educational expenditure exclusive of capital outlay, the amount of money spent for books and periodicals over a period of years; and the annual expenditure for library staff salaries, weighted for enrolment. Standards for the annual salary budget and the annual book budget based on the service load of the library.

No library budget could be prepared solely on the basis of these standards or of any other standards without taking into consideration local factors, such as the cost of living in the community, present status of the library book collection, curriculum changes, and the physical arrangement of the library. They serve a useful purpose, however, in checking the librarian's estimate of his needs and in justifying the recommendations for increases in the library's income it is not already larger than the amounts cited in the standards. The librarian should keep in mind the general limitations inherent in all types of standards and the fact that in many cases they set up figures which are intended to be regarded as minima.

1.5.6 *Budget Process*

The order of procedure, outlined to this point, is to assemble to information; to estimate the expenditures necessary to provide for adequate library service; and to prepare the budget statement with supporting interpretation. In presenting the budget, the librarian endeavours to show its relationship to the objectives of the library and to the educational aims of the organization. The purpose is to show what services the library can render on an adequate budget and the outcome of educational values. When the library budget is approved, it is set up in final form in the librarian's financial records. It may be appropriated in a lump sum or appropriated under the various subdivisions of the budget classification. The librarian would have complete freedom, except in matter of salary, to authorize expenditure from the budget as may seem best. When the appropriation for the library is made in a rigidly segregated budget, a practice common in academic libraries, the object classifications of the budget must be strictly adhered to. There are advantages to both types of appropriation but the ideal lies somewhere between the two extremes. Control must be sufficient to insure efficient administration, but on the other hand, not so rigid as to hamper the library in carrying out its services.

Budget is helpful as it provides a safeguard against unreasonable demands of certain faculty members. It stimulates the faculty to participate more actively in book selection, since it enables departments to feel that there is some money available which they can call their own. It guards the librarian against the possible charge that the expenditure of book funds has been unjust to some departments. It prevents the clash of personalities among the faculty. It curbs the exercise of an excessive degree of discretionary power and arbitrariness on the part of librarians.

1.5.6.1 *General Book Fund*

A basic assumption in the appointment of book funds is that a substantial sum should be set aside for direct expenditure by the librarian. Ordinarily this sum is spoken of as the general book fund and it is intended to take care of the need for general reference books, general continuations recreational reading, duplicates and replacements recommended and purchased by the librarian.

Budget proportions such as these are useful only as a guide. Perhaps a sounder basis of determining the amount of the general book fund is to keep exact annual records on the expenditures for each type of material purchased and to base the estimate on the average annual expenditure over a period of years. Such a method has its limitations, to be sure, but it carried private assurance that local conditions are being taken into account. The greatest variation in the amount of money needed from year to year in the general book fund is likely to be reflected in the purchase of reference sets. In the matter of estimating the budget need for new sets, it is frequently possible to anticipate unusual expenditures by watching for the pre-publication announcement of each set.

Periodicals

The funds for the purchase of periodicals usually considered part of the total book fund, may be administered as part of the general book fund. There are two definite dangers in leaving periodical. The first is a tendency to refer to the librarian, for purchase from the general book fund, many requests for new journals and for costly back files which the department probably would not purchase if the expenditure came directly from its own funds; the second is the lack of knowledge or consideration on the part of departments as to the secondary costs involved in unrestricted periodical purchasing. Aside from these possible objections, the advantages are strongly in favour of maintaining the periodical and binding funds on an unapportioned basis. If periodical funds are apportioned, however, it is advisable to set aside a substantial sum for the purchase of general journals, back files, replacements, and duplicates needed for binding.

1.5.6.2 *Book Funds for Branch Libraries/Departmental Libraries*

In determining the amount of money to be allotted annually to each branch, the librarian usually acts with or through the library committee. The basis of distribution most commonly in effect is that of the personal estimates of the librarian checked by the impressions of the needs made upon the members of the sub-library committee. The average annual expenditure for books, periodicals, and binding of each department over a period of years; the deficiencies in certain branch/department collections which have shown up in requests for material at the loan desks; the use of books by the several branch/departments, and the probable changes in the course programme which may effect the need for library materials.

The following factors not necessarily in order of importance, affect a branch/department's book needs: (1) the enrolment; (2) the extent of use of books; (3) the number of new publications in the various fields; (4) the relative cost per volume of books in the several fields; and (5) the state of the collections in each field in the library. They then attempt to reduce these factors to numerical ratings and to develop a percentage ratio of the book fund for each branch/department. This percentage ratio is then applied to the division of the book funds to be apportioned and the library committee and the librarian make certain adjustments to take care of special factors or conditions not provided for in the distribution formula.

A number of other methods have been suggested for apportioning book funds. All such plans as seek a scientific basis of distribution present many difficulties. They require a great deal of faculty and library time to prepare and assemble the necessary information, and temporary book-keeping records must be set up until the final apportionment is made.

1.6 Library Book-keeping

Different situations require different forms of records, the underlying principles are the same. It is of first importance, therefore, to know the reason why records are kept and their uses.

The fundamental purpose of financial records is to show the amount of money set aside purposes for the fiscal period, the amount spent, the purposes for which it was spent, and the balance that remains. Some of the more important uses to which records are put include the following: (1) to aid in the preparation of the budget; (2) to control the spending of the library's funds in a way that will increase the efficiency of library service; (3) to insure that no funds are overdrawn; (4) to aid in the preparation of the annual report and special reports; and (5) to provide information on library finances for reports to accrediting and library agencies.

Most of the libraries keep their financial records according to a single entry system and do not attempt to record receipts, the expenditure record being the primary transaction in which they are interested. When the budget is approved and set up in the librarian's office, the income of the library remains relatively stationary except for small sums which are received from fines, replacements, and the sale of publications. The single entry system for recording expenditures is, therefore, obviously an incomplete record of the library's financial condition and would not be considered sufficient where great importance is attached to sound principles of accounting. But for all practical purposes, and for the uses for which they are intended, the conventional library records serve their purposes with reasonable satisfaction and efficiency.

The most important function in library book-keeping is to set up control records to keep the budget in balance. By this is meant that the amount of money available in the various subdivisions of the budget for a certain fiscal period equals or exceeds the expenditures and commitments for salaries, books, supplies, and the other categories of expense in the budget. In considering the accounts payable, the total of outstanding book orders cannot be ignored, particularly in the final months and weeks of the fiscal period.

In methods of keeping library accounts there is great diversity. The records should serve the purposes enumerated above and any special requirements necessitated by local conditions. The more important financial records, forms, and files would include: requisition and order forms, the monthly financial report, the subsidiary fund ledger, the record of approved accounts payable, the permanent file of dealers' bill, the readers pay-roll register, and the record of petty cash.

1.6.1 *Monthly Report*

A monthly financial report, which indicates in summary form for the librarian the expenses and balances at an indicated date, is essential in the efficient management of the library. Disbursements are shown for each of the major items in the budget and the departmental book and general book funds are broken down to show how and for what purposes each is spent. This record may consist of a single sheet for each month, arranged in vertical columns. It will be noticed that this form follows exactly the classification scheme of the budget and serves not only as a record of past expenditures but as a guide to those in the future as well.

The Monthly Report provides in summary form a control for encumbrances. The encumbrance balance is determined by using a subsidiary ledger for each object in the budget classification. The encumbrance balance could also be obtained by keeping a duplicate file of requisitions, purchase orders, or order cards. For example, in ordering books it is possible to keep one card file of outstanding orders arranged alphabetically by author for searching purchases, and a duplicate set, arranged by fund, for determining encumbrance balances. When an order is filled and the cards withdrawn from the alphabetical author file, the duplicate cards are also withdrawn and the total remaining provides the balance of book orders encumbrances.

MONTHLY REPORT

Budget Categories
BOOKS
I. Departments
Art
Biological Science
Education
History
Physical Sciences
Social Sciences
II. General
General
Reference
Recreational books
Replacement
Transportation
Library of Congress card
Total of I and II
Periodical
Binding
Supplies
Equipment
Salaries:
1. Staff
2. Statement
TOTAL

1.6.2 *Subsidiary Fund Ledger*

The subsidiary or fund ledger has an account for each object or fund in the budget classification. Each transaction is entered under Date, Vendor, Order number, Encumbrances, and Expenditures. It is to be noted that there are three columns under Encumbrances and under Expenditures. The last figure in the Balance column under Encumbrances gives the total outstanding in orders for books, supplies, etc. At any time, therefore, it is possible to determine if the orders to be placed against any specific fund will exceed the amount budgeted to the fund.

A file of duplicate bills in the librarian's office, arranged first by month and second by dealer and stamped individually with the date of approval, would serve for reference and verification. It would not, however, be so convenient for quick reference as a page-listing. Moreover, most libraries keep their files of duplicate bills in an alphabetical dealer arrangement for the entire fiscal period.

Probably the most satisfactory method of providing a quick reference means of checking on bills is to prepare a monthly record of approval accounts payable. This record is not essential if the library keeps a subsidiary ledger for each fund. It includes entries for all expenditures except salaries and payments from petty cash. It is made up at the time bills are approved and forwarded for payment. The method of recording is alphabetical by dealer, with entries for the date of the bill, the date approved for payment, and other special information required to fit the particular library's need.

ANNUAL RECORD

Months			Source............				Cost.........		
43-44	Cst.	Circ.	Order	Per.	R.R.	Ref.	Res.	Total	Recd.	Balance
July										
Aug.										
Sept.										
Oct.										
Nov.										
Dec.										
Jan.										
Feb.										
Mar.										
Apr.										
May										
June										
Total										

1.6.3 *Permanent File of Bills*

The record of the cost of books may be kept on the order card if it is filed permanently after the order transaction is completed. Alternative places for keeping this record are the shelf list and accession record. This record is useful in determining readily the cost of a book which must be replaced, in adding duplicate copies.

1.6.4 *Record of Imprest Money*

In general, imprest account are handled in two principal ways: (1) in some libraries, fines and replacement money are turned into imprest directly by the library; and (2) in other libraries, the imprest fund is established by a cash payment from the account office. This is regarded as the best practice by most finance officers. In the first case, a special account book should be kept of all income and expenditure.

It is necessary for the library to establish an imprest fund for small items of expenditure by drawing a certain amount of money from the treasurer's office. This sum, amounting to whatever is though necessary to take care of petty cash expenditures for a month or more, is charged against the library's "supply" fund, and a record is kept by the librarian for totaling the amount in the monthly record of expenditures for the particular month when it is withdrawn. The money is placed in a box and vouchers are secured supporting every payment from the fund. When the imprest money is exhausted, a statement of all payments made from the fund together with vouchers supporting same, is turned over to the finance office who pays the library an amount equal to the total disbursements as shown by the statement. In this plan, the fund remains intact after it is created.

REFERENCES

ALA, BLR Committee. *Guidelines for Handling Library Orders.* Chicago, ALA, 1973.

ALA Board of Salaries. Subcommittee on Budgets. Classification and Pay Plan for Libraries in Institutions of Higher Education. Vol. II.

Bach, H. "Why allocate"? *Lib. Resources & Tech. Services.* 8, 1964.

Barues, Frank. "Budget Priorities for Libraries". *Mangmt. in Lib.* Melbourne, Ormond, 1971.

Barr, K.P. "Estimates of Number of Currently Available Scientific and Technical Periodicals". *Jrl. of Doc.* 23, 1967.

Browen, Norman B. "Price Indexes for 1882". *Lib. Jrl.*

Cowla, S.R. "Presenting the Library Budget to Appropriate Authorities". *Minnesota Libraries.* 22.

Drake, Mariam A. "Attribution of Library Cost." *Coll. & Res. Lib.* 38, 1977.

Dix William, S. "The Financing of Research Libraries". *Coll. & Res. Lib.* Vol. 35.

Ehikhamenor, Fabian A. "A Formula for Allocating Book Funds." *Libri.* 33, 2, 1983.

Ellsworth, Ralph E. "Some Aspects of the Problem of Allocating Book Fund for a University Library". *Lib. Qrly.* 2.

Ford Stophen. *The Acquisition of Library Materials.* Chicago, ALA, 1973.

Girja Kumar and Jayaswal, P.K. *Information Needs of Economists* (chapter). N. Delhi, JNU, 1982.

Gold, Steven D. "Allocating Book Budget: An Economic Model." *Coll. & Res. Lib.* 36, 5, 1975.

Gopinath, M.A. "Financial Norms for Collection Development in Libraries". *Lib. Sc. Sl. Doc.* 20, 3, 1983.

Goyal, S.K. "Allocation of Library Funds to Different Departments of a University". *Coll. & Res. Lib.* 34.

Guha, A.K. "Book Prices and Their Impact on Libraries". *ALA Bull.* XVI, Jan. 1980.

India, Ministry of Education. Edu. Commission. Kothari Commission Report. 1964.

ILA Conf. XXI. Jan. 1976. National Wage Policy for Library and Information Service Sector in India. Symposium.

Kapoor, Shabad. Rising Trends in Subscription Rates of Chemistry, Economics, and English Language Journals. *IASLIC Bull.* 28, 1983.

Katz, William A. *A Collection Development.* N. York, Halt, 1980.

Keller, John E. "Programme Budgeting and Cost Benefit Analysis for University Libraries". *Coll. & Res. Lib.* 30.

McGrath, W.E. etc. "An Allocation Formula Derived from Factor Analysis of Academic Department". *Coll. & Res.* 30, 1, 1969.

McGum. "Ground Work in Budget Making". *ALA Bull.* 29.

Mittal, R.L. *Library Administration.* Delhi, Metropolitan, 1982.

Mukharjee, A.K. "Fundamentals of Spl. Librarianship and Documentation". Calcutta, *IASLIC,* 1982.

Muller, Hans, "The Management of College Library Funds". *Coll. & Res. Lib.* 2.

Pafford, J.H.P. "Book Selection in University Library". *Unesco Bull.* Jan. 1963.

Randall, Garden E. "Budgeting for Libraries". *Spl. Lib.* 67, 1, 1976.

Ranganathan, S.R. *Fine Laws of Library Science.* Bombay, Asia, 1965.

Recommendations of the Seminar on Library Resources in University Education and Research No. 25-27, 1982. Osmania University, Hyderabad.

Reeves, E.W. "Administration of Library Budget". *Lib. Qrly.* 2.

Rogers, R.P. *University Library Administration.* N. York, Wilson, 1971.

Saxena, R.S. "Impact of Essential Rate of Growth of Periodicals and Their Cost in Scientific and Technical Libraries" *IL Bull.* XVI, Jan.-June, 1980.

Schad, J.G. "Allocating Book Funds; Control and Planning". *Coll. & Res. Lib.* 31, 3, 1970.

Sitaramaiah, T. "Price Trends in Chemical Engineering Journal". *IASLIC Bull.* 2, 1975.

Smith, K.R. "Serial Agents/Serial Librarian". *Lib. Resources & Tech. Services.* 14, 1970.

Timmerman. "Position Classification and Pay Plans". *Lib. Trends* III, 1965.

UNESCO: Statistical Yearbook. Paris, UNESCO, 1983.

Walwood, R.J. Book Budget Allocations. *Canadian Lib. Jrl.* 34, 3, 1977.

Young, H.C. "Planning Programming, Budget Systems in Academic Libaries". Detriot, Gate, 1976.

2

Personnel Management (Human Resources)

Personnel administration is that part of the process of management which is primarily concerned with the human constituent of an organization. The term 'personnel management' is called by different names *i.e.* personnel management in public enterprizes, also labour management; industrial relations, and manpower management. Management in broad sense is not confined to private enterprize, it is also essential in business, agencies and also non-profit organizations like libraries. In other words, management is a organizational leadership, and one of its central task is effective coordination and utilization of organization. The personal functions of management are a central responsibility of management everywhere. Edwin B. Flippo described the personnel that the personnel function is concerned with the procurement, development, compensation, integration, and maintenance of the personnel of an organization for the purpose of contributing towards the accomplishment of that organizational major goals or objectives. Therefore, personnel management is the planning, organizing, directing and controlling of the performance of those operative functions.

Personnel management is an integral but distinctive part of management, concerned with people at work and their relationship within the enterprize, seeking to bring together into effective librarian, the man and women who staff the library enabling each to make his own best contribution to its success, both as an individual and as a working group. It seeks to provide relationship within the library that are conductive both to effective work and human satisfaction.

Personnel management includes the activities of systematic recruitment and maintenance of the labour force, employees incentive systems, rating and standard, job analysis and job description, employee's training, maintenance of personal records, personnel welfare, policies, procedures and physical conditions etc.

Objectives: It is said to be a specialized function, aimed at releasing the objective of an library's management within certain pre-laid down policies which were based on well-laid principles. The main objectives are twofold:

1. It improves the services rendered by the enterprize to society through building better employees morale;
2. It establishes in the minds of those associated with the library-employees participation, readers at large, the fact that each employee will share the responsibility and the benefits of the results of the library service rendered by them and result drawn out of that.

2.1 Functions

The main functions of personnel management (staffing) can be categorized as under:

1. Personnel management deals with a human factors. The phase of this start with the employment procedure, *i.e.*, appointment of the persons and applying the proper methods of their selection. It collects the information of the staff required in library and fix the wage rates on the basis of rating and standards, necessary procedures for resting, interviewing, checking, are adopted and seek necessary recommendations of supervisors. Personnel department also maintain records of all employees, working presently or formerly.
2. Personnel management is responsible to frame the policies of promotions, and see that the policies are properly followed. It helps in the transfer policies, for the convenience of the libraries, to correct the displacement of employees, to increase flexibility of employees as a part of the work stabilization programme, and to provide the necessary records to carryout the policies.

Library is a technical type of organization, where most of staff engaged or appointed possesses professional qualification and technical training. It will not be suitable and good in the interest of the library to terminate, transfer and replace the employees all of sudden or after a short interval of time. One person working in particular department familiar himself with the situations, resource and the working procedures of the section.

3. Personnel management aids in the formulation of policies governing training of new employees, being upgrades, apprentices and supervisors. Training is provided with all safety provisions and according to the policies of the institution. It accords cooperation in preparation of the special annual report for employees.
4. It also evaluates all jobs and classify them according to the worklines and write job specification. Policies governing payment for suggestions, pension plans, mutual savings programmes, insurance plans, unions, loans and advances.

The library staff has two functions:

1. Acquiring and organizing reading material and to make them available to readers.
2. Maintaining personnel management in which adequate number of staff serves the clientele effectively and with maximum satisfaction. It matters very little of a library has got a very valuable selection of rare books and manuscripts and housed in a beautiful building and provides all amenities necessary for a good library service. But if it has unqualified staff and they are not dedicated to library service and lack cordiality and spirit, the whole library will be of less use. It is, therefore, essential that library personnel should be qualified, trained and possess sweet temperament, cordiality and dedication to service to readers.

Several commission and committees discussed several problems of higher education stated, which vehemently emphasized the need of an organized library for standard educational pattern. Consequently it will not be possible to organize a well systematic library until we have a competent personnel possessing high intellectual calibre and professional competence.

Presently librarianship has acquired a very complex role in the society. The area of work in the libraries is widespread that a big human organization is required to manage it. The librarian, who is head of this organization should have together skilled, devoted and spirited colleagues around him and should give this group of men a form of coherent team in order to accomplish the task successfully. The librarian assumes the role of a manager of a personnel department and look after the administration.

Personnel administration is a method of developing the potentialities of employees so that they will get maximum satisfaction out of their work and give their best offers to the organization. A well qualified and adequate staff of a library is required for effective participation in the instructions to the readers in the use of library tools and bibliographies, carrying out the objectives of the institutions extending the use of the library and the resources in education. A professional must have an advance knowledge of the work which depends on the invention, imagination and talent of the employee and requires constant exercise of desecration and judgment in the performance.

Librarianship

Librarianship is a complicated profession and a combination of various kinds of excellence: as administrator, scholars, technician, lover of book, social worker and overall a social reformer. The librarian should work as manager of a business firm. He requires frequent consultation and close relationship with the administrators and library committee members and should impress them with sound judgment. He also holds confidence of library staff by his ability to develop a systematic organization of library work. The librarian is an administrator and educationist and also an officer responsible to the authority for the executive management of the library. He selects his staff according to the need of the library. He is responsible for staff duties and their performance; for library building, stock and equipment.

2.1.1 *Planning*

A systematic planning is done to achieve the maximum utility of both the resources.

To achieve the maximum utility of both the resources, a systematic planning is done. It may be long-term planning or short-term planning. It is a difficult job to make planning as it leads to future certainty. Planning is essential to establishment and recognition of future job requirements.

Planning can be informal and can be framed without any planning division. It is in mind not in record or in oral discussions. In contrast, formal plans are documentary. Persons are given task of developing plans and assignment identifies the formal recognition given to the planning activities. Planning can be effective only in its influence on operations. It involves Librarian, Dy. Librarian, Asstt. Librarian, Section In-charge and rank and file workers.

Planning: (a) Formation of objectives, developing policies,

(b) Staff recruitment, selection, promotion,

(c) Leadership traits,

(d) Negotiating among resources, coordination, communication, training, evaluation.

There are two factors of planning —

1. Forecasting for personnel planning usually begins with present staffing schedules. Forecasts of future requirements for skilled workers involves consideration of both quantity and quality members and required capabilities. It measures perspective requirements.
2. Programming phase in planning is the process of discovery, identification and preparation. The process is applied both in existing personnel and to new, added recruits. It must continually evaluated, council, assist and direct those who are in process for later stage services. Programming leaves heavily on the accuracy of forecasts.

2.1.2 *Management Policy*

The entire process of personnel management is co-ordinated and organized by guidelines of management policy.

"Policies are statements of the organizations over all purpose and its objectives in the various areas with which its operations are concerned."

A policy is a predetermined, selected course established as a guide towards accepted goals and objectives. Policies reduce the range of individual decisions and encourage management by exception.

There is a difference between policies, procedures and practices. While policy is a predetermined source of guidance, the procedures are the methods whereby the organization is to achieve its stated objectives. They are usually setup by high level librarians and carried out first line supervisors. On the other hand practices are what is actually done in the organization and what rank and the employees do depends almost entirely on the calibre of their immediate supervisors. Policy is a guiding principles. "Policy outlines a long range purpose, based on considered principles of human relations and library objectives."

Characteristics of Policy

1. Policy sets forth the principles and guide the librarian's actions not the actions themselves. Expression of belief provides rule of thumb.
2. The main purpose of the policies is to guide the present and also for future, because policies are stated as broadest terms. Suppose a library provides two weeks' summer vacation to each employee with more than one year service by seniority rotation.
3. Policies should be framed by an active participation of top management. The personnel executive will work in staff capacity. There is a way the staff people may think of their participation also. The librarian should call advises from the supervisors at all levels about the problems, scrutinize it and put before the working committee of the chief executives, *i.e.*, governing body.
4. Policies should be for long period, present and future and even generations to come. Long range policies make the organization more stable and services effective for long period.

5. Policies should not include any exception in any circumstances. If a single exception is admitted, the policy leave its own place.
6. Verbal policies have no solid ground and not believed and should be in writing. When a library write its policies, the librarian and governing board collectively try to put their best foot forward.

2.1.3 *Principles of Personnel Management*

Personnel management can be called as 'Peoples Management' or 'staffing'. There are few principles which proved to be a good guide to the librarians and other personnel executives:

1. The human assets of any library are of immense value. They must be conserve, cultivated and enhanced as the library is to develop and grow.
2. The principle made responsibility of line organization which is unlike as the enlighted use and treatment of people implies a degree of expertise and specialization unlikely to be found among members of the average line organization.
3. The personnel staff counsel and assist the Librarian and the subordinate line executives in the formulation of objectives, plans, policies, procedures and practices relating to maximum effective use of the human resources in the library.
4. Personnel staff is responsible for continuing study, analysis, evaluate, and review all aspects of the library's personnel programmes.
5. No doubt that the chief librarian is surrounded by many secrecies, but when plans are assigned to the subordinate executive to improve the services or the work, it is common to consult the person concerned.
6. Personnel staff is responsible to apply the recommendations of the line, equitably and constantly throughout the library organization.

2.1.4 *Nature and Size of the Staff*

The bricks of an organization are its people. The success of a library depend on the people hired as they increase the opportunity, to expand into new areas and work skilfully with lesser mistakes. The librarian should be fully left to manage the library to see the opportunity, to plan, to capitalize on these opportunities, and decide the action and control with concentration in building the library serviceable.

A library needed a man for the job of issuing books on the counter. It could find no one with these exact qualifications.

It identified the job being named and the required qualification of those who fill them. The process creates staffing schedule. It is worth noting that this assessment of current resources emphasized numbers and qualifications that are required. There are persons whose capabilities, though having high potentiality, are unused and some qualified for a job are not given the same job, while unqualified persons are given skilled and specialized job.

2.2 Job Analysis and Job Specifications

2.2.1 *Job Analysis*

According to Ranganathan "Job is meant an ultimate piece of work which is best done at the single stretch and whose duration is ordinarily short. For staffing purpose, a job is defined as a collection or aggregation of tasks, duties and responsibilities that, as a whole, is regarded as the reasonable assignment to an individual employee. Every employee has a position."

Job analysis can be called as job study, which helps in tasks, processes, responsibilities and personal requirements. A job may require staff, professional, semi-professional and non-professionals. All three type of workers are different in authorities and powers. Semi-professionals are not expected to exercise much independent judgment. While making job analysis of workers at each level — top level, middle level and lower level — is done to determine the nature of work, the qualifications necessary, training required, and the amount of supervisions etc. There are persons of staff role, having various positions and levels: Librarian, Dy. Librarian, Asstt. Librarian, Section In-charge, Unit In-charge and others. Job analysis establish their positions, requirements and relations at a certain point.

Job analysis is a common practice in large libraries. It is also used for multi-purposes and includes following points:

1. Determination of qualifications;
2. Provides guidance in recruitment and selection;
3. Establishment of responsibility, and authority;
4. Evaluations for transfers and promotions;
5. Settlement of salary levels;
6. Judgment of the merits, assignment and compensation;
7. Guidance in the measurement of work standards.

Factors involved in process: Job analysis is determined by a process, which requires many informations as under:

(a) Job should be properly identified;

(b) Distinctive and significant characteristics of a job should be specified. It includes location, physical setting, supervision and association.

(c) Every assignment involves specific operations, tasks, timings, importance, simplicity, complexities and responsibilities for staff members, library material and library finance.

(d) Material used by workers has also due consideration in the process of job analysis as Books, periodicals, films, microfilms, maps, music etc.

(e) How job is performed. The operational nature may be specified for the purpose of job analysis. Performation may be shelf arrangement, lending, photographing, document abstracting, indexing, levelling, cataloguing, classifying and binding etc.

(f) Personal attribute is also helpful, as it proved more effective in job analysis. Personal attributes include job experience, training, physical fitness, sound mind, aptitudes and social skills.

(g) Job relations are also into account in job analysis. The person should have opportunities for promotion, cooperation, proper direction and leadership.

2.2.2 *Job Specifications*

The term job specification is used for the personal

characteristics required for the job. Whether the library is small or large, it has been the responsibility of proper staffing. Once we know what a job is, we must determine what kind of person we need to do that job. It is we call, the main specification. There are differences in regional area, departments within the library, and within the library staff.

It is very essential to consider some specific factors of a person for staff turnover and improvement of library services. These factors are: Age of the person, Education of the person, Mental fitness, Aptitude to the job of the person, Attitude towards authority, Attitude towards working with others, Previous experience, Willingness to learn.

Job specification is also a brief job summary, which reveals the feeling of person about his job. It helps the librarian in many ways: (a) It may stipulate a specified period of experience in a particular job or jobs; (b) It may state physical requirements; (c) It may identify tasks to be taken and state required fores; (d) It may specify general and special educational requirements; (e) It suggests the relative importance of being able to memorize; (f) It makes understand mechanical device, meet readers, speak and write well, plan and make decisions rapidly.

The quantity of the employees depends largely on the type of the job and how each performs the job. However, to measure the quantity requirement, some tools should be used. Measurement may also help the libraries suggesting for the promotions, merit increase in wages and performance of the probationers.

2.2.3 *Job Standards*

Time study: It has been observed that wage incentive system has been developed and based on some tools, *i.e.* time study, motion study, standard time data, and effort rating technique. Job analysis describes the qualities required of worker and the conditions under which the work is performed. The technique of time study is attributed to Fedrick W. Taylor who considered it as the most important feature of scientific management. The main aim of time study to determine the standard time required to carryout a job most efficiently. It functions to subject each operation of a given piece of work, to eliminate unnecessary operation of a given piece of work, to determine the quick and the best method of performing each necessary operation; to standardize equipment, methods and working conditions; to determine the number of standard hours. It is method to find out the one best way of doing the work in libraries.

Dr. Ranganathan has classified the job analysis system in many parts: (a) Job occurs; (b) Job belongs to a distinctive library function; (c) Function of the job; (d) Factors to which job relates; (e) Work in which the job relates; (f) Period of job.

Through the process of job breakdown, each job is outlined as a sequence of tasks or job elements. Standard time hour established of these elements, so that the overall timing for the job may be estimated by combining operations. Time study is recorded on the basis of the time taken in completing the job cycle. This recorded time is averaged. Such standards helps in the measurement of work load and time budgeting studies of the supervisory staff and the librarian. Records are analyzed to discover; how time is spent; efficient utilization of personnel; Estimation of personnel in expansions; Decentralization and other changes.

2.2.4 *Motion Study*

It is a process to determine the work standards. It is very necessary to measure the work and service output per worker or group of workers over a period of time. It analyses the methods, materials, tools, equipments and performance of a piece of work.

In making the motion study, the librarian should select the task for study. A process chart should be prepared and each work place should be studied. New methods should be suggested. In short, the man doing the motion study should be expert himself, and must be well versed in library operations and conditions. Motion study increases the work output, economy, services and the interest of the worker. But on the other hand, it fixes the monotonous motions, destroys initiative of the worker, keep the worker in dark about the usefulness of motion study, considers the differences of workers etc.

These studies comprise of the sequence of purpose of the job, place of the workers, time taken, persons engaged, methods applied, reason of necessarily, developing the methods, submitting the proposals and installation of new methods etc. Several tools are applied, *i.e.* duty list, job description list, activity list, charts, cast study, operational research etc. A job is not a static. It may be changed by altered circumstances or by administrative decision.

2.3 Staff Formulas

The question arises how many jobs in a given time are required in a library or an administrative officer. He makes the judgment and grouping the jobs as under:

Public Library of 5 Lakh Population		*University Library*	
Professional:		Professional:	
Librarian	— 1	Librarian	— 1
Dy. Librarian	— 2	Dy. Librarian	— 1
Asstt. Librarian	— 4	Asstt. Librarian	— 6
Technical Asstt.	—12	Technical Asstt.	—15
		Jr. Tech. Asstt.	— 4
Semi-Professional:		Semi-Professional:	
Sr. Library Asstt.	— 2	Sr. Library Asstt.	— 8
Jr. Lib. Asstt.	— 4	Jr. Lib. Asstt.	— 4
U.D.C.	— 2	U.D.C.	— 4
L.D.C.	— 2	L.D.C.	— 4
Non-Professional:		Non-Professional:	
Book Attendant	— 4	Book Lifter	— 6
Gate-keeper	— 2	Gate-keeper	— 2
Chowkidar	— 2	Custodian	— 1
		Chowkidar	— 2

Adequate staffing is an essential condition of effective library. In general library staff is divided into three categories: Superior (Sr. Professional staff) and professional staff; the middle or semi-professional staff; the lower service or non-professional or clerical or other staff.

Professional and non-professional are shown below:

First expansion	*Second expansion*
Professional	
1. Administrative	*Administrative*
	Librarian
	Asstt. Librarian
	Personal Officer
	Departmental Head
	Special Librarians
2. Technical	*Technical*
	Order librarian
	Catalogue librarian
	Binding librarian
	Bibliography librarian
3. Research	*Research*
	Reference librarian
	Bibliographer
	Periodical librarian
	Special librarian
4. Instruction	*Instructional*
	Reference librarian
	Circulation librarian
	Reserve Book librarian
	Divisional librarian
	Special librarian
Non-Professional	
5. Clerical	*Clerical*
	Book-keeper
	Secretaries
	Typists
	Filers
6. Others	*Others*
	Routine worker
	Janitor
	Cleaner

In view of the above groupings, it can be better said that job-classification is based on the following factors:

1. Distinguish characteristics of work:
   (i) Supervision;
   (ii) Responsibilities;
   (iii) Constant dealings with the readers;
   (iv) Constants of books, tools and methods.
2. Specific duties:
   (i) Training;
   (ii) Referring questions;
   (iii) Selecting books for purchase;
   (iv) Recommending changes in politics.
3. Qualifications needed:
   (i) Background;
   (ii) Ability;
   (iii) Dealing with persons;
   (iv) Professional experience;
   (v) Subject knowledge;
   (vi) Library techniques.

Land Grant Survey recommended some norms for academic libraries: Five full time trained librarians for the first five hundred students, ten for one thousand students and four additional staff members for each additional five hundred students. A more scientific approach to determine the size of the staff is contained in the report of "A.L.A. Classification and Pay Plan."

"3 professional persons for the first 800 service units, plus one more for each additional 500 units, plus the chief librarian. The number of professional positions would be nine or possibly nine and one half in full time equivalent. A number of clerical staff position recommended in the report, ranges from a minimum of 40 per cent of the number of the professional positions to a maximum of 60 per cent."

Ranganathan has suggested the following criteria for estimating the size of staffing in various libraries:

A — Number of volumes accessioned in a year.

B — Annual Budget allotment in rupees.

D — Number of periodical documented — that is abstracted and indexed in a year.

G — Number of Gate-hours for a year (one gate hour one counter gate kept open for one hour).

H — Number of hours the library is kept open in a day.

P — Number of periodicals currently taken

R — Number of Readers per day.

S — Number of seats of readers.

V — Number of volumes in a year.

W — Number of working days in a year.

(X) — X, if x is an integer.

= The integer just greater than x if its fractional part is greater than .25.

= The integer just smaller than x, if its fractional part is not greater than .25.

SB — Number of persons in Book Selection.

SC — Number of persons in Circulation Section.

SL — Number of persons as Librarian and his Deputies.

SM — Number of persons in Maintenance Section.

SP — Number of persons in Periodicals Section.

SR — Number of persons in Reference Section.

ST — Number of persons in technical — that is classification and cataloguing section.

Formula for staff of different sections

SB = A/6000 (one person for every 6000 volumes accessioned in a year).

SC = G/1500 (one person for every 1500 gate hours in a year).

SL = HW/1500 (one person for every 3000 volumes accessioned in a year).

SM = A/3000 (one person for every 3000 volumes accessioned in a year).

SP = P/500 (one person for every 500 periodicals taken in a year).

SR = (R/50) W/250 (one person for every 50 readers in a day for 250 days in a year).

ST = (A + 400)/2000 (one person for every 2000 volumes accessioned and one person for every 50 periodicals documented in a year).

Formula for total professional staff

SB + SC + SL + SM + SP + ST = [3(A+200) = (G + 3P) = 2N (H+6(R/50)]/3800

Formula for Non-professional skilled staff

B/30000+[S/1000]. One person for every Rs. 40000/- of annual budget and one person for every 100 seats for readers.

Formula for unskilled staff

BS/4+SC/2+SL+SM/4+SP/2+SR/8+A/20000+B/500+B/6000–[S/100]/4+V/30000

=(27A + 2) (B+120D)+40(G+3P)+30000 [S/100]+4V+2W (40H+3)(R/50)/120000

During past few years the formula of Ranganathan has been followed even in some foreign libraries. Modern libraries are adopting the methods of science of management. It is based on the actual quantum of daily work.

According to the University Grant Commission, the staff strength should be estimated as follows:

Section	*Strength of the staff*
1. Book Section	— One person for every 6000 volumes added in a year
2. Periodical Publication Section	— One person for every 500 current periodical taken
3. Documentation Section	— One person for every 1000 entries prepared in a year
4. Technical Section	— One person for every 2000 vols. added in a year
5. Reference Section	— One person for every 50 readers (other than the users of the textbook collection) in a day.

(*Contd.*)

Section	*Strength of the staff*
6. Circulation Section	— One person for every 1500 hours for which one wicket gate of the library has to be kept open in a year.
7. Maintenance Section	— One person for every 6000 volumes added in a year. One person for every 500 vols. to be replaced in a day and one person for every 100000 vols. in a library.
8. Administrative Section	— Minimum of one library accountant, one steno-typist and one correspondence clerk.
9. Unskilled Staff	— One cleaner for every 30000 volumes, the library attendant each for every 6000 volumes added in a year for every 500 current periodicals taken, and for each of the shifts in the circulation section, besides unskilled and the semiskilled worker normal to any institution.
10. Supervisory Section	— One librarian and one assistant librarian or Dy. Librarian.
Leave Substitute	— Provision for leave vacancy at the rate of one month in a year for each member in it.

However it is suggested that there should be the following staff size in libraries:

	Small Library	*Big Library*
1. Librarian	— 1	— 1
2. Dy. Librarian	— 1	— 3
3. Section heads (Asstt. Librarian)	— 1 each deptt.	— 1 each deptt.
4. Sr. Assistant	— 1 each deptt.	— 1 each deptt.
5. Technical Asstt.	— 3 each deptt.	— 3 each deptt.
6. Clerk	— 1 each deptt.	— 2 each deptt.

Formula

50000 volumes or an annual loan of 10000 vols.

= 5 persons for each set.

The ratio of staff to users	= 1 : 15 or 1 : 30 or 1 : 50 as per size and services offered by the library.
Total library staff	= Depending on the activities of the library. Minimum 5 persons and maximum as per service points.

The formula submitted by Dr. Ranganathan and others by UGC based on Ranganathan's, have been formed suitable for academic libraries in particular. It cannot be adequately applied to other libraries specially the technical libraries where readers are limited but need vast collection of special material. The formula of Shri Sarkar is vague and does not specifically mention the standards or the staff position in a technical library.

It is suggested that the formula of staff position should be based on the:

(a) Types of libraries;

(b) Type of work in each department;

(c) Minimum needs in a library;

(d) Methods adopted in a library.

The number of readers effected a little to the staff position which varies from library to library. There are one or two departments which are seriously effected by the increase in the number of readers. So far public libraries are concerned, there has been a problem of general readers who need material of common men. This can be solved by increasing few more persons in public dealing departments, *i.e.* circulation and reference service. Other things being equal to other libraries.

Hence the following minimum staff position is suggested:

Medium Size Library

Librarian	— 1
Chief Dy. Librarian	— 1

Asstt. Librarian	— 3 (Circulation, reference and periodicals)
Preservation Librarian	— 1 (if there is a reprography section)
Professional Asstts.	— 1 each section
Jr. Professional Asstts.	— 3 for each section
Sr. Assistant	— 1 for each section
Jr. Assistants	— 2 for each section
Others:	
Book-Lifter Attendant	— One for 1000 books in stack room
	— One for 200 members in reference section
	— One for each section other than the above
Porter	— One for book-budget of 25000 = annual
Book binder	— One for every 100 journalist
	— One for every 1500 book store
Cleaner	— One for every two section Or One for each floor area
Security Staff	— Two for one gate
	— Two for one property counter
	— Two watchmen for night and day separately
Peons	— One for Librarian
	— One for Dy. Librarian
	— One for each section
	— Two for Administrative section
	— One for Dak services.

2.4 Status

Status mean standing and implies rights, privileges, and the same time restrictions on the action of the individual. There are two structures of status in a library organization: (1) Functional status structure; (2) Scalar status structure.

Functional status structure is based on the contribution of the office in organization. It reflects the requirements in terms of skill, knowledge, and know-how. The technical assistant's position is thus placed in a distinctly higher status than that of the common book-attendant. On the other hand, scalar status is based on power and authority.

Status has many significances such as: (a) It suggests need of organization; (b) It contributes sense of security in office holders; (c) It is associated with income and other rewards for performance; (d) It presents a broad perception of the position; (e) It presents standing of each person in the entire bureaucracy.

2.4.1 *Informal Status*

If reflects perceptions of what individuals can do. For example, a medical doctor has higher informal status in military organization than is indicated by his rank. Informations may be related to length of service, age and seniority, although these particular factors may not influence the formal status of the job.

2.4.2 *Formal Status*

It represents the rank evidenced by job titles, various privileges, priorities in work assignments, facilities, equipment, number of assistants, wage and salary are also included in symbols. In a library newly organized, or re-organized, necessary status are assigned. Status can be increased or decreased by re-organization of the library.

The higher a man's status, the greater his influence. The status of a man is also set by the opinion of other people.

2.4.3 *Factors Involved in Establishing Status*

(1) **Title**: A person is also made influential by giving him an impressive title. For example Secretary to the librarian connotes higher status than the Technical Assistant in a library organization.

(2) **Pay**: Pay or salary is also an important symbol as a status. Financial incentive is accounted as status of a employee as it maintains a man to high standard. It is common that a high paid man is listened by all in a society and his opinion is given more weight. The

rate of pay is similar to insignia and rank, which carries much influence in library organization also.

(3) **Office:** The location and size of a man's office are symbols of his importance in libraries. If a office is well furnished and decorated with all facilities, it becomes the symbol of the same.

(4) **Privileges:** In every library certain privileges are accorded to man of high status. It includes the privileges of leave, personal assistant, and vehicle etc.

There are few human needs which also influence the status:

(a) Physical need;

(b) Social need;

(c) Self-expression need;

(d) Security needs.

Academic status implies formal recognition of professional librarians as members of the instructional and research staff in the form of assigned or equivalent faculty ranks and titles along with comparable salaries and privileges.

The lack of such recognition is one of the major obstacles to recruiting a competent library staff. This problem was discussed in Regional seminar on library development in South Asia in 1960. The Seminar passed a resolution as below:

Description of Staff members	Nature of duties	Equivalent to faculty post and enjoying scale of:
1. Librarian	Supervisory	University Professor
2. Dy. Librarian	Sr. Professional work	University Reader
3. Asstt. Librarian	Professional work	University Lecturer
4. Sr. Library Asstt.	Professional Routine work	University Asstt. Lecturer
5. Technical Asstt.	-do-	do-

Carl M. White in his report of Delhi University Library says that the University was the first in India to be in tune with international standard in providing proper librarian's service conditions comparable to those applied to the rest of the academic staff.

UGC

In India UGC appointed a Library Committee in 1964 under the chairmanship of Dr. S.R. Ranganathan which made recommendations for the development of status of the university library staff. The academic and professional qualification prescribed for various categories of library staff are at par with those prescribed for corresponding faculty positions and that the library forms an 'integral part of academic community'.

The service rendered by the library scientists, information scientists are centred round the human intellects which is actually the infrastructure of all-round development of individuals as well as of societies. Therefore, those who are responsible in discharging such services should be given proper and just status.

UGC also took decision on the recommendations of Sen-Gupta Committee, and recommended the following scales. The decision has been taken on the lines of Third Pay Commission. Other commissions and committees relating to academic staff discussed the status of librarians and recommendations were made accordingly.

At one hand UGC has recommended to appoint a scholar of repute on the post of librarian, but on the other hand it has not recommended the scale of such scholar at par with professor. It is further claimed that everywhere the librarian possesses higher qualification than a common lecturer. It is not justified on the part of UGC to give stepmotherly treatment with the library staff as it is also directly related to academic work and in no case contribute less than a teacher in educational expansion and instructional work.

Status is always based on merit and ability. So far

qualifications are concerned, the same qualification as fixed to the teaching staff, may be fixed. It is suggested as under:

1. Librarian	1. M.Lib.Sc., Ph.D. in any discipline. 2. Research experience or published work. 3. Experience of 15 years in the profession including administrative experience at least for 5 years.
2. Dy. Librarian	1. M.Lib.Sc., Ph.D. in any discipline. 2. Research experience or published work. 3. Experience of 10 years in the profession including experience of 5 years as Assistant Librarian or equivalent.
3. Asstt. Librarian	1. M.Lib.Sc. 2. Good Academic records. 3. Net qualifying.
4. College Librarian	1. M.A. II. 2. Good academic record. 3. Net qualifying. 4. Specialization in any of cataloguing, classification or documentation.

A Scene in India

Library is a trinity of material, reader and personnel. The third factor, the library personnel has its own importance and dealt as the link between the two. While reader enter the library and leave out of the library premises, he find directly or indirectly, his relation with library personnel.

During his library utilization, he comes across the following personnel:

New readers —	Property counter	— to deposit his property
	Gate-keeper	— to cross into library
	Reference assistant	— for guidance of the reference Staff
	Lending section	— for loan services

(*Contd.*)

	Stack personnel	— for guidance in stack area.
	Administrative staff	— for enrolment.
Researcher or Senior readers —	Co-operation section	— Inter library loan
	Bibliographic section	— for research work
	Documentation section	— for references
	Reference section	— for enquiries
	Photographic section	— for photographic services

Library personnel in either way contribute their service to readers. Reader may be a student in academic library, public man in public libraries, research scholar in research libraries, technician in technical libraries and a businessman in business or industrial libraries.

Library is a centre of self-education, explosion of knowledge and information. Modern world is at the threshold of modern technology and libraries are real media for scientific, cultural and economic advancement. When we talk of library service, library work, library techniques and operations, it is not the mere brickwalls of library building or the back printed papers in the form of books, periodicals or the other, it is the library personnel who are always alert and active to their services to the community, society and thus the nation.

Library personnel stand by many objectives:

1. Eradication of illiteracy;
2. Explosion of knowledge;
3. Habit of self-education;
4. Guidance to the reader in location of their reading material;
5. Preservation of reading material;
6. Expansion of education;
7. Consciousness towards rights and duties of a citizen;
8. Guidance to scholars in their researches;
9. Comply to the enquiries of research scholars;
10. Cultivate reading habit in the people.

Library personnel perform following types of works:

(a) Traditional work;

(b) Work based on modern and scientific methods channelizing their duties to effective extension services;

(c) Building the proper collection; and

(d) Dissemination of nascent thought.

Several conferences, seminars and discussions have been organized on library personnel by various associations, institutions or the societies. I.L.A. specially organized a seminar in its XVII All India Library Conference in 1968 at Indore on status of librarians. Other associations at state, national and international level have also discussed various problems of library personnel from time to time.

2.4.4 *Categories of Library Personnel*

There are various types of libraries with different functions, nature and the personnel. Library personnel can also be divided in many categories:

I. BY WORK

(a) Personnel engaged in technical work;

(b) Personnel engaged in reference work;

(c) Personnel engaged in reprographic and other specific work;

(d) Personnel engaged in public relation work;

(e) Personnel engaged in administrative work.

II. BY LIBRARY

(a) Personnel engaged in academic libraries: School, College and University libraries.

(b) Personnel engaged in special libraries;

(c) Personnel engaged in public libraries;

(d) Personnel engaged in children libraries.

III. BY MATERIAL

(a) Personnel engaged in collecting the books;

(b) Personnel engaged in collecting the periodicals;

(c) Personnel engaged in collecting the audio-visual aids;

(d) Personnel engaged in special material: photographic materials, music scores, maps, and charts etc.

IV. BY SERVICE

(a) Personnel engaged in reference service;

(b) Personnel engaged in circulation service;

(c) Personnel engaged in technical service;

(d) Personnel engaged in reprographic service;

(e) Personnel engaged in documentation service;

(f) Personnel engaged in administrative service.

In highly specialized libraries, library personnel must be a scholar *i.e.* they must be essentially subject specialists, and must know professional techniques. It is desirability of having highly qualified personnel in university and public library. A qualified librarian possesses the following qualities:

(a) Talent;

(b) Scholarship;

(c) Independability;

(d) Free mind;

(e) Fact interpretation;

(f) Academician;

(g) Competentness;

(h) Bibliographical knowledge;

(i) Potentiality;

(j) Knowledge of professional techniques.

A chief librarian, who is the leader of the library staff, has capability of supervision. He has to perform two types of activities (i) Academic activities, and (ii) Technical activities. A librarian well verse in library techniques, does not claim to be the best academician.

The atmosphere of university is purely academic and requires exclusively the intellectuals in university libraries. The university library necessarily demand a real professional, a true academician, a profound technician and a good human being. The human qualities are essentially the factors which makes the librarian a good organizer, efficient administrator and a true librarian.

They may be professionals, semi-professionals and non-professionals, Dy. Librarians, Asstt. Librarians, Technical assistants, junior technical assistants, U.D.C., L.D.C., Book-lifters, peons, and chowkidars, and other seniors and juniors etc. Library personnel are the various hands and fingers of a librarian which are used for various functions of a library.

Library personnel are judged by his devotion in duty, interest and initiative in professional work, academic interest, dynamism, handwork, co-operative spirit and missionary attitude. Large libraries have six categories of library staff. Professional and semi-professional staff is selected directly by outer sources or internal (library) sources. But there has not been a uniform system of selection for non-professional staff. In some universities, clerical and the fourth class persons are transferred from registrar's office as the Registrar hold the authority of selection for class III and IV. There are universities where the person departmentally punished or found indisciplined or insufficient, is transferred to the library as a award of punishment. This method of inter-transfer scheme in Public and Academic Libraries severely effect the library working, create indiscipline, reduce efficiency and rule out the promotion chances of library staff.

2.5 Library Profession

Librarianship is a profession. The basic duty of a librarian is to help a reader find the book or information he needs, just. The librarian must know books and bibliography and understand people. Even though specialized, the librarian's job is the most general, because his services may be needed by all. The librarian's job is to help all. The only specialization of the librarian lies in his knowledge of the technique of book utilization. As a noble profession librarianship enhances the broadness of vision, increases the sphere of knowledge.

Librarian performs specialized job and needs special training.

2.5.1 *Conditions of Work*

The librarian is supposed as chief of the library staff and usually directly responsible for a considerable number of other personnel matters in addition to the selection and training of the staff, academic rank and salaries which also include the physical conditions under which staff members work, hours of service and work, vacations and leave, tenure and retirement provision, and other matters necessary for the improvement of the all.

Physical Factors

It is important that every consideration should be taken up to provide best working conditions possible for the staff, which includes the layout of the building, building facilities, storage facilities, heating, lighting, ventilation, air-conditioning, floors, communication systems, furniture and equipment etc.

The following are regarded as minimum essentials in working conditions, the most important are as follows:

1. Vitality of the staff is the first condition, which may result maximum output with the minimum expenditure.
2. Work requiring concentration and accuracy should not be scheduled during the time an assistant is at the loan desk.
3. Work sections should be planned in detail to improving efficiency and securing economy of effort.
4. Furniture should be so arranged as to expedite duties without loss of motion or time.
5. Allocation of space is essentially 100 square feet per person which includes space for work. From 3 to 3½ feet should be allowed between the back of one desk and the front of another, and 4 feet should be regarded as the minimum width for aisles.
6. Proper conditions of ventilation and heating are important. The optimum atmospheric conditions for the comfort and health of personnel are a temperature of from 60° to 70° and 40-60 per cent relative humidity.
7. The lighting of work place should be economical in operation, supply sufficient illumination without glare, and give a uniform and nearly shadowless illumination for desks. As much natural light as possible is desirable.
8. Noise is a contributing element to fatigue and should be minimized as far as possible.
9. Each person can have his own outfit of necessary tools, and the proper selection of chairs, tables, supply closets, and other conveniences in the work place.

10. The equipment with which the staff has to work are important. Many scientific inventions not intended primarily for libraries are directly usable or adaptable, and it is well worth the time and expense involved to discover and apply them at the time of building or remodeling; ventilating and air-conditioning systems, passenger and freight elevators, book lifts and conveyor systems, and telephones etc.

Hours of Service

There is considerable variation in the number of hours that libraries are kept open for the use of public and faculty. There are three factors effecting the hours: (a) Size of staff; (b) Number of rooms; and (c) Number of readers. The hours open for circulation service, range front fifty-four to eighty-six, with the median at seventy-seven hours. If to these hours is added the time the library is open for reading and study but not for circulation service, the range increases from fifty-four to one hundred and three, and the median is seventy-eight excluding Sunday.

Most of the libraries are making available the full services of the library during Sunday afternoon and evening. If the library is playing its part in developing reading habits a professional staff member should be on duty at all hours during which the building is open.

Hours of Work

There are also variations in the number of working hours. Hours of work should not exceed thirty-eight a week, and even to the range of thirty-seven to forty-eight and a median of thirty-nine and a half hours per week for librarians in institutions with approximately a thousand enrolment or less. If Sunday duty is extra, this fact should be made clear to the assistant at the time of appointment. Sunday duty may be voluntary on the part of the staff members, and paid for at a fixed rate per hour, or the time may be considered as part of the weekly schedule with commensurate freedom at other periods.

Vacations

There should be a consideration of twenty-four or more working days to all or certain members of the professional staffs. In certain institutions there is variation in the length of vacations based on length of service. As regards the former, twelve working days were allowed for less than one year of service, eighteen working days for one to five years, and twenty-six working days thereafter. The chief librarian and departments heads may be allowed one month and the professional staff eighteen working days.

That six weeks in summer, with time equal to one week during the winter holidays should be granted to the professional staff as a whole. In the case of the head librarian, reference librarian, bibliographer, and for the incumbents of the other posts requiring increasing scholarship, that the summer allowance be extended to the full faculty vacation.

Incentives may be given to library staff. A generous vacation allowance will help to offset the salary deficiency and attract those who might otherwise go into other fields of work. An arrangement of vacations to give the fullest benefit to all members of the professional staff will undoubtedly improve morale and encourage the staff.

The usual general holidays of the college are in addition to the vacation period. Provision should also be made for persons who change positions in the middle of the year or just before their annual leave is due.

2.5.2 *Promotions, Service Ratings, Tenure and Dismissal*

There are standing principles of promotions and dismissal, the methods of measuring personnel efficiency, and the regulations concerning tenure are well understood and applied in educational institutions also. Librarians in libraries have shown remarkably little interest in such matters.

Promotions

Libraries of higher education have a definite programme of promotion. The number of positions available and the size of the personnel budget in the average library are too small to provide for the advancement of staff members who are entitled to promotion on the basis of an excellent service record. When promotions in position are made, they are likely to occur as a result of a vacancy on the staff or the creation of a new position in the library. When it is impossible to advance a staff member in position or salary, it is sometimes possible to show recognition for good work by transferring the staff member to another position offering new experience, placing him in charge of a special experiment, giving him some supervisory duties, or putting him in charge of some general library activity. But in some institutions library staff is transferred to other departments which is a setback to library development and it hampers the work of library.

There are few principles to be followed for promotion:

1. Promotions in position should be made for reasons of merit and not on the basis of years in service. The merit principle is just, stimulates a high performance of work, and encourages the staff member to improve himself in service. Time promotion is never beneficial to library working.
2. Promotions should be based on records of fitness such as service ratings and not alone on the individual judgment of the librarian.
3. The qualifications and experience should be main consideration of the present staff with a view to promoting a qualified person to the vacant position.
4. When new appointments are made on the basis of qualifications to the junior levels of professional service.

Service Rating

It is better if a sub-committee with Librarian should be given this responsibility.

Service ratings of the library staff, are usually informal and are based on the personal opinion of the librarian or the librarian in consultation with the immediate supervisor of the staff member. A service rating properly embraces the factors of efficiency, character, and conduct.

Service rating is useful because —

(1) it assists supervisors in comparing the work of an assistant with the standards set up in the library, which is essential to a fair policy of promotion;

(2) it needs for transferring an assistant from one type of work to another;

(3) it helps in revealing weaknesses which can be corrected at the outset;

(4) it affords a basis for dismissal if weaknesses are not corrected;

(5) it helps to review staff talent and enables the librarian to assign special work to those persons who have special capacities; and

(6) it stimulates interest in self-improvement because the ratings are impartial and are shown to and discussed with the staff member.

Some precautions should be taken while making service ratio:

(a) Ratings should be clear and simple.

(b) Ratings should insure a fair appraisal of the qualifications and work of each person.

(c) Ratings should be uniform for those doing similar work.

(d) Ratings should be made at regular intervals, but not too frequently to allow for change.

(e) Ratings should be made by three raters when possible, or passed upon by a reviewing board.

(f) Ratings should be confined to past or present accomplishment.

(g) A general statement is often the most valuable part of a rating.

(h) Unfavourable ratings should be followed up with definite suggestions for improvement.

(i) Each rating should bear the signatures of the rater and of the department head, the date, and the name of the institution.

The usual frequency of rating is done once in a year or twice a year. Informal discussion between each assistant and his supervisor provides the soundest basis for staff development.

Harrington suggested the following factors for rating: (1) ability to follow instructions; (2) accuracy; (3) co-operativeness; (4) initiative; (5) job knowledge; (6) judgment;

(7) loyalty; (8) organization of work; (9) professional spirit; (10) quantity of work done; (11) reading habits; and (12) relationships with people.

Service Improvement of Library Staff

There are few factors which effect the service of a staff member:

(a) Amount of training;

(b) Quality of training;

(c) Working experience;

(d) Proper planning;

(e) Job satisfaction;

(f) Able supervision.

New Library Staff Member

It is an essential feature in the practice of acquainting the new staff member with the policies of the institute and of the library, with the general layout and special features of the library, and with the functions in the particular division of the library in which the new staff member will work. The new staff member may expect proper supervision. The new staff member familiarizes himself with the staff or divisional manual and with other published library instructions and guides. The new employee is given some opportunity for experience in all or most divisions of the library work.

Need for Staff Manual

Many libraries codify their policies and practices for staff use in what is commonly known as a staff manual. The staff manual is most useful in the large library where there is a considerable turnover in professional and clerical positions, they discovered that "in many of the smaller libraries, the staffs of which often consist of a single professional worker, such manuals are indispensible media of instruction for a constantly changing body of student workers". The size of the library is not the only factor of importance. Staff manuals were found useful where library practice varied from the standard codes and manuals, where student help was used to a large extent, and where members of the staff were frequently rotated from one position to another in a particular library.

The staff manual has five main functions:

1. New staff member is known with library's policies and to the specific duties in the division of service in which he will serve. Failure to follow library practices carefully and accurately cannot be excused.
2. Staff manual not only introduces him to the work in all departments of the library, but it stresses the educational objectives of the library and the proper professional attitude necessary to attain these objectives.
3. Manual is usually a cooperative affair. It affords an opportunity for experienced members of the staff to systematize and organize their work more effectively, to refine procedures, to eliminate duplication of duties, and to determine responsibility.
4. Staff manual promotes efficiency by insuring a proper sequence of work, by securing uniform procedures in routine.
5. It provides an effective medium for interpreting the library to the administration and the faculty.

Few libraries are not in favour of preparing staff manual because —

1. They tended to crystallize action and thought.
2. They allow little freedom of expression of professional attitude.
3. It is expensive and took much time to prepare.
4. Compilation is time consuming.
5. It does not prescribe the action of professional assistant in the instructional phrases of his work where individual judgments are most important.

The essential aim in a staff manual is to eliminate mere personal opinion in routines and in technical detail, to make sure that all elements of library efficiency have been given proper consideration and weight in the formation of a final judgment, and to insure that rules, regulations, and practices are based on a sure foundation of facts and sound educational principles.

Staff manuals are generally in two parts: (1) the general manual; and (2) the departmental manual. The general manual deals with policies and practices in the library as a whole. It is intended to give the new assistant a fundamental background knowledge of the library, its policies, internal organization and clientele, and particularly to inform him of his responsibilities and privileges as a member of the staff. The departmental manual, contains concrete and specific information about the work of the department. The relation of the department to other departments, and the way in which the work is carried on in the department. University library generally prepare departmental manual while other libraries prepare General Manual.

Structure (According to A.L.A.)

Introduction: Brief history of the library, statute or by-law, chart of organization, library committee of the faculty and its authority, and staff roster, with the titles of positions.

Administration

- General regulations: hours of opening, holidays, etc.
- Staff: appointment, tenure and promotion, schedules, vacations, leaves of absence, etc.
- Student assistants: selection, assignments, hours, rate of pay
- Clerical assistants: appointments, vacations, etc.
- Staff meetings: purpose, frequency, etc.
- Publicity
- Publications: annual report handbook, bulletin, miscellaneous
- Building: general regulations, assignment of carrels, seminar rooms, etc.

Acquisitions

- General: checking requests, verifying items, routines of ordering, accounts
- Exchange and gifts, records, acknowledgments
- Serials: records and routines
- Accessioning
- Binding and repairs

Cataloguing and Classifications

- Process: books, serials
- Files and filing
- Shelf-listing
- Inventory

Circulation: General and Reserve Books

- Specific objectives
- Desk routines and schedules, statistics
- Borrowers' register: faculty, students, alumni, and others
- Charging books
- Return of books
- Overdues
- Fines
- Lost books
- Shelving
- Relations to other divisions of work

Reference Service

- Administration and organization of the collection: books, periodicals, maps and atlases, newspapers, and vertical file material: pamphlets and pictures
- Interlibrary loan
- Special aid to faculty
- Records and statistics
- Relation to other divisions of work

Departmental Libraries

- Organization, names and locations, relations to central library
- Routines in cataloguing and classification, circulation, reference, research

Other Services

- Browsing room, dormitory libraries, seminar collections, service to alumni, service to townspeople.

Manuals are not static instruments of managerial instruction; it is revised timely. Thus it is best to prepare and publish the manual in some simple, inexpensive manner with provision for revisions.

Staff Meetings: Staff meetings are held time to time. The library staff meeting has a two-fold function, namely, to facilitate the general administration of the library and to improve the librarians in service. It is used primarily for the discussion of administrative problems and draw attention to the improvement of librarians in service.

The staff meeting provides an opportunity for the exchange of ideas on procedures, services, and problems. It is desirable to hold regular meetings, not less often than once a month, when all staff members can be present. In the medium-sized and large library, it may be possible to use library time for the meeting, arranging the schedule so that only one or two members are absent on regular duty, and providing for a rotation of work so that all members have an opportunity to attend most of the meetings.

The good administrator is interested in the promotion of staff discussion of all aspects of a problem, in the development of all points of view so that out of the exchange of ideas and convictions the very best plans will be adopted and perfected. Such discussions not only provide a balanced consideration of all facts before decisions are made, but promote interest and *esprit de corps.*

The staff meeting is truly effective if — (a) It is held timely; (b) using the meeting as critical approach; (c) aims to develop library activities; (d) fulfil educational objectives; (e) leads to professional ethics; (f) develop the techniques of policy.

In some institutes members of the faculty are invited to speak at the library staff meetings on recent developments in their fields.

2.5.3 *The Continuing Education for Librarians*

Even under the best of conditions, librarianship has a tendency to become routine and stale. There is routine work even in duties which are predominantly professional, and a great deal more of it in work that goes on behind the scenes. There is the ever present danger that the experienced non-progressive staff member, having adjusted himself to these conditions, will see the routines as ends in themselves and will be satisfied so long as his work moves smoothly.

The informal self-education programme of the library staff consists in the main of reading, attendance at every kind of real cultural entertainment, such as lecture and personal and professional meetings.

It is probably true that members of the staff do not keep up with their professional developments. Some devices may be proved useful *i.e.* as the routing of books and journals to each staff member, the allowance of library time for at least an hour of professional reading a week, and the provision for the discussion of professional literature at staff meetings have been found useful in stimulating professional reading.

(a) Facility of reading professional literature,

(b) Discussion on modern techniques and their application in staff meeting,

(c) Discussion on modern techniques by staff members with faculty members,

(d) Staff members should be encouraged for speaking and writing.

Hurt has developed an outline and suggestions: (1) secure a topical outline of the subject content of the field; (2) give brief consideration to the principal encyclopedic works; (3) locate and examine all guides to the literature of the field; (4) prepare a basic list of textbooks and other general works devoted to the entire field and examine some of the outstanding titles; (5) make a similar study of the books and monographs devoted to special phases of the subject; (6) give attention to the sources of printed materials.

There are other opportunities for cultural improvement, more personal and recreative, such as (a) Attending the lecture and music programmes or by organizations in the community. (b) Active participation in local, state, and national library meetings. (c) Inspection visits to other libraries are encouraged as one of the best means of improving staff performance and stimulating further study. (d) Membership in learned and educational organizations may be of equal importance, particularly to the librarian, because such bodies afford stimulating contacts and opportunities for the librarian to contribute to the broader group. (e) Visits to other libraries, publishing houses, and binderies provide opportunities for studying specific problems in actual practice and (f) afford interesting and valuable contacts.

In larger libraries provision is made for staff members to take courses up to a definite maximum limit of course hours each semester and staff members are generally excused from library duties during attendance at classes. In certain instances there are special inducements in the way of reduced fees for course.

2.5.4 *Librarian's Ethics*

The rapid development of library service and the consequent increase in the library personnel have compelled to call attention to the duties and obligations of librarians. Librarians in their working relations are not isolated individuals; they have professional problems in common which can be met most satisfactorily in a professional way. There is national professional association which has attempted to raise not only the level of professional competency and to improve working conditions for librarians but also to define the duties and obligations of its members toward the library governing authority, toward the community and society, toward the library profession.

The library as an institution exists for the benefit of a given constituency, whether it be the citizens of a community, members of an educational institution, or some larger or more specialized group. The term librarian applies to any person who is employed by a library to do work that is recognized to be professional in character according to standards established by the American Library Association.

A code should be prepared and applied specifically to all aspects of library work and to all members of the library staff, a fact which is sometimes overlooked by those who think of ethical codes simply in terms of staff relationships to the public at the charging desk.

Relation with governing authority: The librarian should perform his duties with realization of the fact that final jurisdiction over the administration of the library rests in the officially constituted governing authority. The chief librarian should keep the governing authority informed on professional standards and progressive action. Each librarian should be responsible for carrying out the policies of the governing authority and its appointed executives with a spirit of loyalty to the library. The chief librarian should interpret decisions of the governing authority to the staff, and should act as liaison officer in maintaining friendly relations between staff members and those in authority.

Touch with reading community: The chief librarian, aided by staff members in touch with the constituency, should study the present and future needs of the library, and should acquire materials on the basis of those needs. Provision should be made for as wide a range of publications and as varied a representation of viewpoints as is consistent with the policies of the library and with the funds available. It is the librarian's responsibility to make the resources and services of the library known to its potential users.

Relations within the library: The chief librarian should delegate authority, encourage a sense of responsibility and initiative on the part of staff members, provide for their professional development, and appreciate good work. Staff members should be informed of the duties of their positions and the policies and problems of the library.

The following factors may strengthen the relations among the librarian and the staff —

(a) Loyalty to follow workers;

(b) A spirit of courteous cooperation;

(c) Criticism of library policies;

(d) Acceptance of position;

(e) Contact and agreement are well honoured;

(f) No library resources should be put for personal use;

(g) No library dealing on personal behalf.

The interests of the library should be placed above personal interest. The staff member must bear in mind that it is not personal gain but opportunity for service which makes libarianship a profession.

Relation to his profession: A librarian should encourage only those persons with suitable aptitudes to enter the library profession and should discourage the continuance in service of the unfit. Librarians should have a sincere belief and a critical interest in the library profession. They should endeavour to achieve and maintain adequate salaries and proper working conditions. Librarian should have membership in library organizations and should be ready to attend and participate in library meetings and conferences.

The librarians should secure academic status on their own campuses and recognition of librarianship as a profession co-equal to that of teaching.

Relation to society: Librarians should encourage a general realization of the value of library service and be informed concerning movements, organizations, and institutions whose aims are compatible with those of the library. Librarians should participate in public and community affairs and so represent the library that it will take its place among (other) educational, social, and cultural agencies.

2.5.5 *Librarian and Library Staff*

In 20th century some universities were started with teaching functions in higher education and state libraries and it was found very necessary to establish a rich library equipped with useful material and adequate staff. The development of university requires above all the intellectuals and professional services of man and woman who have been trained for precisely such specific purpose. Hence trained and qualified librarian was desired to acquiring and organizing reading material and to make them easily available to students, teachers and other members of the university staff; and maintaining personnel management in which adequate number of staff serves the clientele effectively and with satisfaction.

It matters very little if a library has got a very valuable selection of rare books and manuscripts. It also matters very little if the library building is beautiful and provides all amenities necessary for a good library service. But if the staff is not qualified and its members are not dedicated to service or they lack cordiality and spirit of public service then the beautiful library building and valuable collection will serve no useful purpose.

Several commissions and committees are faced with several problems of higher education stated in 1917 to Kothari Commission, 1964 which vehemently emphasized the need of an organized library for a standard educational pattern. Dantan says "Librarianship today is highly complex profession requiring specific and detailed knowledge of many kinds; personal, financial and bibliographical". The Head of the library must, in short, be thoroughly familiar with all phases of modern librarianship.

The librarian, who is head of this organization, has together skilled, devoted and spirited colleagues around him and to give this group of men a form of a coherent team so that the task is successfully accomplished. The librarian assumes the role of a manager of personnel department.

A well qualified and adequate staff of a library is required for effective participation in the instructions to the students in the use of library tools and bibliographies, carrying out the objectives of the university in collaboration with the faculty and extending the use of library resources in education.

Baktar Mitra has explained three main functions of librarian:

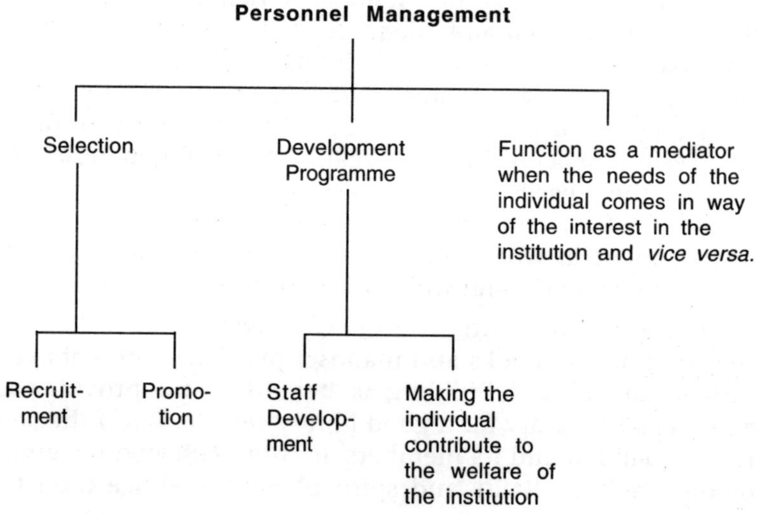

Librarian's Personality Traits

The librarian should have the following personality traits:

(i) Ability to delegate authority, estimate other capacity, and give clear instructions;

(ii) Power to keep the group to a common goal;

(iii) Capacity of the decision-making, habit of applying new methods and freedom from prejudice;

(iv) Courage of patience, accepting criticism, seek suggestions and praise work of the above staff members.

(v) A sense of humour and the faculty of observation of the objectives.

2.5.5.1 *Selection Procedure*

Usually the selection of librarian and the library staff is made by two methods:

1. By promotion;
2. By selection.

The person selected as Librarian should have good educational background, adequate training, professional consciousness, good personality, social ability and practical working experience.

In all the university libraries the post of librarian and the Deputy Librarian are statutory posts whereas the rest of the staff members are recruited by promotion or selection. The idea of recruiting the upper positions by open competitions is to post the best person in all respects at the most responsible position in library management. Though promotion posts are usually filled in by seniority. Efficiency in work comes not purely by seniority, but by Merit-cum-Seniority. Since the librarian is supposed to estimate the merit of the employees working under him, it is expected that he should be objective and unbiased in his evaluation procedure. It is desirable to develop on objective rating scale which could be used for promoting the library staff to some higher positions. The other rating principles were suggested by Harrington based on ability, accuracy, cooperation, initiative, job knowledge, judgment, loyalty, organizational capability, professional spirit, reading habits and social behaviour. It will be wise if no discrimination is made on the basis of caste, creed and sex.

In Indian universities, the selection of the post of Librarian, Dy. Librarian and the Assistant Librarian is made on the pattern similar to teaching staff. A selection committee is formed by the university executive committee. Selection committee consists of two experts, one Governor's nominee, one number of executive committee and the dean of the faculty. Vice-Chancellor act as the Chairman.

LIBRARIAN

Status of Librarian: Academic status implies formal recognition of processional librarians as members of the instructional and research staff in the form of assigned or equivalent faculty ranks and titles along with comparable salaries and privileges. The lack of such recognition is one of the major obstacles to recruiting a competent library staff. This problem was discussed in "Regional Seminar on library development in South Asia in 1960". The Seminar passed a resolution as below:

Description of Staff members	Nature of duties	Equivalent to faculty post and enjoying scale of:
1. Librarian	Supervisory	University Professor
2. Dy. Librarian	Sr. Professional	University Reader
3. Asstt. Librarian	Professional	University Lecturer
4. Sr. Library Asstt.	Professional Assistant	University Asstt. Lecturer
5. Technical Asstt.	-do-	-do-

The graduate staff have equal status with the academic staff. The librarian should be the officer of professional status and an ex-officio-member of all faculties. Whatever method be adopted to enable the librarian to be in touch with the faculties, he should present at or presented at all university meetings at which the annual financial allocations are to be decided. Carl M. White in his report of Delhi University Library says that the University (Delhi) was the first in India to fall in with an international trend to provide properly qualified librarian's service conditions comparable to those which apply to the rest of academic staff.

In India UGC appointed a library committee in 1958 under the chairmanship of Dr. S.R. Ranganathan which made several recommendations for the development of libraries including the qualifications and status of the university library and the staff. Executive Council of Delhi University passed a resolution on 26-04-1974 that "the pay scales for various categories of library staff should be at par with the corresponding scales of the teaching and research staff in the university in accordance with the recommendations of the S.R. Ranganathan Committee. The academic and professional qualifications prescribed for various categories of library staff are at par with these prescribed for corresponding faculty positions and that the library forms an integral part of academic community."

In universities professional staff has been put at par with other faculty members. Library staff has been designated as the library faculty, with all the rights and duties of the academic faculty in the university accruing to it. "In Great Britain, the status of librarians has been accepted at par with academic community." In public libraries librarian is put at par with class I Gazetted officers.

Librarian has academic competence. He is a master of subject, knowledge of effective use of teaching. Ability to anticipate, identify and define area of library service; interaction with colleagues and readers, increased competence in performance, effective library leadership. Ability on a scholar: Published or unpublished research work on a consultant or membership as an investigating or research committee. Effectiveness of library service; membership of university service; interaction with the faculty and studies; active participation in professional and scholarly organization; participation in the conferences, workshops and seminars; formal class study; independent study.

The position of the staff in library service is pivotal. The student body, faculty, and public using the library are peculiarly sensitive to its oversight, judgment, and enterprise.

2.5.5.2 *Qualifications of Librarian*

In discussing the role of the library in higher education, Dr. Louis R. Wilson has stated that it no longer considers the possession of an B.Lib.Sc. degree and the completion of one year of training in a library school sufficient equipment for the librarian who is to become a successful administrator, a wise counsellor in the use of books, and a force in shaping instructional policies. It insists that the librarian must be a person of imagination and initiative, that he must have a sound understanding of library administration and some subject field, and that he must know how to relate the use of the library to the educational programme of the institute. He must be a person of character, integrity. The librarian should possess the highest professional qualification and academic achievements.

Administrative Ability

The librarian should have the qualities of a good administrator; yet so important are the librarian's instructional relations to the faculty that this requirement is not so generally nor so permanently borne in mind as it should be. Dr. Harvie Branscomb correctly states that the administrative problems of the university library are more complex than those of the other type of libraries, but it must be stressed that one of the best services the librarian can render is to be a good administrator and leader in the library. It is essential that the librarian assume a large measure of administrative responsibility, including the supervision of the staff, the proper budgeting and expenditure of library funds, and the oversight of the library building. He must also hold the confidence of the library staff by his ability to develop a systematic organization of library work, to conduct the many types of transactions involving the administration and faculty, and to administer personnel, budgets, and services in a satisfactory manner. If the librarian is to have confidence in the staff, he must first have confidence in his own judgment. Indecision is fatal to good administration. Mutual confidence implies also that the librarian should have full confidence in the staff. The best evidence of his trust is the degree to which he is willing and able to delegate authority in work to be done. To be given a particular job to do and to have the satisfaction of seeing its final accomplishment is a great motivator. The librarian is also responsible for cultivating and maintaining an *esprit de corps*. There should be square deal among staff in matters of promotion and salary, in providing for the physical comfort of workers, in showing appreciation of satisfactory performance, and in being fair and impartial in criticism. Sometimes grievances and friction will show up in the staff for reasons which have nothing to do with the librarian's personal administration. It is then his job to determine the cause of the friction and to eliminate it firmly and openly.

Scholarly Talent

John D. Russell, says that the librarian must himself qualify as a scholar. He must be able to speak the language of scholars. He must know the ways in which scholars and specialists in various fields derive their knowledge and apply it to practical situations. The librarian should be a scholar in the sense of an eminent specialist or researcher. His work allows him no time for the continuous application to a single subject which is essential for the specialist. His working hours are long, he is interrupted at every turn, and his administrative and instructional duties in the library require him to switch his attention at a moment's notice to a new subject. As a librarian his function is not primarily to engage in teaching or research; he exists, rather, to aid those who are teaching, investigation, or writing. He should be familiar with the methods of research; be competent to instruct young people in the proper use of bibliographical tools, and be capable of advising in problems of research. He should be a person of broad interests with the intelligence and ability to appreciate and understand the problems of others.

Ability to Work with Readers

The ability of the librarian to work with reader is a requirement so widely recognized by the profession. The library fails to fulfil its complete function unless the librarian knows the readers' needs, how they may be met, and what readers expect of the library.

In a library, the librarian has a good many personal contacts with readers.

There are factors which greatly effect the success of a librarian in carrying his work:

1. Personal contact with readers. He should explain the library policies and regulations before readers.
2. Lectures should be organized to aware the readers with library working.
3. Servicing every reader equally without any prejudice feelings.
4. Librarian should have wide intellectual interests and a sympathetic understanding of the problems of readers.
5. Readers' opinion about staff members must be reviewed from time to time.
6. Faculty opinion about library staff must be sought by the librarian.

Professional Librarian

There are major criticisms that:

1. Most qualified persons are never keep there staff in confidence and mostly indulge with relations to faculty members.
2. Most academically qualified librarian has been proved less professional applitude until unless he is also fully professionally qualified.
3. It is claimed that librarian often lacks the vision and ability to play as active part in the formulation of the policies of the organization.

Library service is not judged exclusively on the technical aspects of its work. Library service is equally important like reference service, public relation etc. There are four aspects to be considered necessary for a librarian:

1. Reference work
2. Instructions in the use of library
3. Readers advisory service
4. Wide reading
5. Versatility in aiding readers

The librarian is naturally dependent on the various members of the teaching staff, each of whom is an authority on the literature of his subject, for the development of the collections to aid instruction and scholarship.

In other words, a greater degree of personality and mental attainment is required on the part of the librarian and the library staff for appointment to membership on the educational and policy-making committees of the college than for the faculty who have already an accepted place in the academic circle. It is an anomaly of the educational world that librarians everywhere should be actuated by such genuinely high motives of service.

All library science schools have developed comprehensive plans for selective admission, usually based on scholarship records, interviews and counselling procedures, and intelligence and aptitude tests. Higher standards of admission are required for entrance to library schools. A much greater emphasis than formerly is placed on personal qualities of leadership. The responsibility of the librarian and his staff in discovering readers with unusual abilities for library service has been stressed.

The improvement in the quality of library science school graduates by better methods of passing upon the fitness of applicants for admission and by creating greater interest in library service as a career for graduates of exceptional ability has been accompanied by a more precise definition of the requirements for pre-professional training. Fundamentally, this training should consist of a general education leading to a knowledge of broad fields of learning and a real understanding of the relevance of this knowledge to the intellectual and social structure of the world.

Many librarians feel that more than modification of the traditional training programme will be necessary to bring education for librarianship abreast of current library needs and thought. A widespread movement among librarians has sought in recent years to revise the entire programme by placing instruction in library methods on the undergraduate level as a prerequisite for admission to a year of professional graduate study.

For postgraduate work in librarianship, there are also noticeable improvements in the curricular offerings for librarians. One established practice is illustrated by the extent to which the facilities and resources of many departments are brought into the educational programme of the librarian. At the universities, a student may combine a major in library science with a minor in any special subject for which he is adequately prepared. The practice quite properly recognizes the close relationship that exists between librarianship and instruction in the various subject fields, and it emphasizes one way in which the subject field departments can contribute to the education of the superior librarian.

Finally, there is a strong trend toward taking graduate courses in the academic and professional fields which will lead to the doctor's degree. There is no general agreement that the Ph.D. is essential in the work of the librarian, but it is recommended on the ground that if the librarian is to work effectively with a group of scholars, he should have a scholarly training equal to theirs. The opinions of the leading university librarians support this thesis for the university librarian. On the other hand, it is equally necessary to point out that graduate work at the present time suffers from an overemphasis on narrow specialization, and that for the librarian, at least, there is little doubt that breadth of learning in many fields is more important than narrow concentration. It is not the intention here, however, to debate the question.

The pre-professional training of prospective librarians is being emphasized and more specifically defined. The educational programme in postgraduate library instruction is placing more emphasis on the broader aspects of librarianship and less on the training of specific skills, on the acquisition of educational and social understanding on the part of librarians, and on the training of librarians in methods of research. There is considerable pressure on younger librarians to seek higher academic and professional training leading to the doctorate. All these efforts have improved the quality of librarians and are helping to make librarianship a more integral part of education than it has been in the past.

2.5.5.3 *Educational Level*

The fundamental basis of selection is an obvious one: to secure the best person for the salary the library is able to afford. Some of the qualifications taken into account in the attempt to secure the best person are these:

1. **Education**: The minimum training required of a person who is planning a professional career in library work is graduation from a recognized college or university and one year of library training from a library school. Consideration is given to the undergraduate institution from which the candidate has received a degree and the quality of the work he did there. If the work to be performed falls somewhere between the classification of professional and clerical duties and yet calls for a broader educational background than is expected of a clerical assistant.

2. **Experience**: The amount of professional training and experience required depends in the last analysis upon the position to be filled. Librarians prefer experienced staff members for the more advanced positions and for types of work involving instructional duties with students and faculty. There is little danger that they will lack for a chance to gain experience. In the long run, it is to the advantage of the library to fill the larger number of its professional positions with superior library school graduates rather than to employ less able librarians whose claim for consideration is a year or so of experience. Librarians seem to prefer staff members between the age of eighteen to thirty in the initial appointments. The age limit in the original appointment may be extended to thirty-three to forty for the more important positions, but in general, librarians are reluctant to make such appointments beyond this age group.

Methods of Selection

Having that the chief librarian selects and nominates the library staff for appointment and that staff members are selected on the basis of their training, experience, and personal qualifications, there remains for consideration the matter of how the library personnel is employed and what methods are used for insuring the best selection possible for a given position. When a vacancy occurs for which there is no eligible candidate within the library system, the librarian prepares a description of the position for submission to the placement officers of library schools and to other sources of recruitment.

In most of the libraries, where the turnover in staff is comparatively small, there is no urgent need for application forms. When the librarian has selected tentatively what he considers the best possible candidate or candidates from the recommendations of library schools and other placement agencies. The information about prospective candidates is then conveniently at hand and in a form that can be readily scrutinized in the event there arises an unexpected vacancy.

The personal interview, properly conducted, is an important method for getting a line on personal qualities which are difficult to judge on paper. Ordinarily one thinks of the interview as a device of use to the employer only, but the interchange which takes place in the course of the interview and the opportunity for visiting and seeing the library. The average library interview is a less complicated affair, but it is nevertheless susceptible of deliberate planning.

Appointment of the Staff

The final steps in the appointment will vary in different institutions, depending on who exercises the final authority. Generally speaking, however, the process of selection is completed when the librarian's nomination is approved and the chief executive officer of the organization has notified the candidate of his appointment to the library staff. Ordinarily all first-year appointments are for one year only, with the hope and expectation that if the candidate's services are satisfactory and he or she is content the contact will be renewed.

2.5.5.4 *Size of the Staff*

There are certain variables which determine the size of the staff in a particular institution: (1) the rate of acquisition; (2) the number of readers, students and faculty members; (3) the nature of the teaching programme; (4) the hours of opening, the number of service units, and the organization of procedures in the library; and (5) the nature of the building programme.

According to the A.L.A. Classification and Pay Plans, library would belong in Class 4 and would have a minimum staff of three professional persons for the first 800 service units, plus one more for each additional 500 units, plus the librarian. The number of professional positions in the example used, therefore, would be nine or possibly nine and one-half in full-time equivalent.

2.6 Staff Training

The old concept of preservation has gone and now it is considered as a professional which takes into consideration the concept of promotion. Libraries have been compared with growing organism, and therefore, the first thing which must be aimed at is the all-round growth and development of this library-organism. Consequently, library is to be cared for and nourished with the spirit of a human being. Librarian of any university library is, therefore, considered as the father-figure, and is expected to discharge all the duties and responsibilities that a father discharges to his child.

Libraries were few with small collection and felt no need for a professional man. The teachers or the other non-professional persons were made in-charge of library in addition to their own duties. The librarian was responsible to keep the books in safe custody and held personally responsible for the loss of the books. Melwil Dewey could visualise and give practical shape of fundamentals of librarianship. Dewey broke the old tradition and created a class of professional librarians through formal education. He established the first school of library science in 1887 in Columbia College, New York, which expanded to 32 well established branches in U.S.A. In India W.C. Borden, a State librarian at Baroda started a training class in 1911. It was open to working librarians only. The other course was started by A. Dichenson, a Punjab University librarian in 1915. It was a apprentice course and a run part time till 1947. In 1929 Ranganathan started a Certificate Course in Library Science from the platform of Madras Library Association and diploma course in 1931 in Madras University. It was a full-time course and upgraded to a post-graduate course in 1937 and now as B.Lib.Sc. Course, where the course leads to first degree. It nearly always contains a 'general studies' element in addition to the library and information science element.

At present several centres; universities, colleges, technical institutions, associations and private and government bodies are imparting different type of trainings: Master of Library and Information Science; Bachelor of Library and Information Science; Certificate in Library Science Course and Diploma of Library Science and other research training like M.Phil. and Ph.D. etc.

Library have to serve people of any community in their educational development by way of efficient information retrieval. This object can be easily achieved if suitable grades and well trained librarians are produced. Unprecedented expansion of educational institutions, democratization of social life have caused the steady growth of literacy, explosion of knowledge have created a great need for qualified hands in libraries. Librarian provide in-service training to the semi-professionals or non-professionals and train them in traditional way of training which is given by the librarian without conducting formal classes.

Librarianship is not a pure science. It is an applied science of knowledge. Generally speaking library science may be divided in two parts:

1. Formal education;
2. In-service education based on experience.

Formal education is given in two levels:

1. Lower or elementary training:
   (a) Certificate Course (C.L.S.)
   (b) Diploma Course (D.L.S.)
2. High level training:
   (a) Degree Course (B.L. & I.S.)
   (b) Master's Course (M.L. & I.S.)
   (c) M.Phil.
3. Research level:
   (a) Doctoral Course (Ph.D.)
   (b) Post-Doctoral Course (D. Litt.)

During the last decades a number of universities have started courses without providing the essential requirements like academic identifications, fulltime teaching staff, professional books and journals, accommodations etc. But today library education is more specific and conducted in greater number of centres:

1950	:	6 Centres
1960	:	11 Centres
1970	:	45 Centres
1974	:	84 Centres
1984	:	91 Centres
2000	:	156 Centres

There are few centres which are not independent and run under the university library and teaching work is conducted by the library staff. In such centres Librarian has been the Head of the Department of Library Science in addition to his own duties. Library staff is engaged in teaching work in his duty hours or in their off timings. Some centres have engaged part time teachers. "Part-time teachers are an anachronism in Indian Library Education." In some universities no allowance is paid to the library staff for the teaching. It is obvious that the over-worked library staff, if engaged in regular teaching during library hours, would teach not more than pouring out the drale and dried material which defeats the very purpose of higher learning, research and the training. Teaching is an art and successful teaching require sustained layout in accumulation of material from various sources on the part of the teacher and novel of way of delivering these goods to students. It is, therefore, essential that a separate staff should be recruited for imparting successful teaching to students. When the attention and labour is divided, the output is affected to that extent.

As qualified and dedicated teachers are hardly available, the courses are suffering for want of competent teachers. The development of library education depends on the quality of teachers. Even the full time teachers have little experience of teaching methods. It resulted in lowering down the standard of teaching. Absence of qualified teachers and encouragement to part-time teachers have created a vacuum in the country. Universities are taking interest in opening more and more faculties but less attention has been given towards equipping them properly by providing good teachers, sufficient accommodation, reading material and equipments.

2.6.1 *Training Programme*

Training programme is undertaken in three levels:

(i) Training for semi-professionals;

(ii) Training for professionals;

(iii) Training in research.

Training for semi-professional training admission is different at various training centres: At one centre it is High School, while Higher Secondary at the other centre and Intermediate at the third centre. This training is conducted with various types of name of the courses *i.e.* 'Refresher Course', 'Certificate Course', 'Elementary Course', 'Library Assistant Course', and the 'Proficiency Course' etc. Further, there is diversity in the various aspects of training courses, such as duration of training, timings of training, number of students admitted.

The training courses are also different in various centres. Mostly following courses are adopted in semi-professional trainings:

Courses

1. Cataloguing
2. Classification
3. Organization and Administration
4. Library Service

Diploma Course is also conducted by various centres. This course is suitable for the semi-professionals. Diploma course is somehow more extensive than the Certificate Course. It has some detailed course also. Its duration is one year, but its standard is below the Bachelors Course. It is also not recognized by the University Grant Commission and as such by the Universities also. Before 1964 the UGC derecognized these courses and recognized the Degree Courses only. At present there are only few centres which are running these courses.

Training for the Professionals: The training for Junior Professionals should be degree level and the course for the professionals should be of Post Graduate Course. They are called B.Lib.I.Sc. and M.Lib.I.Sc. The objective of university degree course was described by various scholars:

1. Professional training assure ourselves to be fit in the context of society.
2. Laster, Ashiern says that it nobles the librarian to grasp the subject-matter of the library and manage the library intelligently.
3. Education for librarianship cannot be considered in a vacuum, but has to be related to the library development in a particular country.
4. Library education is pragmatic approach. Education for librarianship is shaped on the simple principle as to what is required of them.

In addition to the above objective, degree course is conducted with the objective to prepare the students for advance studies, underlying techniques and skills of librarianship, culture and social relations to undertake the bibliographic control of literature and to give the student an understanding of the basic principles and fundamental laws of library science.

The degree course is generally conducted by the universities or its colleges. Every state have training centres of their own. Before 1965 universities were conducting Diploma courses which were converted into B.Lib.I.Sc. The advise of UGC, Advisory Committee for libraries in its report on 12-11-1958 recommended that "the government of India should set up an expert committee consisting of professional libraries for suggesting complete recognization of the syllabus of library diploma course". University Grant Commission also appointed a library committee in 1957 under the Chairmanship of Dr. S.R. Ranganathan to advise the UGC about the development of libraries and their organization and also consider the problem of teaching of library science in various universities.

IASLIC also had few seminars on "Education for Librarianship in India" under the Directorship of S. Bashiruddin. UGC formed a Review Committee in 1961 under the

Chairmanship of Dr. Ranganathan. This committee was given the responsibility to review the standards of teaching and research in library science. The committee reviewed the necessity of setting up separate full-fledged departments of library science so as to put a stable footing and avoid confrontation with library staff. The committee also laid down the objective of various type of courses and suggested uniform syllabus for the courses to serve as guidelines for library science centres. A seminar was held at the Department of Library Science in Delhi University on "Teaching of library science". Another step in the development of library education was "Survey of University of Delhi", department of library science, conducted by A. Gelfand. The survey laid down some objectives of teaching courses in library science. B.Lib.I.Sc. course is a professional course which is conducted by various universities in India. The minimum qualification for admission is graduation.

The main condition for admission, applicable in various universities, is as under:

(i) Minimum qualification for admission is graduate of recognized university.

(ii) Preference to the candidate having library working experience.

(iii) The candidate serving in any institution or society has to submit the employer's permission to join the course.

(iv) The candidate admitted in B.Lib.I.Sc. is not allowed to join any other course of the university.

Course

The curriculla prescribed in all the universities are almost similar. In almost all the courses, more stress is given on the theory and practicals of classification and cataloguing and nearly 300 to 400 marks are allotted to these subjects. There are some additional papers like "Book Selection and Physical Bibliography", "Reference Service", and "Information Science". Each paper contains 100 marks. The practical papers of cataloguing and classification is a written examination where candidates are examined on practical problems. There are few centres where practical examination by external examiner is held. Some centres have made necessary provision for Viva-Voce examination. In such cases, candidates are evaluated by the department on 100 marks (50 marks for Viva-Voce and 50 marks for class work). The B.Lib.I.Sc. examination comprises 800 marks. Information Science as separate paper has not been prescribed by most of the centres in B.Lib.I.Sc. course.

M.Lib.I.Sc. Course: The M.Lib.I.Sc. course was started in 1948 for the first time in India. It was in 1946 when Government of India recognized librarianship as an academic profession. M.Lib.I.Sc. is a postgraduate degree conducted by the university. It is open to the students holding the bachelors' degree in library science. So far professional training in library science is concerned, M.Lib.I.Sc. Course is the highest degree in Indian universities. The advisory committee for libraries states the following objectives of M.Lib.I.Sc. course:

(i) To train the librarians for administrative posts in one of the major types of libraries, large public library systems, university libraries, special libraries — by objectives, principles and special problems of organization and administration.

(ii) To offer specialization in different fields of librarianship.

(iii) To train the persons in method of research.

(iv) To provide teachers of library science for the universities.

The aim of this course is not merely to teach the established techniques and practices, but to prepare the students to meet the new situations with new library techniques and practices. Assimilation, adaptation and application are the basic aims of imparting knowledge and instruction in M.Lib.I.Sc. They should be so equipped in the modern methodology in library science as to become library engineers rather than simple mechanics.

Dr. Ranganathan in his report of Review Committee, has stated that M.Lib.I.Sc. course should be conducted with the aim to acquaint the students with organization and development of universe of subjects, research methods, knowledge of reading material, documentation list, advance library techniques, management of selective type of libraries and Information Systems.

Advisory Committee is of the opinion that M.Lib.I.Sc. course should be limited to some type of jobs and kinds of libraries while Review Committee does not refer, to any particular job or kind of library but various techniques applied in various kinds of libraries.

In view of the syllabus of the M.Lib.I.Sc. course being quite extensive specialized knowledge is expected. In the degree course, topics like library development or library movement are included. But in postgraduate degree the following subjects are included in syllabus:

(i) Advanced classification : theory and practice;

(ii) Advanced cataloguing : theory and practice;

(iii) Universe of knowledge;

(iv) Information science/technology;

(v) Information technology: Automation in libraries; and

(vi) Specialization in public libraries or special libraries in academic libraries;

Or

(vii) Dissemination of knowledge/Archival libraries;

Or

(viii) Library service or Literature survey;

(ix) Viva-Voce.

Doctor of Philosophy or Research in Library Science: Library science has become a specific discipline and several centres are conducting researches in various fields of the librarianship. Universities are offering research training with the objectives of imparting knowledge and skills in research methods. The minimum qualification for admission in this programme is Master's Degree in Library Science. Ranganathan started doctoral programme in Delhi University for the first time and produced one Ph.D. The research programme is conducted by qualified permanent faculty Professor.

Organization of Library Science Department: Library science department has discrimination with other departments. It is a department similar to science and other technical departments. It has its specific character. Library science is not mere a art.

It is a science. The organization of the department requires the following prerequisites:

(i) Teachers Chamber;
(ii) Classrooms;
(iii) Practical laboratories;
(iv) Seminar room;
(v) Display room (demonstration room);
(vi) Departmental library;
(vii) Reading room.

The UGC Review Committee has laid down the following minimum condition for well-equipped department of Library Science:

1. The Lecture rooms;
2. One practical and laboratory room;
3. One reading room;
4. Staff room for individual teachers;
5. One room for demonstration and use of library equipment;
6. One office room.

Field work: Library science students undertake field work *i.e.* practical library administrative and operational work in university or the attached libraries. Mostly trainees are deputed to the various wings of university library for practical work under the direct guidance of library staff. In some centres trainees are directed to work in local big libraries. This programme impart practical training to the trainees in the field of library service.

2.6.2 *Selection Procedure*

It is a common experience that in all types of professions and occupations some are brilliantly successful and some are miserable failure. Why is this so? Because many of them are 'misfits' for the occupation they are employed in. If for example, a man of ordinary skill and intelligence is employed in job which calls for high degree of these qualifications, he will develop nervous incompetence and will be constant fear of exposure and dismissal. On the other hand, a highly capable man, if he is employed in a job which does not suit him temperamentally may shirk the work. All this will lead to poor production both in quality and quantity and to high labour turnover.

The heart of personnel management is the selection and appointment of notably good new staff members. Each poorly qualified person lowers the morale of the staff and effectiveness of the library. Administrator should make all efforts to free the library from persons who impede it and learn from the mistakes.

Usually the selection of library staff is made by two methods: (1) by promotion and (2) by selection.

The person selected as librarian should have good educational background, adequate training, professional consciousness, good personality, social ability and practical working experience. Though promotion posts are usually filled in by seniority; however, efficiency in work comes not purely by seniority, but seniority-cum-merit. The librarian should be objective and unbiased in his evaluation procedure. It is desirable to develop an objective rating scale which could be used for promoting the library staff to some higher positions. Harrington suggested rating principles based on ability, accuracy, cooperation initiative, job knowledge, judgment, loyalty, organizational capability, professional spirit, reading habits and social behaviour.

Basis of Selection: It is to select the best suited candidate within the allotted and afforded salary. The selection is made, taking in consideration, on two main factors: suitability and the salary. The suitability of the candidate is based on the following basis:

1. **Education**: Candidate should be more educated. Education mean the higher qualifications or the academic background of the candidate. Each job has its essential and desired qualifications.

In academic libraries, the education varies from posts to posts and institution to institution in various states. The librarian should essentially have the knowledge of library operations and techniques, principles of library administration and organization, library reading material, objectives of higher education and research methods, professional training should also be considered while selecting the librarian. So far semi-professionals are concerned, the candidate should possess bachelors degree and non-professionals the first stage educational degree respectively.

(a) *Academic qualification*: Library employee cannot be but similar to office clerk as the qualifications of library staff are much more and specific in nature. The qualification of library staff should be at par with teachers. The librarian, the reference librarian, the classifier and the documentalists in a university library taken together should be fully familiar with the highways and byways of knowledge in every subject.

(b) *Professional qualification*: The librarian and his professional staff should also have professional qualifications of an equally higher order. The standard of professional qualification is indicated by the directorate, the M.Phil., M.Lib.I.Sc. and B.Lib.I.Sc. degree attained now-a-days by a successful persuit of post-graduate study in library science in a university.

The UGC committee further recommended the following qualifications:

UNIVERSITY LIBRARY

Post	Status	Qualification	Desirable	Grade
Librarian	Professional	M.Lib.I.Sc. II Class or M.A. or M.Sc. II; and D.Lib.Sc. or B.Lib.I.Sc.	Ph.D. in Lib. Sc. or in other subject	I
Documentalist	"	"	—	II
Dy. Librarian/ Asstt. Librarian	"	"	(UGC Net)	II
Reference Librarian	"	"	(UGC Net)	II
Chief Classifier	"	"	(UGC Net)	II
Chief Cataloguer	"	"	(UGC Net)	II
Maintenance	"	"	(UGC Net)	II
Librarian	Junior	B.Lib.I.Sc. and B.A. or B.Sc. or B.Com. II	—	III

(*Contd.*)

Post	Status	Qualification	Desirable	Grade
Asstt. Classifier	Junior	B.Lib.I.Sc. and B.A. or B.Sc. or B.Com. II	—	III
Asstt. Cataloguer	"	"	—	III
Accession Librarian	"	"	—	III
Periodicals Librarian	"	"	—	III
Circulation Librarian	"	"	—	III
Sr. Library Asstt. (in any section but not in reference section)	Professional Assistant	"	—	III
Jr. Librarian Asstt. (in any section but not in reference section)	Semi-Professional	C.Lib.Sc./D.Lib.Sc. Higher Secondary Certificate	—	IV

State University, New York has fixed the following criteria of the qualification:

1. Master of "Subject matter" (Lib.Sc.).
2. Effectiveness in teacher (*i.e.* effectiveness of performance as librarian).
3. (a) Ability to anticipate, identify and define area of library service;
   (b) Interaction with colleague and readers;
   (c) Increased competence in performance;
   (d) Effective library leadership; and
   (e) Competence to perform in positions of increased responsibility.
4. Ability as a scholar:
   (a) Published and unpublished research; and
   (b) Work as a consultant or membership as an investigate or research committee.

5. Effectiveness of library service:
   (a) Membership of university bodies;
   (b) Interaction with the faculty and students; and
   (c) Active participation in community affairs.
6. Continuing growth:
   (a) Membership and participation in professional and scholarly organization;
   (b) Participation in the conferences, workshops and seminar;
   (c) Formal class study; and
   (d) Independent study.

The academic status has been granted to professional librarians in the universities in many countries abroad. U.K. in 1962 has accepted the academic status of a librarian at par with academic community. In 1974 an agreement was signed between Department of Education and Science and the UGC in U.K., in which new scales were also applied to librarians similar academic related scales. UGC in India accepted the status of Library professionals at par with teachers since 1979.

Fixation of the qualifications for the recruitment of the library personnel are not uniform on all India basis. However, some universities has adopted their own qualifications set aside the UGC qualification. On the other hand some universities have adopted higher qualifications.

2. Experience: In addition to professional and academic qualifications, there are other important factors to be considered necessary for the selection of library staff. Persons having an experience of library working are required on senior and technical positions as well as the positions of instructional duties dealing with students and the researchers. In India most of the libraries are understaffed and pull-on the work with inadequate staff. To run the library satisfactorily and providing service to the maximum satisfaction of the readers, the libraries prefer an experienced librarian and library staff. In many libraries trained graduates are appointed on apprentice basis and made regular after an experience of 2-3 years in the same library.

3. Personal Traits: Each person has some general traits and some specific traits. In a business enterprise, personality counts much as it attracts the customer. Similarly librarian with impressive personality traits are preferred. Personal traits include intelligence, integrity, good health, pleasing voice and manner, attractive appearance, pleasing personality, interest in people, imagination, dependability, courtesy, energy, dignity, ability and forcefulness. More important traits are distinctive cultural background, physical health, sympathy and imagination, spiritual comprehension and tastes, and genuine interest in the profession.

Reader wants sweet voice and helpful attitude of the library staff and as much any worker with good habits and helpful nature gain success and up the image of the library.

2.6.2.1 *Selection Methods*

Generally there are three fundamental methods of selection which may prove more traditional, natural and career testing.

1. Traditional Methods

(a) **Self selection method**: The boy himself expresses his desire to serve a particular type of job. But it is rare that a boy of today is able to say what he wants to do in future. When we ask any boy, he says, "I don't know my future." But in some cases, boy instinctively like certain jobs and express his aptitude for them. Thus boy's emotional make-up, the choice of his job can be ascertained.

(b) **Guardian selection method**: Guardian select the job of their choice and give little care to the choice of the boy. They don't take in consideration the liking of the boy. On the other hand, all educated and enlightened parents provide all facilities of education and training of the job well suited to their children.

(c) **Teacher selection method**: The third testing method is the teacher who knows the student for a long time and make a psychological reading of the liking of the student. Teacher is also to discover some special qualities of his student, but his guidance will be more effective in scholarly achievement being the examination as a last valuation method. But it need to near contact between the teacher and taught. But the present educational system is not suitable for the career selection of a boy and need great modifications.

2. Scientific Methods of Selection

Every person has some inward talents and also certain outward environment of fortune and a combination at the two. There is the doctrine of determining which is based on three factors: (i) heredity, and inheritance; (ii) environmental circumstances and (iii) influence of family, religion and race.

There are various tests applied in scientific method:

(a) **Intelligence tests**: These tests are devised suitable to ascertain the mental alertness and capacity to grasp things in employees. With the help of such tests, the suitability of the employee for a particular task is traced. They possess value in indicating the probable relative native abilities of individuals who have experience about the same environment and school opportunities. They are thus helpful in appraising man's qualities and placing him in a suitable job. General intelligence tests are devised to find out intellectual capacity. For proficiency tests, the questions of practical nature are put. Questions should sufficiently be given in order to fair and accurate measurement of ability and capacity.

When a vacancy occurs and the librarian finds no eligible candidate within the library, the librarian calls for the candidates through several sources and asks the candidates to be present for interview. The personal interview is an proper method to judge the personality qualities, while the written test helps in judging the intellect and capability.

There are few tests apply for measuring the intelligence of the candidate:

1. SRA Adaptability tests. (Merit ability)
2. Thurstone mental alertness test. (Learning ability test)
3. Wesman Personnel classification test. (Mental ability test)

(b) **Aptitude test**: Aptitude tests are devised to findout the particular aptitude or special ability of a person in a particular job. A job analysis is required to conduct the test. It is easy to find out the technical ability, cataloguing, classification, photography etc. but very difficult to find out the aptitude or inner desire towards a particular job. There may be circumstances that a person has adopted a job and properly skilled for, but it does not mean that he likes the same job. Aptitude test find out skill in working, perception, physical endurance and meanness in work. These tests have been very popular in business enterprises but less practiced in libraries.

(c) **Psychological tests**: There are chances that a person have a high degree of intelligence and special aptitude, but not necessarily the proper temperament to suit the job. Psychological test help in finding out self-confidence, aggressiveness, sensitiveness, determination timidity, assertiveness, honesty, cheerfulness, cooperativeness, and sociability. We may trace out the misfits by applying this test. Generally these tests are taken where mass recruitments are made.

(d) **Merit rating**: Merit rating is usually used in placement of workers on the job suited to their talents and in promoting the staff to higher position. Rating method help in evaluating the quality of work done, job knowledge, cooperation, accuracy, loyalty, productiveness, creative ability, relation with fellow workers etc. It betters the morale of the workers because they are rewarded for their superior qualities. This method recognizes the merit, skill and rightly recompensate by promotion to higher posts. Moreover, librarian has full knowledge about a person and apply it at the time of promotions and recruitment of staff. But merit rating system, being a pure technique, is carefully handled.

Rating systems are of two types: Informal and formal. Informal procedure is based on the personal opinion of the librarian who finalizes his opinion after consulting the supervisors. Informal rating also involves the holding of timely meeting of the supervisors, librarians and the administrators and discussions are made on the abilities of various members of the staff. Formal system involves questionnaire of objective type questions asked to the individual and thus ability is checked.

2.6.2.2 *Selection Sources*

This is an age of specialization and few jobs have specifications that cannot be met from the inventory of present skills. Personnel department should follow such policy which may look forward and contact outer agencies outside the library. They are enumerated as under: (a) Employment agencies; (b) Advertising agencies; (c) Field trips; (d) Training schools; (e) Professional meetings and conventions; (f) Executive search; (g) Internal search; (h) Foreign sources.

1. **Employment agencies**: Employment agencies are working everywhere and in every country. These agencies in position to put an employer in contact with a selected number of prospective workers. From a survey it has been found that libraries are taking services of exchanges in the recruitment of Class III and Class IV employees. But professionals are not available in exchanges. Hence, more of semi-professionals and non-professionals selected through exchanges. But now employment agencies are being avoided and the post is advertised for open selection.
2. **Advertising agencies**: Most of the libraries follow the sources of advertisement. Posts are advertised with their qualification, salary, condition of service, method of selection etc. Advertisements may be more useful if they are placed in professional magazines. Generally newspapers are popular media, but several journals are also used for the purpose. Advertisements also reveals the status, goodwill and the position of the organization. This source is very useful to the persons seeking job independently and of his choice.

   Library being a technical organization requires technical hands which cannot be pooled by local efforts and such all posts of technical nature in particular are advertised in popular magazines and newspapers. The main advantage of advertising in newspaper is that a large number of replies may be received, out of which it is possible to interview only a few.

3. **Training schools**: Recruitment from training institutions is the well established practice of thousands of libraries in developed countries. Libraries that require large number or a single person for continuing or apprenticeship programme usually request the training school. Selection out of the schools successful professional, differ library to library. Some libraries call applications from the applicants undergo training, while other book their advance request for recruiting the meritorious candidates in the list of successful candidates.

In Indian Libraries no uniform pattern of selection sources is followed. Training schools neither provide any such service, nor the libraries are taking any help from them.

Professional meetings or conventions: Meetings are another over related source of professional employees. There are clever librarians who utilize a chance of consulting other colleagues at a professional gathering and try to select the best, out of many attending the meeting or on the recommendation of other librarians. They realize that good and senior professionals attend such a meeting in order to participate in its work not to find a job. Librarian personally attend these meetings or send other senior members of the library to represent the library. They may well pickup new employees. In India, there are few librarians who take advantage of meeting and conventions for selection purpose. Most of the librarians are not empowered to select any person individually or offer appointment officially. They are recommendatory officers.

2.6.2.3 *Selection by Promotion*

Libraries should frame a selection policy. Promotion is a good media of selection. It has been a healthy tradition in big concern to give a chance to its old and experienced persons to serve on immediate higher posts. Promotion policy is accepted in clerical, supervisory and even managerial ranks in many organizations. A promotion plan must be definite, systematic, fair and adhered to rigidly. The basis of the promotion should be functional-organizational-statement developed after a systematic job analysis, his position, his line of promotion, requirement for the next job and the salary.

The promotion should not be provided only on the basis of the opinion or assessment of the officer, it should be based on objective data. Personal data of every employee should be prepared which includes the points: (a) age; (b) marital status; (c) education; (d) experience; (e) special ability; (f) physical condition; and (g) behaviour and dealing with other employees.

Promotion is movement to a position in which responsibilities and prestige are increased. It involves an increase in rank and regarded as a change that result in higher earning. But it is not always essential. Gilbreth has suggested "three position plan". Each position is related to other positions — one from which employees are promoted and another to which promotions are made and still others to which incumbents may be promoted. In many libraries, sophisticated psychological tests are being used to observe and evaluate rank-and-file employees in order to locate future managerial ability. Other criteria, such as recommendations of supervisors. Seniority, and excellence of technical skills are still given appropriate weight, psychologically patterned series of tests are becoming more popularly need in an attempt to locate supervisory and managerial ability among non-supervisory employees. They are conducted in three ways:

(a) **Voluntarily**: Where employees voluntarily participate in the personal assessment programme that consists of one and half days lists and group discussions.

(b) **Group discussion**: Where actual managerial situations are stimulated. A group of the employees of executive positions are given problem and told to make its own decisions and find its own solutions.

(c) **Expert observation**: Where a professional expert evaluate good appraisal of leadership skills.

Variables to be considered for promotion policies:

1. **Attitudes and actions of employees**: More employees are likely to feel more secure and to identify their own long-term interests with those of the library when

they can anticipate first chance at job opportunities. On the other hand, general application of the promoted from within policy may encourage mediocre performance.

2. **Level of specialization**: In many libraries, the principal source for qualified employers may be ranks of present employees who have received specialized training.
3. **Participation by employees**: In a library emphasis is given on participation by employees at all level as a general man-power policy. New employee from outside fails to handle the position being unknown and unexperienced in the work and service of the library and his participation become ineffective.
4. **Need for originality and initiative**: A library prefer his own employees for a training which suits to the library. If facilities to the employees are assumed, new persons can be imparted.
5. **Seniority principle**: In most of the libraries, if the employee is given a promotion from within, seniority is considered.

2.6.2.4 *Seniority as Basis*

The policy of promotion from within be implemented through the practice of seniority. Seniority means length of service. It may be calculated as the time elapsed since the employee's name first appeared on the payroll, or it may be measured as the number of days of service since that date. Frequently, absence from the payroll for extended periods caused loan of seniority, and an employee laid off who fails to respond or is available for employment when he is called, loses his seniority. Seniority is frequently a basis for promotion and probably should be since it is based upon the principle that those who have served loyally for a long period merit recognition; seniority must not be adhered to rigidly because it is an arbitrary check on the younger worker and if continued, may result in a somewhat stagnant staff.

Seniority is established by provisions as consideration of range of seniority rights. A seniority may be: whole library-wise, department-wise or section-wise or trade-wise. Some practice goes so far as to provide rate bracket seniority, in which seniority employees in each rate range or salary classification enjoy seniority rights with respect to work assignments, layoff and recall and promotion.

Merits: Seniority-policy is suitable because it frequently play an important role in layoff procedure. Employees with heavy family responsibilities and favourites received preferential treatment and it provides a fairly objective decision rule.

On the other hand seniority creates many problems for the librarian and administrators as it encourages half-hearted performance and inefficiency; it seriously interfere in necessary reductions to discontinue unprofitable operations; it creates chaotic as members of unions negotiate for their seniority; and it encourages the retention of older employees.

2.6.2.5 *Ability-vs-Seniority (Seniority-cum-Merit)*

Both are important. To follow a single policy cannot be a rightful action. But on the other hand they should be qualified for such jobs. Hence, seniority governs when other relevant qualifications are equal.

There are several methods applied to determine the ability of employees *i.e.* (a) written test; (b) performance test; (c) cautions and warnings; (d) commendations; (e) age; (f) experience; (g) production records; (h) meritration; (i) education and training; (j) physical examinations; (k) absence and tardiness records.

Though seniority is widely accepted as a major consideration in promotions, but it is not the sole determinant. Generally it is decisive only if the senior applicant is qualified or is equal to any other qualified applicant.

Transfer: Transfers are an important source for internal recruiting. Some librarian prefer the policy of promotion by transfer. Transfer solve many problems. A self-request transfer should not be given importance, as it encourages indiscipline and irritate the supervisor. Transfer should take up as solution in case an employee is unfit and disobey supervisor.

Promotion — an evaluation: Libraries are technical centres when all functions are conducted by technical personnel. Staff members have specialization in various aspects of library science. Moreover every library in addition to universal systems, methods, techniques and operational methods involve local variations. Any change in his work may create difficulty and desperation. Sometimes if there is suitable staff but the librarian is not pleased with his work. In such cases, outsider is appointed. Sometimes seniority is determined by the date of joining service, and not by the efficient work and higher qualifications. When the promotions are made only by seniority and not by qualifications, it naturally effects the efficiency of the work of library.

To remove the difficulties and problems the method of 50 per cent : 50 per cent is more appropriate. There are university and college libraries where this method is applied. In some state universities, a particular percentage has been fixed. Some libraries are adopting 50 per cent : 50 per cent method. It enables a library administrators to make the best choice among the staff members and from outside.

2.7 Library Education

Proper training not only increases the self-confidence and improves the morale of the worker but also increase service, reduces initial errors, and improve the quality of the new employee's work. It further, standardizes the methods of doing the work, reduces the amount of supervision necessary, reduces the turnover caused by unsatisfactory adjustment to a new job, corrects mistakes judgments as a result of hiring interview, and increases the interest in the job because of a more thorough understanding of the work and its relation to that of other employees.

The development of libraries and the continuous growth in the readers and the production of reading material has put a challenge before the library profession. Barmley has mentioned four silent characteristics of a profession:

1. The possession of a body of theoretical knowledge upon which professional practice can be based;
2. The need for extensive education and training;
3. The organization of practitioners into a formal professional association;
4. The imposition of a test of competence which

practitioners are required to pass before they can be elected to the ranks of qualified members.

Since libraries have been developed their bibliographical and reference services to meet the day-to-day needs of common man in a society, the library staff with well qualifications and academic competence is essentially demanded. Libraries, today have been the adequate source of spreading of education in certain countries as it speedily propagate the new knowledge.

Librarian is a wide term. It includes all persons working in a library at all levels: schools, colleges, universities, research centres, public libraries of all categories, technical libraries and the business libraries etc. It includes the top administrator as well as the lower incumbents at the professional ladder, in any type of library techniques and also not qualified to the level needed.

General education is imparted to the general public which means the language knowledge and the mental development to understand others' views and able to express his own views on others. It includes the knowledge of learning, reading, verifying and differentiate between the good and the bad qualities. Academic education is imparted to the person or group of persons who seek detailed knowledge of discipline and a faculty as a whole or specific aspect of the same. The professional education is imparted to the person or groups of persons for the purpose to achieve knowledge of the techniques applied to a particular professional trade of technology.

Objectives: The main objectives may be described as under:

1. To acquaint the person with the diffusion of knowledge;
2. To understand the co-relation between various fascicles of knowledge;
3. To ensure the fitness for the profession;
4. To assure the society of the competence of the person in a particular discipline;
5. To make the person known with the responsibilities and the duties of the librarian;
6. To develop the grasping power of the librarian;

7. To make the librarian more active in dealing with the professional activities and apply more intelligentsia;
8. To discharge duties in meeting the growing needs and requirements successfully;
9. To develop the sense of services to the citizen, society and nation;
10. To make the librarian realize that books are for all and every reader is a master to be served with zeal and jest;
11. To develop self-education and personality traits;
12. To ensure satisfactory job performance.

Education improves the working skill of library personnel and teach new methods or utilization of new technology.

The general objectives of training for librarian should be to acquaint the student with the Universe of knowledge in all of its forms: the historical as well as comptemporary role of libraries as agencies for the selection, acquisition and organization of knowledge of effective use: the principles and practice of librarianship and their application.

Library education is pragmatic in approach. Educational patterns are determined by the professional experts and fit the training to the needs or what is required. Education's shape is determined by the professional demand.

2.7.1 *Philosophy of Library Education*

Education is a wide term and when we think of a good education it includes the librarian on the top administration as well as on the lower ladder persons who have:

(i) No knowledge of library work;
(ii) Little knowledge of library work;
(iii) Sufficient knowledge of library work.

Out of them a large number of librarians have not undergone any library training; few have undergone elementary, certificate or diploma training; some have degree of library education, while some are engaged in research. 'Librarian' and the 'education' are two multilinked concepts. Librarian has no real meaning if he is unknown with the library techniques. Librarianship has two parts: (i) Physical part,

(ii) Mental or intellectual part. Men without intellect is a raw hand. Librarian, without library education is a storekeeper.

19th century was the period of manifestation of library science when the librarian was recognized as a man of techniques by virtue of his work in the profession. The concept of librarian was that of an expert and specialist in updating and maintaining the catalogues of libraries and accordingly extend his knowledge of bibliography. Librarianship is the eventful creation in the field of education and librarian a person of profound knowledge in the field of literature, history and information science. Its necessity was experienced in the rapid growth of library collection. It did not find a place of special training, but need of a scholar who could organize a collection in a systematic way. Thus some eminent librarians started professional education.

Thus librarianship was emerging gradually because of scholarly traditional confict and explosion of knowledge and the reading community. The further developments fielded have been the continuous recognition of the status of librarianship and the library education. This has also given a necessity of a framework of professional cooperation and practical procedures of library working.

The library education gave a new turn to philosophy as the technical routines emerged. Librarians stressed for a need of acquaintance with the books, the readers and the society. Carl M. White emphasises on bookman oriented curriculum in library schools. It was also a need of inclusion of applied bibliography service, book selection, cataloguing, classification, in training school's curriculum. Rogers gave a simple logic that library education should be directed to the objectives of providing right book, to the right reader, at the right time. This may be achieved by the acquisition of knowledge, intellectual discipline, sound judgment and operational activities of the librarian.

In modern scientific age professional librarians are busy in clerical or routine work which can be done by the semi-professionals or non-professionals. This has lost the intellect power and energy of the professional librarian thus a set-back to the library education and training schools lost sight of the professional and scholarly foundations of education.

Ranganathan has stressed on universe of knowledge which draws relevant disciplines and provides understanding of knowledge background. It needs a thorough library education with modern techniques of information retrieval. Library education should aim at producing scholars, educators and library theoreticians of the highest level. It should produce semi or junior professionals, imaginative administrators, and intelligent practitioners in addition to library technicians.

2.7.2 *Principles of Library Education*

All types of training courses or programmes are aimed at 'developing' people springs, much of the current disillusionment in library with systematic programme is due to recognition of fundamental law of life. I do not know any library which is fully satisfied with the way it found fostering individual growth. Researches were carried out in this field and much of its fundamentals are followed in right way. The final shape of the library education is still to be searched and framed in the light of human growth.

(1) **Individual's development**: Individualness is uniqueness and development in his continuous character. It follows successful development programme in the form of full time courses, part time courses, seminars, in service training, refresher courses, correspondence courses, conferences, and workshops. No library can manage courses to its all employees. To develop the individual is efficiency, not once, but many educational programmes are needed for the development of profession. Library education covers all these programmes at one or many places.

(2) **Ideal personality traits**: During last century many libraries have tried to evolve training programmes to fit idealized personality traits, but the programmes do not work very well and their implications have seldom been thought out very carefully. Personality traits are developed by professional education. Thus the focus of developmental and educational activities must be upon the work rather than upon the individual. A library is a group of persons with one purpose to

serve the clientele in return of satisfaction of job and personal.

(3) **Universal approach**: Many library educational programmes are based on the idea of selecting the "high potential men, picking some out of many and saying these are the librarians to be developed as professionals". Others are not put on any educational programme. Every profession has potentialities and these should come out and manage the affairs of the libraries. Library science field have many persons of potentialities which be listed and put active training and sharpen their intellectual and managerial capability.

(4) **Librarian a distinct profession**: Librarianship involves managerial techniques. There are two aspects: Professional and managing. Professional is a specialist of a work technique or routine in a particular field, but not necessarily he can be manager or administrator of a library. It is of pivotal importance to judge accurately from sensitive observation of his work, whether he has the desire and capabilities that fit a professional for managing. It needs a managerial education in the field of library science, which has not been included in library educational programme.

(5) **Decision-making education**: Our librarians fall in personality traits and find difficulty in taking any decision independently. Learning and professional skill make the librarian self-guided, confident and courageous. Library education gives the concept of decentralization. It gives relative autonomy to many men at different levels. Educational pattern of librarianship needs a thorough checkup and remodeled as to make the librarians more decision-maker. They would have more responsibilities and therefore more opportunities of developing good judgment, a prime requisite of management.

(6) **Development of moral and spiritual values**: Library education has got a developing stage and includes library ethics in its curriculum and make the librarian more spiritually and morally strong. ALA has prepared

a code of ethics for librarians. America has a job-oriented society. There the librarianship is given due place and holds a key position of international leadership.

2.7.3 *Historical Development*

The thought of library education no doubt emerged in ancient period but its actual growth started in twentieth century when three universities — Calcutta, Mumbai and Chennai were founded and a need for library professionals was experienced. The rapid growth in the number of students has been the main reason behind the thought of first class librarianship. Library education was formerly started in India in 1911 when ruler of Baroda state Maharaja Jiyaji Rao Gaikwad recognized the librarianship and experienced the importance of qualified professional librarian. William Borden, an American librarian was called to give his valuable services in Baroda state to organize the libraries and frame a library system. He agreed to the opinion that the success of library service would be dependent upon the supply of an adequate number of trained American system of library science and stressed a need of a training to the librarians working in the state. He wanted a chain of trained librarians to give more impetus to library movement. Consequently, training school was started in 1911 under the directorship of Borden. It was a short-period course and included a line of "Jack of all" system. This course was started on the lines of the Columbia library school and influenced by Melvil Dewey, a library science teacher. This training course covered the following fundamental or professional skills:

1. Library Hand-writing;
2. Book-binding and repairing;
3. Issue-system;
4. Safety of books; and
5. Cataloguing methods — an outline.

In the other corner of India, Punjab University, Lahore invited another American Librarian Mr. Asa Don Dickinson. He came on the request of Indian Government to organize the university library. His services were also taken for cataloguing purposes. He started a library school in 1915 with special training in library methods. Dickinson was also the pupil of Melvil Dewey and hence followed the Dewey pattern of library education with few changes regarding library methods. It was a apprentice training and continued until the partition of India in 1947 and the school was divided in two. The course was more on ambitious lines and its curriculum covered the basic subject of a professional course:

1. Classification;
2. Cataloguing;
3. Bibliography; and
4. Book selection.

It was a two months course followed by three months practical library experience in all aspects of library work. There were 24 students in first examination in 1914. The course was held in alternative years. Librarians when trained were absorbed in better jobs in academic institutions. He published a book "The Punjab Library Primer" in 1916. Perhaps he was probably first librarian in India who published a book on library science. The course started by Dickinson was very popular.

The next effort was made by Dr. S.R. Ranganathan when he started a certificate course in Lib. Sc. Under the auspices of Madras Library Association in collaboration with university of Madras under the guidance of Dr. Ranganathan. It was a summer course of three months. In 1937 University of Madras offered a full time one year course leading to a diploma in librarianship. It was the first full time course in India which was interduced in university. Later on this course was made Post-graduate Diploma course. This school carry ideals of Dr. Ranganathan's thought has enlightened the world with profound colon classification, chain indexing and fundamental categories etc. This course was changed to B.Lib.Sc. in 1960 and the centre became a place of library research.

Bengal Library Association joined this revolution in 1937 when he started a library training camp at Banserbia under the leadership of Kumar Muninder Rai, President of the Association. It was a certificate course and regularly conducted under the auspices of Hooghly District Library Association.

The step taken by Bengal Library Association encouraged other associations and result was many training centres started by library associations of Bombay, Delhi, Hyderabad, Maharashtra and Gujarat. These courses were mostly Diploma courses continued till degree courses were started in universities of the areas. The Imperial Library also started a part time training course in 1935 under the leadership of the National Librarian K.M. Asadullah. It was a summer course and continued up to 1945. At the beginning this course was summer course and later on changed to Diploma course. In 1945, with the joint efforts of Asadullah and Mr. Syama Prasad Mukherjee, the Vice-Chancellor of the Calcutta University, the training course was transferred to Calcutta University in 1945.

Since the demand of librarians increased due to unprecedented expansion of knowledge and social changes, more training schools were started by academic institutions in particular universities played a leading role in this country and started professional training, *i.e.* Andhra University in 1935, Banaras Hindu University in 1942, Bombay University in 1944 and Delhi in 1947. All these Universities started Diploma courses. Andhra University followed the courses of Madras University. Training schools at Delhi, Varanasi credited to Dr. Ranganathan who was librarian in these universities.

Baroda, Aligarh, Nagpur, Vikram, Osmania, Rajasthan, Punjab, Kerala, and Saugar also started library training schools in 1951, 1956, 1956, 1957, 1959, 1960, 1961, 1963 and 1964 respectively. At present there are more than 145 training schools which are imparting degree courses, 75 centres imparting master's course, 35 centres imparting research programmes, and several other centres imparting diploma and certificate course.

2.7.4 *Association's Role*

2.7.4.1 *India*

Library Associations, amongst professional agencies came forward first to start library schools. Madras Library Association and Bengal Library Association have been the leading units participating activity in professional development. Dr. Ranganathan and Kumar Munindra Rai, the stalwart of library science, were the President of Madras Library Association and Bengal Library Association respectively. These associations started refresher or elementary courses and later on diploma courses. Bengal Library Association is conducting certificate course. Andhra Library Association is a old association and counted first in the field who started training course at local level and served the professional of the area.

Bombay Library Association, Maharashtra Library Association, Gujarat Library Association, Hyderabad Library Association, Delhi Library Association, and U.P. Library Association started certificate course run by their State Central Libraries. Delhi Library Association started its first course in 1955. It has its school of library science. It is a certificate course and still continuing. Now the course is run in two shifts. Association has also started diploma course of one year duration.

Mysore Library Association started a Refresher course in Library Science from 25 Aug. to Sept. 9, 1968 under the guidance of Course Director Prof. A. Neelmeghan. The course was open to trained librarians.

U.P. Library Association started a certificate course in Library Science at many centres: Allahabad, Kanpur, Agra, Aligarh, Lucknow, Varanasi and Gorakhpur etc. This course is registered by U.P. Government and its examination are conducted by the Registrar, Departmental Examination of U.P. Government.

Government agencies: State Governments have shown active interest in the development of library profession and professionals. There are several governments which have started training courses in their departments: academic or technical centres. Punjab Government has started a diploma course in Government Polytechnic, Chandigarh and Jalandhar in 1970. Similarly, Haryana Government started diploma course in their Polytechnic at Ambala. Other governments started training courses are: Orissa, Karnataka and Andhra Pradesh. Training courses are also run by government academic institutions.

Polytechnic Institutes in India are contributing a lot in library profession by imparting library training in basic library skill. Many of them are conducting full time course in library techniques, with texts, tests, and credits. The courses run by Haryana, Orissa, Punjab, Maharashtra, Mysore, Bangalore governments are 1 to 2 years diploma courses. Bihar government runs two courses: one for undergraduates and other for graduates. The course has duration of 3 months under the guidance of Superintendent of Librarians of State's Government.

Public libraries: There are public libraries; State, district and regional libraries, who have started training courses in their libraries at their own decision. Some are not recognized schools by any university or government, while others are recognized. State Library, Hyderabad; Regional Public Library, Gwalior; Bhasha Bharti, Jabalpur & Raipur; Aminuddaula Public Library, Lucknow and Delhi Public Library have started library training courses of elementary knowledge.

Academic institutions: Academic institutions, schools, colleges, and universities are the better centres to impart training to the professionals excluding polytechnics. The history of library training starts with certificate course started in Punjab University in 1915, which was later on upgraded to Diploma Course in 1960. Similarly Madras University started Diploma Course in 1931 which was later on upgraded to degree course in 1946. Banaras Hindu University started diploma course in 1941 which was upgraded to degree course later on. There are more than 250 training centres being run by the university, colleges, associations and other private and government organizations.

2.7.4.2 *United States of America*

The library education in U.S.A. developed at different lines than U.K. American Universities, had never been active in playing out important role in the development of education. Educational pattern has its deep-root and long planning. Professional trainings were given due importance. America developed its own system of training with democratic ideals and conviction of self-development of an individual in his own way.

American universities have always regarded the supply of highly trained, skilled professional men and women as being one of the prime function. Yale and Harvard Universities followed British pattern but it was discouraged and declared as unsuitable for a right product. American developed a new pattern based on hard practical skills. Government passed a Land Grant Act of 1862, which made reactionary provisions for the development of vocational training for the professionals and the trades. These courses were introduced and linked with the basic vocations and could not be separated particularly in case of apprentice method of training. Though such courses were low rated and had no influence in university affairs.

The first revolutionary step towards library education was taken by Melvil Dewey in the later part of nineteenth century. He preferred first to start apprenticeship method as it could be more better to train the young librarians and give elementary knowledge of the profession. This apprenticeship was a form of instruction in connection with some important libraries managed systematically by professional eminents. He started this course in 1879. But he was not satisfied with this effort as he wanted to start a full time course or course which could give a thorough knowledge of the professional techniques. He started a step by step plan to start a central library school.

The delay in work was the reason Mr. Dewey himself. He could not made it clear whether the librarianship is a profession or trade. His statements were concessive and bitterly criticized. He was agreed with Tedder and disclosed his ideas in Buffalo conference organized by American Library Association in 1883. In conference, he was convinced to accept the librarianship as a profession. The conference was divided in two groups: American Libraries with Melvil Dewey, and British Libraries with Tedder. There was difference of opinion. Dewey gave more emphasis on instructional method based on practical training in important libraries, while Tedder stressed on written examination. But no doubt both were agreed on establishment of professional training. Tedder wanted to start a training course for British Library Assistants, while Dewey wanted customary apprentice method.

Dewey's opinion was seconded by many but the reaction of Britain effluent in U.S.A. and a section opposed Dewey for his instruction pattern. William F. Poole, a well-known librarian disagreed with Dewey and retain this theory that education should be based on —

1. Good practical training.
2. Good school educational background.

He also made it clear that librarian of eminence had no time to lecture and thus the training should be imparted by the full time training school. Dewey also proposed for a full time course in a college or university. This controversy continued for few years. At later stage both Mr. Poole and Dewey agreed that librarianship is a skill and technique not an art. It is said that Dewey submitted his proposal before the College Managing Board to start a library training, but the board rejected the proposal. But Dewey was very interested and he persuaded Mr. Barnard, the chairman of college board. The board however, under controversy, forwarded the case to college committee who finally gave its assent in 1884. It took 2-3 years in preparation to open the library school. The building committee put the further hindrance when it expressed inability to supply any special accommodation and furniture. Dewey brought furniture from his house and ultimately started school on January 5, 1887.

There was a need of expansion and Dewey engaged some of his students for instructions and this made the school facing the demand of more trainees. But the trustees of college did not cooperated Dewey and instead put a proposal to close down the school and dismiss Dewey. However, Dewey joined as Director of New York State Library and got the school transferred to State Library and remained up to 1926 and later on shifted to Columbia University. The step to start the library training at university level was appreciated by librarians. Alhamy also started a course in 1890 but based on theoretical instructions. There was a criticism of this school that it has not got the same standard as the university maintained. This course was started at first for library assistants. Its curriculum was different of the New York State School.

The other important school was Amherst Summer School, which was established in 1921. The school adopted primitive standard methods and without lecturer. Public library, Los Angeles started training on apprentice scheme, while the course started by Philadelphia Drixel Institute in 1892 was a course on technical instructions. The school stressed more on handwriting, typing, statistics and book-repairing. The course of Amout Institute, Chicago began in 1893. It was a practical technical course. Later on this course was shifted to Illinois University and the duration of course was increased to four years — Two years Bachelors course and two years specialized library course. A.L.A. prepared some instructions given at library schools. It also organized a conference of librarians held at New York in 1893 to discuss the effect of professional and practical training. Among several participants Mr. Dewey vehemently emphasized on theoretical instructions and said that practical training is not suitable for library schools. The conference passed the following resolutions:

1. Universities should run the school of librarianship;
2. An examination board should be setup with all powers;
3. Minimum qualification for admission to the course should be graduate;
4. The internal assessment or examination should be conducted by the external body.

A.L.A. agreed to the suggestions of Williamson and setup a Board of Education. The board devised a new system of two categories of training in 1953 which resulted to —

(1) Master's Degree course in Library Science in California, Michigan, Columbia, Illinois and Chicago universities for duration of 2 years. Chicago University took one further step and started Ph.D. faculty, and;

(2) Bachelor of Science in Library Science (B.Sc. in Lib.Sc.). Some of these centres continued Diploma Courses in addition to Bachelors course. There were few centres conducting the course in teaching institutions.

There was a change in library education during period when studies were made and published.

1. K.D. Metcalf, 1943 : The programme of instruction in library school.
2. Ernest J. Beace, 1943 : Programmes for library schools.
3. Joseph Wheeler, 1946 : Progress and problems in education for librarianship.

Board of Education (ALA) also published some standards in 1951 and propounded four principles:

1. The course should be for 5 years beyond the secondary school level;
2. The professional contents should be developed within 5 years period, but it should be of one year;
3. The objective of programme should be the development of professional ground of the person and a common knowledge of all types of libraries;
4. Special library training programme should be added in basic programme but not at the sacrifice of general, academic and professional education.

In 1957 the number of library schools raised to 35 as accredited by A.L.A. There were other schools run with their institutional programmes. Board of Education published in 1952 its standards for library science programme in teaching education institutions. In 1954 a new body, the National Council for Accredition of Teacher Education was founded. The undergraduate programmes were limited to the persons who wish to work in school libraries.

There are two basic doctoral programmes in library science in U.S.A.:

1. D.L.S. : Doctorate of Library Science, two years course equivalent to Post-graduate degree.
2. Ph.D. : Doctor of Philosophy. It is awarded to those who have distinguished themselves scholastically and who have published dissertation which makes a substantial contribution to a specific field of research.

In 1962, A.L.A. established a commission to prepare a national plan for library education and a report was published in 1907. It suggested that:

(a) The earlier pattern requires basic changes;

(b) The significance of specialization in various fields of librarianship should be considered;

(c) The redefinition of the goals of library education is required;

(d) Technical training into framework of professional education should be considered;

(e) Internship programme and refresher courses should be valued;

(f) Research programmes should be evaluated;

(g) Standard of library education should be developed.

U.S.A. felt need to change the programme of Ph.D. as to complete with other countries and give more emphasis on research. Some formulas were suggested by prominent educationists; Bernared Belelson in 1960, Liver Carunichoel in 1961 and Stephon Sphur in 1970. Later on many schools were started by Associations.

Other Developments

1972 : Liverpool Polytechnic has decided to offer B.A. Degree in Lib. Sc. With three years duration;

Special course by the Inter-American School of Librarianship, Antioquia University, Modellin, Columbia.

1971 : State University of New York at Albamy: 3 years undergraduate and graduate programme of M.L.S. and B.L.S.

1973 : School of Lib. Sc. Course in Western Reserve University, Cleveland : Educational programmes in Information Science and/or library automation : Non-Degree programmes; and 2 degree programmes.

1995 : There are many more universities and associations started B.L.I.S. and M.L.I.S. courses.

2.7.4.3 *United Kingdom*

Henry Rechard Tedder was the introducer of library education in 1880 when a resolution was put before the Library Association. The resolution was to consider the training of library assistants in the general principles of their profession. Bolten Public Library took initiative and started a apprenticeship of two years. Liverpool Public Library extended the period of training to 5 years of their training centre. The system of examination in 'General English' and 'Professional Knowledge' was proposed for admission in the annual conference at London. But it was not acceptable. In 1882 Tedder reiterated the librarianship as profession and declared the prevailing apprenticeship training in municipal libraries where librarians were unlike called for. He suggested the examination system as to distinguish the profession with other trades.

The course was conducted in 1885 in three ways:

1. Preliminary examination in Arithmetic, English, grammar, and composition, History, Geography and English literature;
2. Second class certificate examination: English literature, one European language, principles of classification of sciences, element of bibliography including cataloguing, library management, and administration;
3. First class certificate examination: Advanced knowledge of 5 subjects listed in second class certificate course and in addition general literary history.

The main features of 1904 syllabus were appreciated by traditional librarians also as the course had three states:

1. Written test of six papers;
2. Oral test; and
3. Thesis on the subject.

The syllabus continuously followed until the outbreak of war in 1914. The preliminary course reintroduced in 1916. The other revolutionary step was the registration register of the association's members, which was suggested by R.B. Predeaux in 1906 and also recommended in seminar by L. Stanley and W. Berwick Sayers at annual conference. Association discussed the matter that a uniform system for the training and testing librarian should be adopted. Whosoever enrolled as member of the association was necessarily joined diploma course. This provision was exempted in case of any one joins the school of librarianship at London University. Library Association considered other suggestions to conduct summer schools. The Education Committee submitted outline of the course and took responsibility for the organization and management of the classes. Summer schools were started at

Manchester and Birmingham, and other 35 centres at municipal and public libraries.

Post-war Period

After world war, the Library Association reviewed its educational policies and thought of starting a full time school of librarianship. The first full time course was started at University College London in September, 1879 with Dr. E.A. Baker as Director. It was not postgraduate school and had one year duration for graduates, two years duration for non-graduate, 3 or 4 years to part-time students.

Library schools were faced setback as private concerns and employer's of public libraries were slow to recognize the diploma of Library Association. University libraries were also less impressed by educational policy of the association. The other setback was the death of Tedder in 1924. Young librarians formed their own association and special libraries also took steps to be united and founded the Association of Special Librarians and Information Bureaux (ASLIB) in 1925. The differences among librarians resulted to many new organizations at regional and national level in 1926 *i.e.* Birmingham and West Midland Library Association and Scottis Library Association.

Henyan Committee

Library Association reviewed the position and formed a departmental committee to give suggestions to strengthen the influence of the association.

The problem was discussed between the Vice-Chancellors, college principals, and the association representatives and the chairman of University Grant Commission. It decided to reopen the school of librarianship at University College, London in October 1945. Other schools started were:

> School of Librarianship, Glasgow, Loughborough, Leads, Manchester, City of London of College, Brighton and New Castle, in 1946.

Library Association reintroduced Registration examination before final examination in 1951. In final examination, the following subjects were allowed: (a) Modern literature; (b) Literature of philosophy; (c) Literature as social sciences;

(d) Literature of science and technology, (e) Literature of fine art; (f) Literature of music. Specialized papers introduced were: advanced cataloguing and classification, paleography and archives, work with young people, or historical bibliography.

Exchange of Views

Library Association in 1950 appointed 'Moderating Committees' to discuss the syllabus. Library school tutor and the examining bodies were invited to exchange their views. A Joint Committee of Library Association and ASLIB was setup in 1957 which recommended the uniformity of standards for library schools. Certain uniform standards were laid down in 1960. It was further recommended that the one year course leading to the qualifying examination in librarianship should be extended to two years.

The library schools joined their hands and founded Association of British Library Schools in 1926. Mr. Kenyon was the chairman and hence committee's report is popular with the name of Kenyon Report, 1930. Its main recommendations were the growth of inter-library cooperation. It gave more regards to the association and the membership raised to 4260 in 1934 from 832 in 1927. Education Committee put new syllabus in 1933 and introduced three new concepts.

W.B. Paton was the main critic of the Kenyon Committee report and enumerated faults included lack of intelligence and education, bad grammar, spelling and writing, undue verliage in answering questions. Earnest Savage also expressed dissatisfaction on the report and criticised the course as below standard and aimed at quantitive education. A committee was setup with Mc Colvin as associate which recommended that universities should be persuaded to provide theoretical aspect while teaching libraries should provide practical training.

The most significant development in the field of library education took place in 1963 when the young librarians entered the rank of the profession determined to obtain the qualifications necessary for personal advancement. Library schools were expanded. College started variety of courses at all academic levels. Certain colleges declared colleges of advanced technology (CAT). The library schools were attached to lower rank colleges. But this step was opposed. 'National

Council for Technological Awards,' drew a code of standards and examined the college and its course in light of those standards. The council was empowered to award the degree also.

In 1964 Library Association introduced a new syllabus especially designed for a full time two years course. New examination had two parts:

Part-I: Four papers: (1) The Library and the Committee, (2) The governments and control of libraries; (3) Organization of knowledge; (4) Bibliographical control and service.

Part-II: (A List) — Alternative papers: (1) Academic and legal deposit libraries; (2) Special libraries and information Bureau; (3) Public (Municipal and country libraries);

(B List) — One out of six: (1) Theory of Classification, (2) Theory of cataloguing, (3) History of libraries and librarianship, (4) Handling and dissemination of information, (5) Hospital libraries, (6) Archival Administration.

(C List) — One out of thirty papers on the bibliography and librarianship of a number of subject fields.

Both examinations were conducted by Library Association.

As a natural result, the training institutions are teaching and not examining bodies. The Library Association prepared to depart from this system. It persuaded university of Sheffield to setup a Post-graduate School of Librarianship. In 1965 at Sheffield, and Belfast Universities in Northern Ireland the schools established were:

1. Glasgow College of Commerce, 1964.
2. Strathelyde University, 1966, B.A. in Librarianship.
3. New Castle College of Commerce: B.Sc. in Information Science.
4. Leeds College of Commerce: B.A. in Librarianship.
5. College Librarianship, University of Wales: Independent degree course.
6. Loughborough School of Librarianship, Loughborough University of Technology — Independent degree course.
7. Deptt. of Librarianship of Strathelyde University — Independent degree course.

Other Courses

College of Librarianship, Wales — 10 weeks course (1967). Leads College of Commerce — Workshop on Medical Librarianship, 1963.

2.8 Learning Conditions

Librarianship is not a pure science. It is an applied branch of knowledge. Learning is a relatively permanent change in behaviours that occurs as a result of practice or experience. Training does not always ensure the trainee's learning. He makes little use of the insight he developed in classroom. Training is of no use if the trainee does not use his learning in his work. The library school programmer should ensure that —

(a) What is taught in training is relevant to the participant's experience;

(b) The trainee gains sufficient understanding of what he learns to be able to use it in his library work.

Best training is justified when an equation is established between what is taught in the classroom and what the trainees use at work.

Conditions: Proper training depend upon the three factors:

1. The trainee's receptiveness;
2. The trainee's report with the trainers;
3. The climate of training.

The person goes under training, shows his motivation to learn. There are also library employees desired to undergo professional training, sent by the library authorities influenced by his perceptive of learning.

Motivation Theory

Motivation theory attempts to explain 'How behaviour gets started, energised, sustained directed, stopped in the organization while all this is going on'.

The following aspects of individuals behaviour can be seen while discussing psychological constructs:

1. An individual develops his sense of right and wrong from association and experiences of only childhood.

They are governed by his intersection with parent, school, communication. At later stage, the individual interprets and evaluates people's action and behaviour. However, the trainee likewise, perceives his world through his own system of values, attitude and experience etc.

2. What an individual aspires is unique to his own personality. The trainee's aspirations are directly related to his history, his concept of his abilities and his goals. These characteristics are not static. They are constantly influenced by his immediate environment and by his contiguous experience of success and failure. There is a continuing processes of evaluation and adjustment through successive experience by retaining what is pleasant and rejecting or repressing the painful.
3. Thus motivation is an individual phenomenon for the trainee. He directs his behaviour in the direction that enables him to reach his perceived goal. For example: If the supervisor has the authority to reward him in a way that brings him closer to a balance between the directorates of the union and those of his supervisor.

Motivation Theory

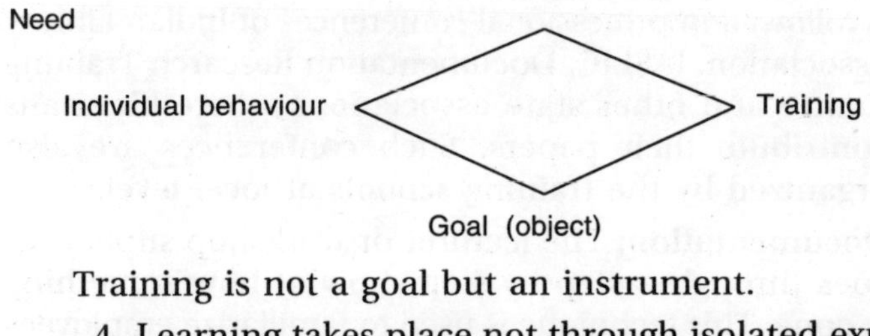

Training is not a goal but an instrument.

4. Learning takes place not through isolated experiences but by enforcement of some experiences or similar one in a relatively permanent change if the individual's work, after training, provides reinforcement of the ideas used in training.

2.8.1 *Teaching Techniques*

There are wide varieties of training techniques:

1. **Lecture**: The lectures talks in a group from prepared

notes on the outline and presents information on given subjects. This technique is particularly good when few trainees are familiar with the subject or capable to understand and grasp the subject.

2. **Written Exercises**: The lecturer gives the trainees an exercise and ask them to write out the problem as they see it. He returns their report to them with his comment. This procedure is continuously followed during the tenure of the training.
3. **Penal Discussion**: One or more specialists discuss a subject and then answer questions posed by each other or from the audience. There is free conversation on the problem of the interest of both or all.
4. **Work Project**: The lecturer will assign one or more trainees to handle a special project, or to find the answer to a problem. This technique requires the giving of clear instructions and has proved quite effective in developing the ability to solve problems. This technique is followed in M.Lib.I.Sc. or Research work.
5. **Conference**: A leader or Librarian serves as guides in discussing problems common to the group. Solutions can often be reached by the pooling of group experiences. In library profession such type of technique is followed in professional conferences of Indian Library Association, IASLIC, Documentation Research Training Centre and other state associations where librarians contribute their papers. Such conferences are also organized by the training schools at local level.
6. **Documentation:** The lecturer or workshop supervisor goes through a step by step show of how something is done. This technique is used to familiarize employees with the details of their job. Library training centres apply this technique.
7. **Exhibit:** Trainees are shown exhibits of specimens, models, mock-ups, pictures of things with which they will be doing. Library centres demonstrate the samples of various circulation systems through their workshop of the practical cell of the centre.

8. **Individual coaching**: The teacher works directly with the trainee to make certain projects, observations etc. that he understands what is expected of him. In M.Lib.I.Sc. course trainees are put under the individual guidance of the teacher.
9. **Education tour**: Trainees are taken on educational tour to learn about the other libraries and their management, technical methods and operational methods. They are told in advance what they will see and will have their questions answered by the guide or supervisor.

2.8.2 *Training Process*

Training must be tailored to fit each position in a library and must not be overlooked. Library is a organization of technical work and also busy business of circulation, reference and reading work at all times during opening hours. Employees are changed to any job when any one of them proceeds on leave or shifted to other responsibilities. On the other hand if new employee is engaged in a work of skill, and not sure of his comfortable work. That is not training. Training is a carefully planned and timely programme.

Four steps of training:

1. **Preparation**: It refers to the readying of trainee's mind for new ideas. It means knowing the new techniques and try the previous experience. Actually trainee's mind is being prepared to receive new ideas. It applies the sharp mind of teaching staff. There are both types of trainees in librarianship training *i.e.* Freshers and in-service trainees.
2. **Presentation**: It should be the practice of a library science teacher not to try to teach too much at one sitting. It is also important to explain why things are done the way they are. It will be poor show to say that it was something a policy or practice. Teaching presentation in library science is purely a process to be clearly explained before the library science trainee.
3. **Application**: Application of teaching process is more important step in which the trainee has the opportunity

to use what he has been taught. He must have plenty of time to absorb and use that he has learnt.

4. **Appraisal:** It is constant part of training and must go on as long as a person is in training. This step is also applied in case of employed trainees. Smart librarians continually took for weaknesses in any employee and then act to correct these. In some cases they keep a checklist on each person, analysing what must be done and which training is needle-in-service training, the elementary training or higher and fulltime training.

2.8.3 *Planning for Training*

Planning is the first phase of training. The following points should be considered while thinking of a sound planning for training:

1. **Location of training activities**: Library science departments are run by many institutions, universities, colleges, polytechnics, public libraries and library associations at various levels. The location of the training activities should be within the campus of the institution and particularly in teaching departments. It will be more suitable if training centre is run in the building of library though its entity will be separate. It should be the effort to locate all types of training at one place C.Lib.Sc., B.Lib.I.Sc., M.Lib.I.Sc. and research.
2. **Coordination of training activities**: Training activities includes, the teaching department, teachers workshop, seminars, seminar library, departmental library, educational tour and cooperation of central library of the institution. All such activities should be coordinate to the main aim of training. Central library services should be available for practical work. Departmental library and workshop should also be well equipped and should have a skilled instructor.
3. **Recorded at training centre and planning of programme**: Each library training centre should keep proper record of each trainee. The record includes:

   (a) Academic record of the trainee;

   (b) Professional activities of the trainee;

(c) Professional experience of the trainee;
(d) Trainee's interest: administration or teaching;
(e) Subject offered: specialization field;
(f) Nature, behaviour and understanding;
(g) Future programme of the trainees;
(h) Employment details, if employed after training;
(i) Trainees unemployed after training.

The head of the department maintain above training record and maintain it even after the person completed the training. It gives opportunity to teachers to give encouragement to the trainees and suggest them in their problems in their work. It also keeps in touch with trainee.

4. **Evaluation of effectiveness of training**: Effectiveness and relevance of training should be judged by the training head. There are two ways to evaluation:
   1. The teaching staff under whom the trainees work.
   2. The trainee: It will be more better to serve the trainee with questionnaire, three months after completing the training course.

2.8.4 *Sample Questionnaire*

INSTITUTE:

COURSE: SESSION:

DIRECTIONS:

1. You have by now undergone the.......... Course of library science at the institute.
2. Your frank and honest observations in retrospect will be of real help to this institution while planning such course in future. *Please make sure that you answer all the questions without any reservation.*
3. Please do not write your name anywhere in the proforma.

1. Quality of the Lectures

(a) What is your opinion about the quality of the lectures in general?

Excellent	Good	Not-sure	Fair	Poor
5	4	3	2	1

(b) What is your evaluation of the lectures who delivered in different papers in this course? Please give their names in the order of priority;

(c) You might not have found all the lectures delivered in this course useful and interesting to the extent. Please indicate the lectures which you have found:

(i) The most useful and interesting (mention in the order of priority);

(ii) Moderately useful and interesting;

(iii) Not at all useful and interesting.

2. General Aspect of the Course

(a) What were your expectations about this course before coming to this institute?

(b) In what many would you rate the course as whole in terms of the following aspects?

	Very much	More	Average	Less/not at all
1.	Satisfying your expectations			
2.	Enriching your knowledge			
3.	Improving your attitude			
4.	Creating further interest			
5.	Any other (specify)			

(c) Do you feel that this course was useful for you?

Very useful	useful	undecided	non-useful	not at all
5	4	3	2	1

(d) If you were organizing a course of this kind, what modifications would you think of in its scope, coverage and topics?

3. Specific Aspect of the Course

(a) Course content and sequential arrangement.

(b) What is your general reaction to the content of the course?

(c) What are the reasons for your reaction?

(d) What is your reaction to the 'Practical classes' arranged in the course?

(e) Do you like the present method of practical classes? If not, what should be the method?

(f) Individual assessment:

(i) What is your reaction about assessment? Do you think it is more useful?

(ii) Do you think that the assessments have helped your orientation for librarianship?

4. Departmental Library

(a) Do you think that you were able to utilize the library to the extent you desired?

(b) Do you think that library facilities were adequate to meet your requirements?

(c) Do you have any suggestions to the functioning of the library for the sake of participants in terms of timings, assistance of library staff etc.

2.8.5 *Training Programme*

Training programme is undertaken at various levels:

1. Training for the semi-professional librarians (Certificate or Diploma course) conducted by state central libraries and academic institutions.
2. Training for professional junior librarians (Degree course) conducted by universities or colleges.

3. Training for professional senior librarians (Post-graduate, Masters course) conducted by universities.
4. Training in research (Ph.D.) conducted by universities.

C.Lib.Sc.: Training for the Semi-Professionals

1. **Objectives**: The librarian working or desire to work in small libraries of middle schools, panchayats, block libraries or at lower level in big libraries undergo the training of certificate course in library science. This course has main objects to:
   (i) give the person/librarian elementary knowledge of library profession;
   (ii) train the person/librarian in routine library working;
   (iii) prepare the person/librarian to run the small library independently.
2. **Various courses**
   (i) Elementary course;
   (ii) Apprentice course;
   (iii) Certificate course;
   (iv) Diploma course.
3. **Duration**: Duration of courses differ from school to school.
4. **Admission qualification**: Qualifications for admission in C.Lib. and D.Lib. are ranging between high school to graduation. Those who have passed the high school examination may also be admitted provided they have at least one year's experience in library work. At few library schools the minimum qualification for admission is high school or intermediate particularly in U.P. and Bihar schools, while higher secondary is in Delhi, M.P., Punjab, Orissa and Karnataka. In polytechnic centres the qualification for admission includes 'a knowledge of English' in addition to basic qualification.
5. **Course of studies**: Most of the centres conducting C.Lib.Sc. have prescribed four papers:
   (i) Classification — Theory and Practice
   (ii) Cataloguing — Theory and Practice

(iii) Library Administration and Organization

(iv) Reference service, bibliography and book selection.

Few centres have specifically limited the organization paper to school and public libraries. 'Library Routine and Reference Work' has been prescribed.

There are other papers prescribed for the proficiency tests: Sessional work, Viva-Voce. Viva-Voce has been given the status of an independent vocal paper in addition to four papers and sessional work.

Diploma course has 4 to 6 papers:

(i) Library classification — theory and practice

(ii) Library cataloguing — theory and practice

(iii) Library administration

(iv) Library organization

(v) Reference service and document bibliography

(vi) Book selection and physical bibliography

Other

(vii) Viva-Voce

(viii) Sessional marks

The paper Nos. 7 and 8 are not applied in all schools.

6. **Valuation point**: Total marks fixed in C.Lib.Sc. are 400 marks (100 marks for each paper) and 50 marks for Viva-Voce and 20 marks to sessional work. The marks for Viva-Voce are fixed to 100 marks and for sessional marks to 25 marks in practical papers in some of the centres. However, total marks of all papers and tests have been fixed to 500 marks in all.

Paper I	—	Classification — theory and practice		100 marks
Paper II	—	Cataloguing — theory and practice		100 marks
Paper III	—	Lib. Administration and Organization		100 marks
Paper IV	—	Reference service, bibliography and book selection		100 marks
Paper V	—	Viva-Voce		50 marks
Sessional marks:				
Classification practice			25 marks	50 marks
Cataloguing practice			25 marks	
Total marks				500 marks

So far *Diploma course* is concerned each paper has been allotted 100 marks and thus reaches to total 600 marks. Most of the schools conducting diploma course have allotted 500 total marks : 400 marks for examination papers and 100 marks for viva-voce test. On the other hand few schools have stopped the viva-voce tests.

The passing marks out of the total marks have been fixed between 33 per cent to 36 per cent as per choice of the schools. To pass the examination a candidate shall require to secure a minimum of 40 per cent marks in the aggregate of all the papers and 25 per cent marks in each paper. Minimum marks for the second division and first division shall be 50 per cent and 60 per cent of the aggregate respcctively. Each paper shall be of 3 hours duration.

Comments

Certificate courses in library schools have been stopped forthwith in universities on the recommendation of University Grant Commission in 1964. The Department of Library Science in university should not ordinarily take responsibility for conducting a course for certificate in library science organized for non-graduates. Such a course is of sub-university standard. It should ordinarily be left to the care of the departments of libraries and the library association of each state. As a result majority of the universities have discontinued C.Lib.Sc. course and diploma courses and started degree courses.

Evaluation

C.Lib.Sc. course as not standardized by any organization and the government has been playing in the hands of many for profit making business or ego of the librarian. This has led to lack of unity, standard and facilities. Most of the courses being part time courses have engaged part time teachers on petty remuneration or honorarium. Teachers teaching in their busy hours usually fails to be regular in class. The trainee even could not have elementary knowledge of library working. Library schools could not provide sufficient seating arrangement, qualified teachers, practical training of methods applied in various sections of the library. There are centres where the librarian run the course on his single shoulder? Regular classes are not run in schools. They take 2-3 periods per week and somehow complete their courses in haphazard way and take their final examination with the same staff.

On the other hand some schools maintaining good standard at lower level, such training can be ticked on fingers. These schools no doubt paid a good heed and achieved standard and imparted theoretical as well as practical training to the librarians. But they are also facing staff problem, separate accommodation problem, practical workshop problem, and mainly the financial problem.

Each school is beating his own drum at its own convenience and way. There is not uniformity of syllabus among the library schools. Some private colleges have been starting the course for the last many years without any recognition of the library associations, government, the universities and the education board. This has put the trainee in uncertain future as they fail to convince the employer regarding validity of the course as well as institution imparted training. This is a severe wastage of money, time and energy, good for nothing and producing several hundreds of librarians with no standard. It is suggested that a library examination board should be constituted at national level to conduct the training courses other than university courses. Indian Library Association may perform the work of examination board but it will be a little success being its political nature.

Correspondence Courses

Few universities are conducting correspondence courses of B.Lib.I.Sc., M.Lib.I.Sc. and earning a lot of money producing below standard candidates. They complete their course by organizing a lecture series of 10 to 15 days in a year during summer and teach all eight papers of these advance courses, while normally the regular University Departments even fail to complete their courses within seven to eight months. UGC is also not taking any interest to close such courses or standardize these courses up to a level which can produce the qualified, talented and knowledgeable librarians.

2.9 Courses

2.9.1 ***Bachelor of Library Science***

There is continuous establishment of educational

institutions, new industrial research institutes, commercial units, government departments, national research laboratories, and other social, political and religious institutions all over the world. It needs a network of libraries: academic, public and special or technical libraries. Several libraries are in existence, several are in making and several are to be established and under planning process. The management of these libraries needs persons with good academic and professional qualifications. Library work is primarily a social service and therefore, needs young men and young women with a sense of dedication and spirit of service. Those intending to enter library profession should satisfy themselves that they possess the necessary academic qualifications that would enable them to work successfully as librarian.

The training for the professionals should be of the university standard... the basic general knowledge and the maturity of mind of the students needed to draw benefit from a university course for the library profession are such that can be expected normally in post-graduate students only. As in the case of education there are two degree courses in library science also. The first is called Bachelor of Library and Information Science (B.Lib.I.Sc.) and the other is Master of Library and Information Science (M.Lib.I.Sc.).

1. Objectives

The objectives of B.Lib.I.Sc. degree course may be mentioned as under:

(a) To give the students an understanding of the basic principles of library science;

(b) To train him/her in the technique of librarianship and the management of libraries;

(c) To acquaint him/her generally with the social, cultural, educational and communicational framework of the library.

The Advisory Committee described the following objectives:

(a) To provide comprehensive training in general librarianship and to prepare the students for advanced work in librarianship in the second year;

(b) To emphasize the teaching of the basic principles

underlying techniques and skills of librarianship, in addition to description of routine practices, etc.;

(c) To acquaint the students with the social, educational and communicational role of the library in modern society;

(d) To give the students adequate bibliographical control of literature, at least, in one department of knowledge, with particular reference to Indian materials.

2. Duration

Duration of B.Lib.I.Sc. course is one year and followed in all Indian Universities.

The illusion of master's degree attracted some young Indian librarians to U.S.A. rather than U.K. Because they could return with master's degree just in a year's study, which was really a first professional degree. Before 1950 it was B.Lib.I.Sc. (B.L.S.) in U.S.A. as first professional course. But since 1951 American Library schools started master's degree (M.L.S. or M.S.I.S.) as first professional degree. Canadian Library school continued B.L.S. degree of one year's duration after basic bachelors degree.

3. Admission Qualification

(a) **Essential qualification**

At least graduate/bachelors degree of any Indian university or equivalent degree of foreign university.

Similarly in all other universities the minimum qualification for admission in B.Lib.I.Sc. is Bachelor's Degree in arts, commerce and science and minimum II Division. The minimum percentage of marks in graduates ranges between 45 per cent to 55 per cent in various universities.

Delhi University in its prospectus has further clearly mentioned that "candidates are advised that in their own interest they should apply for admission only if they have a first class pass degree, or at least a second class honours degree". This suggestion is perhaps given to minimise the crowd of admission.

(b) **Other desirable qualification**

(i) Deputed candidates and librarians with a minimum experience of 5 years. Those who are sponsored by government or university or approved colleges of Public library authority as candidate with pay deputed allowance under rules and are already ordinarily working in a library;

(ii) Science graduate with minimum of II division.

(c) **Written test**

Some universities conduct written and oral test of candidates for B.Lib.I.Sc. admission. B.H.U. conducts written test consisting two papers: (i) General knowledge; (ii) an essay in English. The final selection is thus made in order of merit out of the candidates who qualify in this test with a minimum aggregate of 45 per cent. Oral test is generally conducted by most of the universities.

Order of Preference

(1) Deputed and sponsored candidates with Master's degree II Division;

(2) Deputed and sponsored candidates with Bachelor's degree with II Division at least 50 per cent marks.

(3) Fresher with Master's degree II Division with aptitude test;

(4) Fresher with Bachelor's degree II Division and C.Lib.Sc.

(5) Fresher's with Bachelor's degree II Division with 3 years experience.

(6) Fresher with Bachelor degree with honours after aptitude test.

Evaluation of Admission Test

There is controversy over conducting admission test for admission in B.Lib.I.Sc. and other training courses. Admission test consists of the following objectives:

(a) It leads to fair selection;

(b) It helps in judging the proficiency, reading habits, brilliancy, academic work, medium of instruction, local standard of the candidate;

(c) Aptitude towards library service is judged;

(d) It limits the number of students.

It is based on written test, personal interview and aptitude test. Admission test has been proved to be the best organ in selecting the candidates for various sources of library science. It has been experienced that in Varanasi centre even the Ist class degree holders has not been able to qualify in the test and second divisioners have been qualified in the test and proved better and suitable candidates for this profession. There are many merits of admission test: (a) It attracts the higher qualified candidates and helps in assess out of all young personality, (b) It makes possible the student-teacher ratio.

Previously the trend of admission was purely the merit. The number of candidates was also limited. In modern age library science has been adopted as a popular profession and attracted huge crowd for admission for trainings. Library services have been the necessities for human life and librarians are required.

4. **Seats**

Universities have fixed total seats for B.Lib.I.Sc. course at their own discretion and convenience. The number of seats differ from university to university. The number ranges between 25 to 80. Majority of the universities conducting B.Lib.I.Sc. course have fixed 35 to 60 seats.

5. **Course of Studies**

Fundamentally the training courses should be service-oriented and logic-oriented based on five laws of library science propounded by Dr. Ranganathan. From courses offered by various universities, it has been found that they are similar in subjects except a few changes in terms. For the first time Library Advisory Committee, 1958 considered this problem and suggested that Government of India should appoint a committee of experts to organize the syllabus of teaching programme and conduct of examination. Consequently University Grant Commission appointed a Review Committee in 1961 under the chairmanship of Dr. Ranganathan, which recommended that:

1. There should be separate department of library science with full time teachers;
2. Various kinds of courses in Library Science and uniform syllabus for various library science schools in India.

UGC Library Committee recommended the fundamentals of library teaching programmes. It has mentioned that library training courses should be prepared in light of changes taking place in the universe of knowledge, social purposes of the library, documentation, and established techniques and practices based on practical and observational work.

Ranganathan has explained that library science teaching is a system based on experience, observations and familiarization with idiosyncrasies of reference books and bibliographical tools in particular. He compared the library science with mathematics and physics and henceforth made efforts to collect the scattered material of our library technique/ concept/theme in one place through his books:

(a) Library classification, fundamental and procedure (1944)
(b) Library catalogue, fundamental and procedure (1950)
(c) Reference service and bibliography (1940)
(d) Theory of library catalogue (1938)
(e) Library Book Selection (1952)
(f) Social bibliographer; Physical bibliography for librarians, authors and publishers (1952).

This has given a base for syllabus. Most of the universities adopted the common curriculum of B.Lib.I.Sc.

In addition to the theory papers, there will be a sessional test of 20 marks in each, a viva-voce examination of 50 marks and study tour report of 10 marks.

Evaluation

Found from the syllabus of Indian Universities that there is no uniformity and they adopt the following paper in all:

1. Library classification (theory)
2. Library classification (practical)
3. Library cataloguing (theory)

4. Library cataloguing (practical)
5. Library organization *b
6. Library administration *b
7. Reference service and document bibliography *a, *b
8. Book selection and physical bibliography *c
9. Library management
10. Documentation *a
11. Comparative librarianship.
12. History of libraries
13. Library organization and administration *b
17. Library organization and management
18. Bibliography *c
19. History of libraries and physical bibliography
20. Information science

Item 5 and 6 = Item 13

Item 7 (Part II) = Item 16

Item 7 (Part II) and Item 16 = Item 10 = 9

Item 12 and 8 (Part II) = Item 18

It is evaluated that universities have not reached to a concrete decision of uniform pattern. Moreover, they could not workout the final limit of a particular subject. The main lacuna in the courses could be noted as follows:

1. The more emphasis has been given to classification and cataloguing. These papers have been treated separately and moreover in two parts — theoretical aspect and practical aspect.
2. Universities could not justify the clear meaning and shape of three papers — (1) Organization (2) Administration, (3) Management. All the three papers have been mixed in some way and made a hotch-potch of it. Now these papers have been changed to (a) Library and society (b) Library management.

Practical Aspect of Training

There are two practical papers of classification and cataloguing prescribed in all the universities. Most of them treat them like a theoretical papers. Titles are printed in examination papers and student has to solve it with the help of concerned classification scheme and catalogue code provided by the library school for the purpose. It is clear that so many informations are to be gathered from back of title page, introduction, and other parts of the book or so. The details in examination paper is not sufficiently provided or cannot be provided. This has lost the practical concept. Moreover, students are not questioned out of the rules and procedures of the classification schemes and the cataloguing code. Simple titles are given for constructing the classification number. This is no practical aspect and training centres are unnecessarily giving such in practicable training.

This system should be modified to the applied practical method. The student should be given books or periodicals to construct the number and preparing catalogue cards. No doubt student will not be able to solve more titles, but whatever is solved, it will be accurate, and actual valuation of the student's knowledge.

There is a need for practical demonstration of classification, cataloguing, reference service, book selection, preparation of bibliographies, indexing, abstracting, reproduction and Information Science. A teacher is expected to be acquainted with techniques of handling audio-visual aids etc.

Views

There are grades and classes of Library Assistants — 'Professional Specialist' and 'Librarian' as requiring for adequate education. B.Lib.Sc. should include instruction in the fundamentals of library practice may be obtained in a variety of ways; through on-the-job training and guided experience, through course work following the bachelor's degree offered by graduate schools as a prerequisite to the Master's programme, or for courses offered at the undergraduate level within B.A. programme (Hingway).

Library education must have social relevance. Social requirements, of a system undergoing processes of socialization are bound to change with the advent of time. Library science courses are quality subject to the changed circumstances. It is surely not going to be enough to limit postgraduate library science courses to Bachelor of Library Science and Master of Library Science degrees. In fact, the Bachelor's degree can have no place in the future scheme of things. The Bachelor's degree forming part of the postgraduate degree is a contradiction in terms. Radical orientation of library science courses is called for at the latest. It is high time that consideration is given to the possibility of integrating B.Lib.I.Sc. courses with undergraduate courses at the college level. The some course should be speed over years immediately after schooling and taught along with other subjects. Library science need not be considered purely as a professional course at this level.

One year courses are certainly not enough to train professionals in the real sense of the term. The induction of Library Science courses at the undergraduate level may train, in addition, a large number of undergraduate students in the methodology of how to use the libraries. The core of librarians to be trained at the undergraduates, with at least as much competence at the present, be sufficient to take care of the requirement of library personnel at junior level in all types of libraries.

Training for librarianship may be imparted at three levels. Out of the several universities imparting library training from any single state, only one, possessing adequate training facilities, independent and full time teaching staff, adequate financial support should be choice for training candidates who are likely to occupy responsible posts such as Librarians, Deputy or Assistant Librarians. Remaining universities from the same state may be entrusted with the task of training personnel for the second level *i.e.* Sectional Heads, Senior Assistants and persons who expected to execute work of technical and administrative nature. Regional library associations may be persuaded to conduct short-term courses, in vernacular languages, for a period not less than three months and not more than four months. The object of these courses should aim to a training personnel whose services can be utilized in small public libraries.

The duration of the courses at the first level should be two years and the medium of introductions should be English.

Only such candidates possessing good academic qualifications, good organizing capacity, interest in library work, leadership, and having interest in every human activity, know to get on with authorities, colleagues and public, be admitted to such courses. More academicians not mere technicians do not necessarily prove good and effective librarians. The first year's training should be restricted to the technical aspects of librarianship such as classification cataloguing, Reference Service, Administration, Organization etc. Attempts should be made to build up the total personality of the candidate instead of making him just a scholar or just a technician. The other year should be restricted to Information Science, network and computer application.

The library school curriculum could provide the common base. It should always be remembered that at the Association level or at the high university level accredition is a process whereby an organization recognize a college/university association training centre study programme as having met minimum qualifications standards.... The University Classes have to be properly accredited by the UGC and the basic professional, pre-professional graduate and postgraduate and research work is to be similarly accredited and proper standard maintained. Now come to the various courses that required to be introduced. Preparatory education — Pre-professional education, general and liberal education — Education for Public Librarianship, General education for Public Librarians — Specialization in professional education, graduate study and the Public Library — Education for Academic Librarianship — pre-professional education for academic librarians, Education for library service to children and youth — Basic professional education — Professional training for the Teacher — Librarian — Education — for Special Librarianship — Subject specialization — Advanced study and research in Librarianship — Training of clerical and sub-professional workers — Programme for library technicians.

UGC Review Committee: The committee recommended the following syllabus for Bachelor's degree:

1. Library Organization
2. Library Administration

3. Physical Bibliography and Book Selection
4. Document Bibliography and Reference Service
5. Library Classification (Theory)
6. Library Classification (Practice)
7. Library Cataloguing (Theory)
8. Library Cataloguing (Practice)
9. Record of Practical Work.

The committee did not give more emphasis to classification and cataloguing.

M.A. Gelfand: He suggested the following course for Bachelor's degree at Delhi University:

1. History of books and libraries
2. Library classification: theory and practice
3. Library cataloguing: theory and practice
4. General bibliography
5. Reference service
6. Library organization and administration

7 & 8. Bibliography and literature in humanities, social science and natural science (A choice of two out of three).

2.9.2 *Master of Library Science Course*

Objective: According to UGC Committee the Professional course implies the need for keeping close to what has to be done to make a library function effectively. The course should train the students to —

1. Alert to improve the library practices from time to time in the light of the changes in the —
   (a) Universe of knowledge;
   (b) Social purpose.
2. Intensify the socialization of books and fulfil the demand of democracy to give a chance for everyone to use them in the measure of his capacity and needs.
3. Conserve the research potential of humanity and intensify research so as to enable the libraries to supply human wants in spite of continuing increase of population.

4. People them to meet new situation with new library techniques and practices.
5. Practical and observational work of library working.

UGC Advisory Committee for libraries mentions the following objectives —

1. To train students for administrative posts in one of the major types of libraries — large public library systems. University libraries, special libraries — by offering them opportunity for study of objectives, principles and social problems of organization and administration.
2. To offer specialization to students in the different field of information technology.
3. To train persons in method of research.
4. To provide teachers of library science for the universities.

Review Committee enumerates the objectives as under:

1. To acquaint the student with —
   (a) the organization and development of the universe of knowledge.
   (b) research organization and research methods.
2. To give the student specialized knowledge in respect of —
   (a) kinds of reading and kindred materials, and documentation lists;
   (b) Information products.
3. To make the student proficient in —
   (a) advanced library techniques in the information technology;
   (b) advanced management and administration of selected types of libraries.

Mittal has narrated the following objectives:

1. To give the student an advanced and intensive training in librarianship with special reference to the organization and administration of National libraries,

and other research and special libraries, so as to enable to head any one of the other types of libraries.

2. To prepare the student to:

(a) work as teacher of library science in a university.

OR

enable him to gain specialization in one of the specialized techniques of library science.

(b) prepare him to conduct advanced research in library science.

Banaras Hindu University has described the objectives as below:

1. To give the students specialize knowledge in respect of:

(a) type of libraries; and

(b) libraries materials.

2. To acquaint him with organization of universe of knowledge and scientific method and

3. To make him proficient in the advanced techniques of library classification and cataloguing and methodology of documentation and bibliography.

The Master's course must provide the foundation for further academic study and future intellectual growth. It must acquaint the student with the fundamentals of the intellectual disciplines thus enabling him to think about and deal with substantive intellectual problems, particularly as they relate to society. It must train him to use language skilfully and reason judiciously. It must awaken in the student an understanding of man and the relationships that connect man to man, and it must foster that which will eventually flower as wisdom.

Duration

The duration of course of M.Lib.I.Sc. has been one academic year in every Indian University. The course at six-year level is called Master's degree in Canada MLS, and in U.K. M.A. in Library science. In India M.Lib.Sc. (M.Lib.I.Sc.) second professional degree of one year after B.Lib.Sc. (B.Lib.I.Sc.)

U.S.A. post M.S. or advanced certificate of styled master degree, *i.e.* two years professional study after a basic Bachelor's degree.

U.K. Master degree at Sixth-year level of FLA.

Canada MLS second professional degree of one year after BLS (up to 1971) and first professional degree of two years study after basic Bachelor degree onwards.

Admission Qualification

Vikram University	:	1. Degree or Diploma in Lib.Sc. 50 per cent marks.
		2. Admission test.
Banaras Hindu University	:	1. Degree in Lib.Sc. IInd Div. 50 per cent marks.
		2. Three years Library Experience.
Rajasthan University	:	1. Degree Course or Postgraduate Diploma in Lib.Sc. — 50 per cent marks.
		2. Admission test in Lib. Classification, cataloguing, and general knowledge — 50 per cent marks.
Delhi University	:	1. B.Lib.Sc. — 50 per cent marks.
		2. Written test.
Bombay University	:	1. Degree in Lib.Sc.
		2. Service in a responsible position in an approved library for a period of not less than 3 years.

Vikram, Rajasthan and Delhi Universities conduct admission test and test the proficiency in library classification and cataloguing and also general knowledge of the candidates. University admits even fresh candidates having no library working experience, if he has qualified the test. On the other hand B.H. University and Bombay Universities allow admission on preferential basis to the person having 3 years working experience in an approved library.

Student-fresher, when passed Master's degree fail to seek better jobs in accordance with his higher qualification and student in his career at initial stage in library where B.Lib.I.Sc. student also gets chance. It made no use of the specialized qualification and candidate become outdated or forget what he practiced or learn in his advanced course. On the other hand if candidates having 3 years working experience allowed admission without any test, it will not be a wisely step as nothing could he judged of the proficiency of library techniques learned in degree course. There are chances of admission of unsuitable persons though they have worked in a library in lower capacity or the other.

It suggested that M.Lib.I.Sc. Course should be allowed to the following candidates:

1. Bachelor's Degree in First division, or
2. Bachelor's Degree in Second division with 5 years working experience.
3. Written test in —
   (a) Administrative problems of library;
   (b) Library service;
   (c) Library Technical-knowledge (Classification, Cataloguing and Information Science).
4. Preference should be given to the librarians or same professions working in administrative capacity or in-charge of any Departmental or College Library.

Courses of Studies

1. Some universities have made the paper "Advanced Cataloguing and Advanced Classification" as optional, which is not justified since the cataloguing techniques studies in bachelor's course were not sufficient for proficiency particularly in micro thoughts field as well as interpreparationary ideas. University has not given any importance to both the subjects for their advanced studies. India is a developing country and libraries are poorly financed. Even the librarian himself does the work of cataloguing or classification. Moreover, in these libraries micro-documents are catalogued and classified for documentation purpose which requires

advanced knowledge of classification and cataloguing and even modifications in classification and cataloguing codes on the basis of local variations.

2. Library system is an important paper which has been adopted in all schools except few. But some schools have unnecessarily divided it among various libraries while many of them have the same characteristics and can be studied together. It is suggested that there should be three or four categories of libraries:
   (a) Public library system;
   (b) Academic library system;
   (c) Special libraries; technical, Medical, Law, Agriculture;
   (d) Historical libraries: Archival, Museum, Central record and manuscript libraries.

Treatment of Classification and Cataloguing Paper

From a survey of various syllabus of universities, it has been clearly mentioned that classification and cataloguing have been expanded to Master's course. Degree course is first degree course and librarian need to be work in technical job with the same degree. Committee also recommend that more weight should be assigned to classification. 'Professional Expectations' demand that a new entrant should be grounded in such studies which are likely to be his or her basic or routine requirements in the later period of his or her career.

When we talk of professional expectation, we mean professional duties and functions towards library techniques, organization and service to the society.

Professionals are mainly appointed to organize the library properly. Since organization retrieval require a good knowledge of classification of cataloguing in most of the libraries, particularly small libraries, it is necessary to impart good professional training in all subjects to the librarians. Moreover there are several subjects which can be learned without any specific instructions or formal training. But classification and cataloguing requires proper formal teaching by the qualified professionals. Since one of the objectives of the one year course is to prepare the students for advanced work in librarianship, it is all more imperative that the incumbents get adequate training in both the subjects. On this concept has been changed in 20th century, when automation is the need of the tune and forwarding towards paperless library. Various networks are applied for library services. Information technology, network, Information sources and Information Organisations should compulsorily be taught.

2.9.3 *Inter-School Cooperation*

The present position of library schools is not encouraging. Every library school is beating its own drum and self-centred. There should be a effective cooperation among library schools maintain standards and implement development programmes in order to serve the society to the maximum. The inter-school cooperation may be maintained by:

(a) Formulating a national policy with the cooperation of Government of India and UGC at national level and UNESCO, FID and IFLA at international level;

(b) Collaboration among themselves and with other agencies through professional associations;

(c) Drawing up guidelines for different types of course, curricula, and specialization useful to the nation;

(d) Allowing specialized courses in addition to core subjects to produce specialists in particular area;

(e) Starting research programme, *e.g.* doctoral research;

(f) Implementing teacher-exchange programme, it will facilitate the teachers gaining teaching experience in different contents and methodology adopted in different schools. It will also help teacher exchanging their ideas and strengthening the friendly ties among the schools;

(g) Organizing seminars, workshops and conferences jointly or separately avoiding overlapping of programmes;

(h) Sharing the school resources, particularly costly like computer services. It can be possible to the schools of particular area.

Library school cooperation may be effective at regional level. World, a continent, a sub-continent and a country should be divided in regions. Library schools of one region should be called a "Regional Group of Library School". Region may be geographically, language-wise and based on region, climate, and social structure or combination of all these varieties. The other categories may be Group of underdeveloped countries, developing countries and developed countries etc.

Cooperative efforts among library schools should be aimed to the following factors:

1. It should be a national policy so that effective steps may be taken to maintain harmony.
2. In-service training or on the job training should be made available.
3. All programmes should lead to the promotion of library and information service.
4. There should be joint efforts for collaborating development of programmes.
5. There should be adequate resource sharing of school for advancement of research.
6. It should promote cooperation in the preparation of course material and teaching aids.
7. It should encourage inter-exchange programmes; *e.g.*:
   (a) Exchange of information,
   (b) Exchange of teachers,
   (c) Exchange of students,
   (d) Exchange of library staff,
   (e) Exchange of resource-material.
8. It should provide regional centres to discuss the problems at regional levels.

2.9.4 *Modern Trends in Library Science Courses*

In the present age of Information Science and Technology libraries should be a helping hand in the development of library administration and techniques to provide CAS and SDI services as to serve the people at the same time. The B.Lib.I.Sc. and M.Lib.I.Sc. should be advanced and modern applying modern techniques to cooperate and coordinate the research work in the field of science and technology.

This is an age of technology and mass communication. The courses should be equipped with modern appliances like computer laboratory, fax, e-mail and also audio-video techniques to provide better services. Every department should be well established, well equipped and well staffed. All such training centres which provide guidance for mere 15 days or 1 month a year should be either closed or rationalized. There should be no place for correspondence courses in Library & Information Science or the admission conditions should be strict to the professionals working in any university for 5 years at least.

Correspondence Courses, a Curse

UGC is empowered to deal with such training centres. It should think seriously in this matter. Many universities are imparting distance education in the field of library science. It organises guidance of 2 days a week in mostly in evening hours. It is surprising and surveyed that hardly 35 per cent students attend these classes though they are given qualifying attendance. So far teaching lectures are concerned, most of the professionals are not basically teachers and teaching part time after their regular service period. On the other hand courses are more advanced, which cannot be taught without regular teachers and computer laboratory. It has resulted to below standard trainees. I suggest that all correspondence courses of such type of programmes should be discouraged. Such courses should be allowed in degree courses having theory papers only.

REFERENCES

Allen, Gulchrist. "Work Study in Libraries". *Jrl. of Librarianship* 2, 1970.

Belcher, D.W. "Job Description: Guidelines". *Personnel Journal.* V. 45.

"Education for librarianship in India". *IASLIC Seminar*, 1965.

Gapp, Kameth S. "The librarian's Taste in Improving Personnel" *Coll. & Res. Lib.* 8, 1947.

Galfand, M.A. *University Libraries for Developing Countries.* Unesco, 1972.

Harrison, J.C. "The Staff Problem". *Lib. Asso. Rec.* Vol. 30.

Howard Paul. *Library Staff Manuals and a Theory of Library Management.* Univ. of Chicago, 1939.

Hammill Harold L. "Selection, Training and Staffing for Branch Libraries. *Lib. Trends.* 14, 1966.

Hurt Puyten. "Staff Specialisation: A Possible Substitute for Departmentalisation". *ALA Bull.* 29.

India Advisory Committee for Libraries. *Report.* Delhi Manager of Pub., 1959.

Kaser David. "Library Development in Eight Asian Countries". Metuchan, Sarecrow, 1969.

Karla, P.N. "Lib. Education and Asso. of Teachers in Lib. Sc." *Herald Lib. Sc.* IX, 1970.

Khurshid, Anis. "Lib. Education in South Asia". *Libri.* XX, 1-2, 1970.

Koh, Thong-Ngee. "Library Conditions and Library Training in Singapur". *Libri.* XX, 1970.

Lehrer, R.N. *Work Simplification.* Eaglewood Cliffs, 1968.

Mangla, P.B. *Level of Training in Lib. & Inf. Sc.* Delhi, Macmillan, 1981.

Martine, Lowell. *Personnel Administration in Libraries.* Chicago Univ., 1946.

Maslow, A.H. *Motivation and Personality.* N. York, Harper, 1954.

Mitra, Bankatar G.W. "A Management Problem in Librarianship. "*Herald of Lib. Sc.* Vol. 10, 2, 1971.

Mittal, R.L. *The Library Administration.* Delhi, Metropolitan, 1964.

Neelmeghan, A. "Education for Librarians and Documentalists in India." *Ency. of Lib. & Inf. Sc.* V. II. N. York, Dekker, 1974.

Neuner, Joher. "Office Management." Bombay, D.B. Taraporewala, 1970.

Parkins, John W. "Job Description of Non-professional Library Employees." Englewood Pub. Library, 1967.

Penna, C.V. "Planning Library Services". *Unesco Bull. For Lib.*, 21, 1967.

Russel, K. "Professional Education for Librarianship": *Lib. Qrly.* 12.

Saunders, W.L. "Guidelines for Curriculum Dev. in Inf. Studies". Unesco. 1978.

Sivraman, K.M. "Team work, staff council and Renaissance in Lib. Sc.". *Lib. Sc. Today.* Bombay, Asia. 1968.

Sharma, C.K. *University Library: Management & Org.* Delhi, Metropolitan, 1977.

Thomson, James. *Intro. to University Library Administration.* London, Clive Buigley, 1970.

Tucker, H.W. *In Service Training in Large Public Libraries.* Chicago Univ., 1952.

UGC (India) Review Committee. "Lib. Sc. in Indian Universities." New Delhi, 1965.

Wasserman, Paul. *The New Librarianship.* N. York, Bowker, 1972.

Wingir, Howard Woodrod. "Aspects of Librarianship". *Lib. Qrly.* 31, 1961.

Yadn, Dali. *Personnel Management and Industral Relation.* N. Delhi, Prentice Hall, 1975.

3

LIBRARY BUILDING

3.1 Need for Library Building

Library building is one of the important factors needed for the development of the libraries. Library is a growing organism. It grows in all spheres of service and resources, *i.e.* staff, collection and buildings. The space requirement is a primary need and it is determined by its purpose. Two questions come in mind — what work is to be done in the building, and what service it renders. Even constructing our private house, we consider the family members, householdings, functions of the family members and the future programmes, *e.g.* sleeping, eating, bringing up a family, recreation, quiet and noisy space, indoor and outdoor and various likings of the persons. Different families of different types have different tastes. Similarly, libraries have different nature — public, academic, children, adult, research, business etc.; different collection — reference, non-book material, photographic equipments, different services — reference service, computer service, photographic service, landing service, inter-library loan service etc.; different readers — scientists, general public, research scholars, blinds, general students, labourers, childrens, women etc.; different staff — technical staff, non-technical staff, semi-technical staff etc. It is very difficult to estimate the space requirement from the point of one aspect, by visitors or readers, but from various point of views.

There are different works — on the screen and behind the screen, services — indoor or outdoor. Architect cannot draw an exact line of space demand until unless he consults the librarian and the persons attached to the library services.

All libraries have basically similar library pattern of organization, which makes the library functional. Library differ in these functions. The functions of children libraries will be different with that of adult libraries and the college libraries. If a college library needs a reading room, a university library needs a seminar room in addition to more reading rooms.

Library has its own method of service — open access or closed access. It also effect the space factor in a library. For each task a required amount of space is needed. Departments should be accommodated in such a way that each may be related conveniently to each other.

A good library building is always purposeful for the following:

1. **Efficient function**: Library has its own nature. It may be public, academic or special, but its basis purpose lies with the maximum use of the reading material housed in its building. There are various functions of a library. More functional activities leads more efficient services. It is a research library, photographic, computer, bibliographic and other documentation services including reference services are main function. Each service will have its separate department or division containing the special concerned material. It could be possible, or say, functions can be activised only if proper accommodation and space is provided. Efficient functioning, the first purpose of a library, more or less depend on infrastructure of a library, *i.e.* a functional library.
2. **Maximum service**: It is the effort of each library to serve the reader with maximum facilities and more in number. Library building help in achieving this goal. If library building is well planned based on requirements of a library and equipped with all appliances, equipments and furniture needed for smooth library services, library can serve the reader with high potentiality and capacity.
3. **Conserve reading material**: Library collect reading material and house it systematically so that readers can get their books easily and without losing

unnecessary time. Material is divided at many points; stack rooms, reading rooms, reference rooms, periodical rooms, textbook rooms, and reproduction rooms, and made available for consultation according to the needs of the readers. It avoids crowd at one point.

4. **Specialization:** There are specialists in library staff, readers for which special services are facilitated. Library building help in providing the special services and manage sufficient space for each activity so that specialized activities may not be disturbed by other general works.
5. **Departmentalization:** Departmentalization makes the services more quick and accurate. Library work and services are divided among various departments with their supervisors and the subordinate staff. Each department has its own task and directly related to the executives, which increases discipline, maintains hierarchy and chain of command. Library building proves more helpful and effective to departmentalization if it is built with proper planning.

3.2 Function of a Library Building

Library is a social organism. It serves the society and work as a centre for the dissemination of knowledge. It promotes learning and contribute to the maximum in the development of education. A library has no special consideration for any cost, creed and colour and render its valuable services to all equally irrespective of any distinction and denomination. Informal education is much more provided by the self-learning centres like libraries, where people come and consult the reading material with his own efforts, minds and the ways. No doubt they need initial guidance, but they retain self-education. Library does not engage any subject teacher and never organize class teaching like colleges, schools and universities. Its teachers are the reference tools *i.e.* catalogue, reference books, audio-visual aids and the library staff. It is obvious that functions of a library are centralized to efficient and prompt service to the maximum number of readers on economic measures.

Generally a library does the following functions —

1. It collects the reading material, preserve it, conserve it and make all possible efforts to develop it to a large number. Knowledge is wider term and includes the material of different variety, nature, size, colour, quality. A reader is a knowledge seeker. He has little knowledge of the material produced in huge number. Library apply various methods and acquire it, arrange it systematically.
2. Modern libraries are not storehouses. Their work is not complete after collecting the material. It keep in close watch with latest publications and specific nature of the stored collection. It disseminate the knowledge out of it.
3. Lending is an important function of a library. It distribute the material among the knowledge seekers on demand. Library provide circulation services and makes the material available to the readers.
4. It provides guidance in consulting and locating the desired material through reference service. Reference service is an important function of a library, which relates the reader with the reading material for a particular purpose.
5. A library has a team of workers with their special qualities. Staff is professionally trained in library work and services and known with tactics to deal with the readers and possess the qualities of a gentleman, friend, teacher, guide, administrator and a scholar.
6. It protect the reading material from sun and rain, heat and cold and safeguard our well-being during the hours of work, and rest.

We can enumerate main library functions as under:

1. **Accommodation for reading material**: Reading material includes books, periodicals, reprographic material, bibliographic material and audio-visual aids etc. Library collects material according to its nature of work, size and mainly objectives. A designer or architect, first consider just what kinds of work are done within a

library. But there are basic process behind the preservation nor operation of work pertaining to the collection of reading material — printed or handwritten documents, records including pamphlets, maps and drawings. We call them various devices of knowledge.

The collection work of reading material involves various processes, *i.e.*:

(a) selection of material;

(b) access to lists and indexes;

(c) ordering material;

(d) accessing the material;

(e) returning the material;

(f) cataloguing and classifying the material;

(g) levelling and numbering of material;

(h) displaying the material;

(i) stacking the material;

(j) repairing and binding of material;

(k) reproducing the material.

The above process is a 'Behind the screen process', which is not directly concerned with readers. This is production or work process:

The above process can be categorized according to their related groups:

	Group of work		**Group of workers** **Acquisition Department**
1.	Access to lists Checking of demands Selection of material	→	Book Selection Division Sr. Professionals Subject specialists Attached staff
2.	Ordering Checking on receipt of material	→	Ordering Division Supervisor Assistants

No.	Work		Section / Staff
3.	Accessioning Returning the unwanted material	→	Accessioning Division Supervisor Assistants
4.	Cataloguing Classification	→	Technical Department Supervisor Specialist in ___ & Classi.
5.	Levelling Numbering Displaying	→	Preparation Department Supervisor Assistants
6.	Book arrangement or stacking	→	Stack room Supervisor Assistants
7.	Binding Repairing	→	Binding Department Supervisor Specialists
8.	Reproduction or material or Photographic process	→	Photographic Studio or Reprographic Department Supervisor Specialists
9.	Bibliographic work or Documenting the non-book material	→	Documentation Deptt. Supervisor Assistants

The above categorization or groupism of various works done before library service require sufficient accommodation as per their load of work, size of work, size of collection and the staff engaged in each work. Library building is constructed considering the book-preparation and book storage activities. Building makes the activities effective.

2. **Accommodation for reading community**: Readers are served by the library building in many ways. They are of three types: New readers, enrolled readers, and

the alumni readers. When a new reader enters the library building, he is served with rules and regulations displayed on the board or, walls or on a display desk. Catalogue also help them. It is generally seen that catalogue cabinets are housed or placed near the entrance and the reference desk. A separate accommodation is provided for him. Catalogues are consulted by readers whether public man, student and the scholar. Various forms of reading materials are provided in separate reading rooms. Generally the choice of readers is different. Some readers want microfilms, while other wants books, periodicals etc. Some libraries serve the readers through lectures, seminars or exhibitions.

Reader's activities effect the library building. Library building also serves the readers through various departments, furniture, equipments, and other various facilities.

Reader's activities and the library building both are interrelated. They can be categorized:

Reader's activities	Building accommodation
1. At initial stage — entering the library, the reader:	
(a) deposits his personal property	- Property counter
(b) See book display, and display of rules and regulations	- Display room or the Entrance hall
(c) Consult the catalogue	- Catalogue cabinet or Lending department
(d) Consult library staff or reference staff	- Reference desk
2. At second stage, the reader —	
(a) Consult reference material	- Reference department
(b) Enrolled as number and borrow books	- Circulation department

3. At third stage, the reader —
   - (a) Consult periodicals - Periodical department
   - (b) Demand reproduction of some thoughts in the form of microfilm, photostat copy etc. - Photographic department
   - (c) Use computer for solving some statistical problems - Computer department
   - (d) Demand translations, bibliographies, and documentation lists on some specific aspects or study - Documentation department
4. At fourth stage, the reader —
   - (a) Debates
   - (b) Seminars
   - (c) Lectures
   - (d) Exhibitions

   - Seminar room and Exhibition hall
5. At last stage, the reader —
   - (a) Consult books and makes writing - Reading rooms

3. **Library Staff**: Most of the library staff need to separate accommodation as they work and serve in the departments must for reader's service and the reading material. But the activities of library staff help in extension of the library building.

There are few among the library staff, who need separate accommodation. There are top liner, *i.e.* Executives like Librarian, Dy. Librarian and Assistant Librarians in large libraries, Librarians and Dy. Librarians in middle class libraries, and Librarians in small libraries.

There are other staff activities which are directly or indirectly related to staff, and need separate accommodation and space: *viz.* Administrative office, cubicles, staff canteen, staff meeting or recreation room, lavatories, cleaner's room and cupboards.

3.3 Highlights in Constructing a Library Building

Generally, problems come in engineering field. It has been experienced that proper coordination is not maintained while planning a library. There should be proper coordination between the librarian and architecture. Librarians are not given due consideration and less consulted. Librarian is the right person who spend his most part of his life in the library with library staff. If building is not suitable and well planned, everyone settles down to several years of embarrassing, distressing, frustrating though they are not at fault, but because of the engineering failures.

More, artificiality in building is troublesome. Air conditioning and forced ventilation is not everlasting or even for a long period. It does not work properly and resulted to a wastage of money. The failure of air conditioning causes humidity and require separate maintenance and damages to the building.

Flexibility is a must for library building. Library is a growing organism. It grows and changes made with the time. Any misuse of mezzanine decreases the flexibility. Moreover, "Changing requirements of the not-too-distant future would cause tremendous hardships, as well as some impossible situations. Bearing walls, plumbering, air conditioning and electrical systems, to name a few, would provide 'road blocks' flexibility were not made a part of the design programme".

Situation effect the library service. Location of staff public service is an important factor. Proper situation for a librarian's seat, reference desk, charge desk — should be fixed. The main stack area should be on the appointed side of the main reading room.

There should be no poor relationship between, public service desks and staff work-room, changing stations or checking points and main public exit, as it result to less service to the public and considerable loss of books.

Over departmentalization should be avoided in smaller or medium-sized libraries.

Provision for future expansion of the building should be made. All precautionary and preventive measures should be taken.

There should be no shortage of land. It should have sufficient space for parking, exit and expansion.

Proper coordination among the architectural, electrical, and mechanical element should be established and each element should be well experienced, full of knowledge and whole-hearted interested in the building construction.

Building should not be too monumental in character. Material of low maintenance adjacent to public walks and entrances should be used.

Building should not have too much duplication or overlapping inter-communication system. Telephone should be placed at a place of less noisy.

There should be proper diffused lighting. High quality diffuser can be more useful. Lighting switches should be in the area of the library staff not the public. A current fire-sprinkler system should be used.

Carpeted floors are more useful, but the carpet should have rubber backing. Hard floors should be avoided particularly in the noisy and rush area. Furniture — chairs and tables, should be rubber base.

Library should be well furnished. Children library is given more place for modern and easy furniture.

Planning is an art, not an exact science. What is good for one library, can be bad for the other. It is because of the nature of reader, material and the staff, site and location, finance and other factors involved in the construction of library building.

Wheeler says, "A satisfactory library building can be evolved only through long, careful, joint study on the part of the architect, the librarian and the building committee of the library board." He further formulated some general principles as under:

1. The library should have a librarian appointed before the planning of a library.
2. In case of experienced architect, a advisor, expert in library planning, should be engaged. He may be from the library profession or the architect.

3. ILA also says that the librarian and the architect should make efforts jointly. Before giving the final shape of planning, both should visit some important and functional library buildings.
4. All efforts should be made to construct the library building independently and separately with other buildings.
5. The building should be designed as to attach the readers. It should be convenient access to the readers.
6. It should be economically designed and constructed so that reader and the staff can make communications with each other.
7. It should have a plain level to facilitate the transport of books by book trolleys and travelling racks.
8. It should be the main consideration of providing more convenience to the library users. Moreover, it should be well beautified and special provision should be made to make the building a modern beautiful place where reader can concentrate on his studies.

   On the other hand, building should not be a art piece or over decorated as it will be a wastage of money and less convenient.
9. If funds permits the building should be air-conditioned.
10. If artificial lighting is provided, it should be scientifically planned.
11. Shelving accommodation should be planned seriously as to easy shifting of books from one stack to the other.
12. Consideration should be given for expansion and anticipated development in future.
13. The main study area should be close to book shelves and stacks.
14. **Finance**: Bible says that the love of money is the root of all ends, but the lack of it also presents problems. Library building is constructed once, with minor extension time to time. Hence, maximum effort should be made to make provision for sufficient finance. The

cost should be overestimated due to changes in prices and cost of material and labour. If cost is underestimated, the building construction may be stopped, cut short, or partly left for future. There are also chances that the most useful accommodation is effected by the underestimation. Sometimes, it may effect the quality of construction.

15. **Functional basis**: It will be better if library building is functional. Monumentality and aesthetic problems are also considered. A library building may many good points, but also drawbacks as well. None is full in itself. Everything has merits and demerits at his credit. Monumentalistic structure should be given less importance than the functional, as it effect the financial situations. Metcalf has suggested:

    "Books, readers and staff 55 per cent of the total area, with 45 per cent should be used for architectural space. But in modern libraries, the estimate is different in different ways. Assignable space has been 75 per cent to 80 per cent in many buildings."

Prof. Marla has suggested some points to be considered at the time of planning a library building:

(a) Work-flow of users, material, service, operations, storage, and control.

(b) Display area near the entrance.

(c) Circulation counter in central position with easy access *i.e.* public catalogue, book stacks and reference.

(d) Main catalogue with the easy reach of the users and the reference staff.

(e) Reference area near the public catalogue with a central reference desk.

(f) Main study area near the book stacks and periodicals.

(g) Multitier stacks.

(h) Technical staff activity to be on the same floor of the processing department.

(i) Modular concept to be used in construction.

3.3.1 *Type of Plan*

Building plans are prepared in many types. They may be:

1. **Classical plan**: Which was adopted in antiquity and Renaissance. Earlier libraries were monumental, big pillars decorated with sculpture, alloys etc. There were wall almirahs and raised from floor to ceiling. This type of buildings were built between 4th century AD to sixteenth century and continued in the concept up to nineteenth century. The library is housed in a single hall with palacial decoration. We found such libraries in Greek civilizations, ancient Rome and even in middle age.

   Though, the plan was modified to some extent during medieval period, but it was remained a single hall library. These libraries were founded in Chruches. So far reading facilities are concerned, there were reading desks with double sided sloping. At later stage (in 16th century) reading tables took big sizes and the wooden almirahs were used for shelving the books.

2. **Closed access plan**: During 19th century, the separate rooms were built to house the books and readers were kept separate from the stack room. The plan was adopted because of the continuous growth of the books.

There were libraries in double stories. The stack room on ground floor and the reading room on upper floor. This plan was suitable to the readers because there was enormous daylight in reading room. The passage of reading room was separate from the stack room.

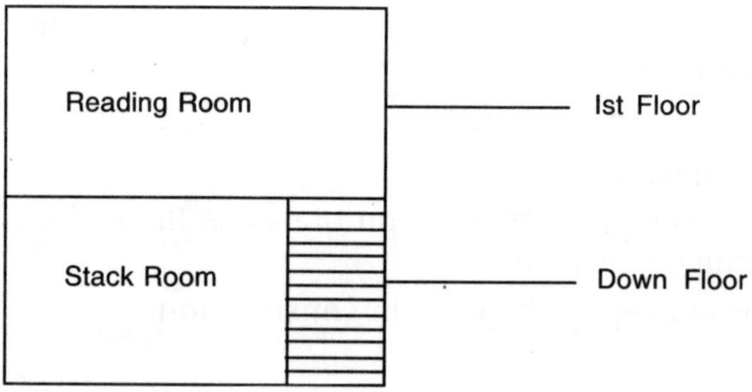

Closed Access System

On the other hand, another plan was adopted in which study area was near the stack room and some places surrounded by the stack room or the reverse.

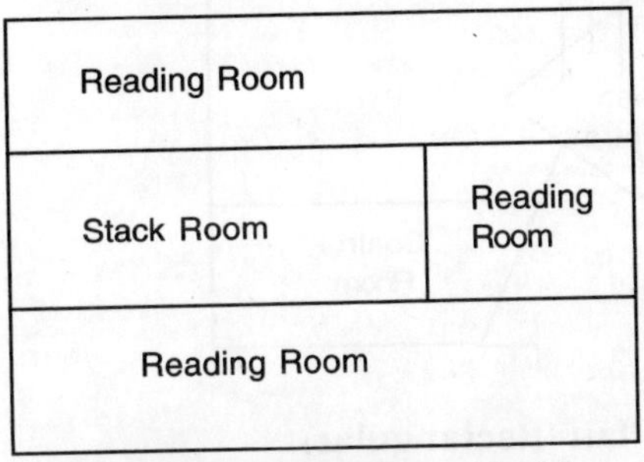

Stack room surrounded by Reading area

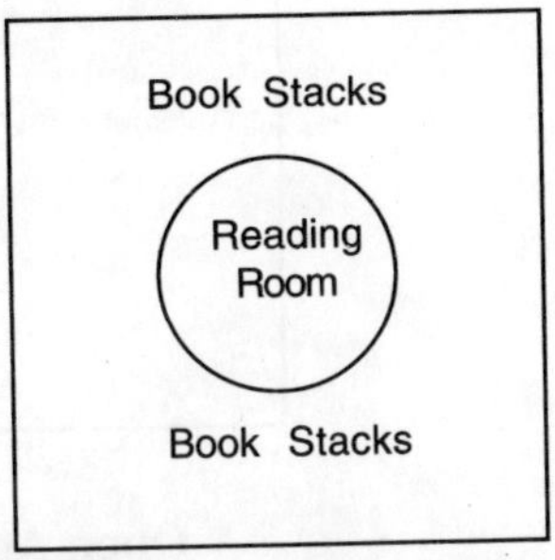

Reading room surrounded by stack room

Single floor libraries were having reading room and the stack room at one place. But they were separated with a wall.

3. **Open access plan**: One hall or one room has been the first outcome of library plan. The books are open and shelved on all side. The book area and reading area are at the same place and mixed in a room. In some libraries talking or reading area and the stack area are partitioned with glass screens.

   The other plan may be the division of one rectangular room. It is divided at the centre line from the entrance. At the centre point the control and loan counter is established. This plan is clearly followed on H, U, L and V shaped type plan. It is the most common plan and followed in most of the small and one room library.

   The large libraries of open-access character, adopts different plan. They follow flexible or modular plan in which main floor is used as stack room of most used books and various departments are divided by the class screen or book cases. The other alternative form is the subject department plan. Each department is formed on the basis of the subject books. This plan is very well-known as subject division plan. Some libraries manage all subject departments at one floor or separately on different floors.

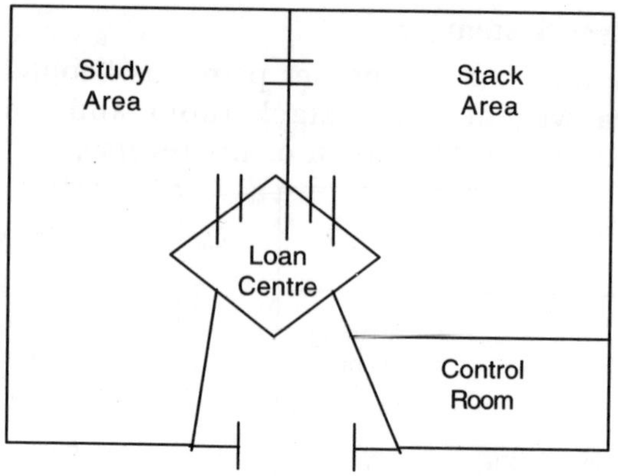

Open Access Plan (Rectangular)

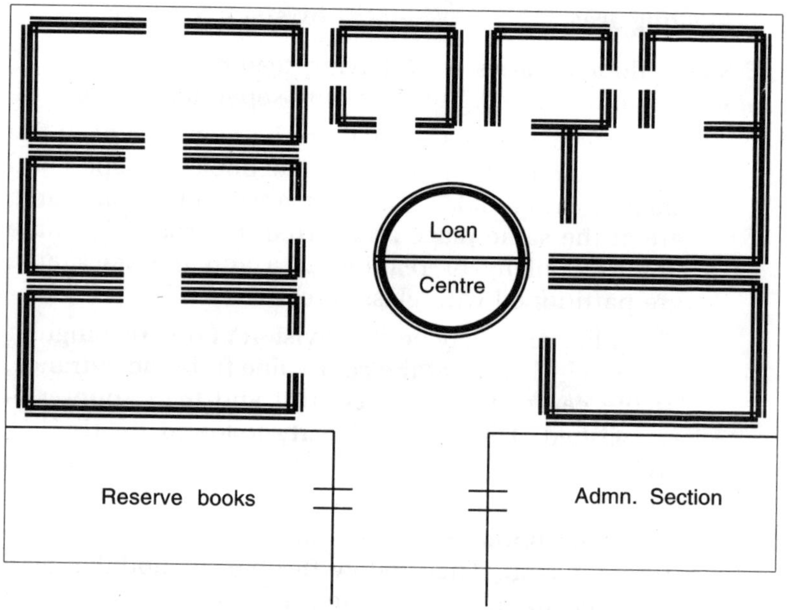

One room large library. Partition by glass screen or book cases

The other plan is drawn on the basis of departmentalization. The building is built according to the needs of the library. Accommodation is allotted to each department and building is equipped on the basis of the library activities. A large library may have multiple story plan.

Departmental type plan is effected by the following factors:

1. By reading area
2. By collection
3. By staff
4. By expansion area

3.3.2 *Librarian's Responsibility*

Librarian deals with the whole process of the library building. He is supposed to be a man of good knowledge of it. At every stage of building planning librarian is consulted.

A librarian should know:

1. What type of building he wants?
2. What need he has?
3. How a building can be put to maximum use?
4. What should be the accommodation and space for every aspect of library activities?
5. What functions are to be undertaken in the building?
6. Which accommodation is given preference for special attention?
7. What will be the chain of communication in building?

Metcalf has suggested seven point programme for librarian:

1. A librarian should know about library building as much as he can.
2. He should learn the educational programme of the institution and the relation between the library and the educational programme.
3. Librarian should take decision about the philosophy of library service.
4. He should consult the administrative officers of the institution for all problems thus arises.
5. He should make careful study of a site, and select the most suitable.
6. He should have an elementary knowledge of architects, and select the best architect for his library building.

Moreover, he should be well versed about the relations with the architect.

7. He should estimate the building costs on the basis of a realistic plan.

In view of the above, it is clear that the librarian should prepare plan in brief and provide it to the architect. This brief should include the accommodation and space required for each department and their relations with each other. Thompson has suggested the lines of planning in a library building.

Each library has general functions. Each function is undertaken in a department. Some departments deal with more number of readers and the readers of general nature and thus make noisy scene, while other serve the readers of specialized nature, and make talking or quiet scenes.

The atmosphere, therefore, is divided in three points:

1. Noisy part of the building;
2. Talking part of the building; and
3. Peace part of the building.

Building

PEACE AREA

1.	Stack room	4.	Photography section
2.	Reference section	5.	Periodical room
3.	Reading room	6.	Professors' reading room

TALKING AREA

1.	Bibliographies	5.	Seminars room
2.	Lending section	6.	Exhibition hall
3.	Administrative block	7.	General reading room
4.	Building section		

NOISY AREA

1. Entrance hall
2. Property counter
3. Catalogues

In view of the above, the responsibility of a librarian is increased. We can categorize the responsibilities of a librarian in planning as under. A librarian should —

1. decide about the convenience of the readers. The entrance or the way to various departments should, in no way, be a disturbing factor to the working of the library or other library users.
2. have knowledge about the nature, objectives of the parent institution to which the library is attached and the building is to be designed.
3. take decision about the space to be allotted to various sections and the reading community. There are readers of various nature, liking, demands, who demand for separate space for reading. We can categorize them as individual reader, faculty readers (as community), group readers, seminars, lectures etc.
4. decide about the special features of library activities. Each library provide some special service for which special space is required *i.e.* audio-visual aids area, photographic area, automation area.
5. determine the number of library personnel to be served in various departments of a library and engaged in operational work.
6. apply and use various formulas and standards approved by the standard institutes for determining the space and accommodation for building purposes.
7. foresee the future requirements and all possibilities of future expansion.
8. make clear and final decisions and make definite recommendations on each major points. No point should be left controversial.
9. make specific recommendation about the furniture and fittings to be used in each area of building.
10. make proper outline, complete in all respect and submit for further action.

However, the librarian, in making the design of the library building, should consult the architect and finalize the matter with full confidence. He should also guide the architect at the time of construction and also furnishing various areas.

3.3.3 *Architect*

An architect works out the plan and prepares the design on paper. He is a person who represent the ideas of the librarian on a paper and draw and sketch the same with architectural features, material and site. Architect is "a person skilled in the out of building. He is supposed to form plans and draw up designs. Specification for buildings and to superintend then execution".

An architect who is well versed and possesses a satisfactory experience of constructing a library building, should be contacted. No doubt that architects of library building experience are rare and not easily traceable, but a fresh architect may also be engaged for library building construction, for which he should be allowed to visit some modern libraries at various places so that he may get the knowledge about the specific nature and type of construction, library working and the library organization.

There should be proper coordination between the librarian or librarian-expert and the architect. An architect cannot design a library building until unless he consults the librarian and aware himself with all the points to be necessarily considered. Architect prepares drawings and sketches for all major functions of a library. In other words we can describe an architect as a "graphic representative". The graphic representation or drawing is followed for construction purposes.

Architect is an important link in the construction of building. He is among the trinity responsible for the successful building a library: Librarian + Administrator (Financer) + Architect. Architect is the last and the final link and give practical shape to the financial ideal and theoretical planning.

An architect provides the following functions:

1. He consult the librarian and the administrator.
2. He draws the final graphic representation according to the specifications of library functions.
3. He draws preliminary sketches and drawing on the

basis of the details worked out by the librarian consultant or the librarian.

4. He supervises the construction work and provides technical information in the use of material and other devices.

Architect is the keyman whose single mistake or carelessness can make the building misfit and non-functional. There is a urgent need of good relations between the architect and the librarian. Any difference or conflict may give a bad-shape to the building and the purpose of effective and efficient service by the library will fail. To avoid any conflict, library building committees are constituted.

3.3.4 ***A Team Work*** (Library Building Committee)

A team is described as "the number of persons associated together to work or activity as a group of workmen each completing one of a set of operations". A team may consist of general persons, specialists or the scientists functioning as collaborative unit.

For library building a team, consisting of few persons, is constituted. It includes —

(1) Librarian

(2) Library-expert or consultant

(3) Architect

(4) Engineer expert or consultant

(5) Administrator or governing authority of the institution.

In some institutions only three persons: the librarian, architect and the administrator constitute a library committee, while in other institutions finance officer or the financer is also included in the list. The administrator acts as chairman and the librarian as secretary of the committee.

A library building is a product of many ideas and of many persons. Hence, it requires a warm cooperation of each person of building committee.

The preliminary duty of the committee includes:

1. A thorough survey of the requirements;
2. A study of the objects of the institution;

3. A meeting with all persons related to the library directly or indirectly;
4. Prepare a questionnaire with several type of questions which can reveal the opinion of the people regarding the design of the building;
5. Inviting suggestions from the readers' community, library staff, administrative staff, the members of governing body, library committee and the faculty members.

Individual Responsibility

The committee members meet together periodically and give and take their ideas in order to reach to a definite result. Each member of library building committee is equally responsible for the success or the failure of the building plan. Each member is responsible for the following acts:

(a) Give-and-take the views of each other.

(b) He must not accept the solution the first stage or the first proposal of a single member. He must hear the views of all members.

(c) Conversion or discussion should be free and frank and nobody should be pressed to follow others' suggestions or solutions.

(d) As each member has specific qualities, abilities and skill, each has a very specific responsibility.

3.3.5 *Librarian*

(e) Librarian is a information media from one member to the others. He is also responsible for preparing the written building programme.

(f) He converts the architect on the furniture and the interior furnishing.

(g) Normally librarian represents the institutional head in library building committee. Hence, he should know the building and to speak what he wants.

(h) He is also responsible for suggesting the area to be covered for library functions. He must explain the operation of the building to the architect.

(i) He must be concise, knowledgeable and specific and a prompt communicator.

(j) Librarian is more nearer to the people than other members. Hence, he must call the suggestions of the people and put before the committee.

(k) Generally library building committee is final authority to finalize the plan. Even then the librarian's role is inevitable and more responsible.

3.3.6 *Library Building Committee*

(l) Building committee being the authority on the subject, is responsible to collect the finance. It may be by Government grant, donation or a resolution.

(m) The committee makes necessary selection of a architect suitable.

(n) It selects the site and finally approves it.

(o) The committee allow discussions on the planning problems and hear each member and thereafter approve preliminary plans.

(p) Everywhere, there has been a problem of a suitable contractor. Library board decides and approves the contractor to whom the construction work is entrusted.

Architect

(q) Architect is most responsible person in library building committee. He contributes a lot in the design of a building. An architect is recognized by his status and repute. An architect evaluates the need of the librarian and reviews the building programme.

(r) He is responsible for both the problems: What will be the looking scene and how it will work?

(s) He advises regarding the technical effect of climate on building to be constructed on a particular site.

(t) He follows the building codes, acts or regulations of the local governments and suggests for the real financial requirements.

(u) He establishes the beauty of the building and advises on accommodations required for each function.

(v) He prepares detailed working drawings and specifications.

(w) He suggests for the better contractor and help you in the selection.

3.4 Principles of Planning Library Building

Whether it is a necessity to design a public library, academic library or the research library, it is based on some fundamental principles of planning. In other words it is also called with the name of structural planning. The important principles which are popularly considered in planning process, can be enumerated as under:

(a) Thc building should be utilized by all without any consideration for caste, creed and sex. Library is a social organism and every body whosoever is the member of the society should be free to use it. Hence it should be planned accordingly.

(b) There are contradictory nature in ornamental or the functional. Ornamental design may be good looking, costly and can be appreciated by a layman. But until unless the building is functional, it cannot be put to effective and sincere service to the community. Hence, building should be designed on functional basis.

(c) Building should be simple in construction, but effective for efficient service.

(d) Reading area, the reading rooms should be near to the stack area. It will help in easy approach to reading material.

(e) The building should be designed to economy the administrative working and all other operations done in a library.

(f) An foresight outlook should be applied and expansion programme should be given due consideration. Library grows continuously and thus future anticipations should be kept in mind while planning a library building.

(g) A detailed study should be made about the overall activities of a library and a brief statement of concerning data should be prepared in the light of proportionate future growth.

(h) Physical facilities should be provisioned in proportion of the reading community and the library staff.

The planning is based on some data which are of much value. The broad principles also consider these data. Each library has some objectives and functions accordingly. Functions include library work and service through various departments and sections. These data are taken from the working at various points in a library. We can call them statistics of library working. These are as under:

1. The total collection of the library. It includes books and bound periodicals.
2. Journals which are currently subscribed.
3. Total number of specialized collection, *i.e.* manuscripts, rare books, out of print books etc.
4. Total number of non-book material, *i.e.* microfilms, micro-card etc.
5. The number of books added in a year.
6. Work involved in acquisition programme.
7. Type of technical work and its programme *i.e.* cataloguing, classification etc.
8. Statistics of circulation desk, *i.e.* number of issue and deposit in a day.
9. Type of reference service provided. Data regarding the number of persons to be served.
10. Reading capacity and number of reading rooms.
11. Specialized services provided. Data regarding number of reproduction.
12. Number of library staff in various capacities *i.e.* professional, semi-professional and non-professional.
13. Stack room capacity, *i.e.* number of shelves, capacity of shelves and future programme.
14. Rate of growth in each section, *i.e.* growth in readers, material, service, storage, operation and staff.

3.4.1 *Planning and the Standards*

There are institutions working out the standard specifications for library buildings. These standards are run in both capacities: private and public. In most of the countries the standard institutions have been established at national level. The main functions of a standard institution can be enumerated as under:

1. They form standards for productive output produced in various industrial and commercial firms.
2. They form quality standard to bring the commodity at high level in a competitive market as well useful for the public.
3. They, by standardizing the quality, bring economy in output cost and conducting researches in this respect.
4. They control the quality and bring uniformity in all concerns of similar nature.

Standard institute constitute a committee for work out and for the quality standard of a particular type of commodities. There are separate committees for specialized output. These committees consists of scientists, specialists of a specialized field. Several committees, consisting of professional experts in library science and building, have been constituted by many standard institutions.

British Standard Institute, London constituted a Library Building Committee. Likewise, USA and USSR Standard Institutes formed committees on library buildings.

A standard institute has been established in India also. It is known as 'Indian Standard Institute' with headquarter at New Delhi. This institute has formed standards on library building and allied aspects. It has two committees:

(i) Documentation Sectional Committee

(ii) Committee on library buildings, fittings and furnitures.

Dr. Ranganathan acted as chairman of the committees. The committees laid specifications and formed standards for:

(a) Documentation techniques,

(b) Primary elements of buildings,

(c) Elements of furniture and fittings.

The ISI committees for documentation and building, furniture and fittings consists library professionals, architects and the engineers. ISI is a national institute and committees constituted by it mainly deal with national standards and specifications on a particular output. Specifications laid down for library building have been the efforts of all the member which are supposed to be the experts of this field. Whatever decisions are taken, they are with serious discussions and consultations of all experts.

Indian Standard Institute has published the following standards:

IS:1553-1960	Code of Practice relating to Primary Elements in the Design of Library Buildings.
IS:1829 (Part-I)-1961	Library furniture and fittings; Part-I Timber
IS:1661-1964	Libra cline (Mobile library)
IS:2662-1964	Packages for the libraries.

There are standard institutions which functions at international level. There is a International Standards Organization (ISO). It has laid specifications on documentation. Some associations are also forming standards, such as Special Library Association, New York, F.I.D., UNESCO and British Library Association etc.

3.4.2 *Library Building Programme*

It is the duty of Library Building Committee to work out the details of requirements. The requirements should fulfil the objectives of a institution. It includes site of the building, preparation of design and construction, distribution of space, lighting and furniture and equipment. There will a quantification of each factor. It will be based on —

1. quantity of material;
2. quantity of readers;
3. quantity of staff;
4. type of function service;
5. kinds of communication between material, readers and the staff and among the departments.

The more responsibility goes on the shoulders of the librarian, was, only, has knowledge and experience of library working and techniques. He advises on many technical problems of space capacity, arrangement and utility involved.

Dennis has enlisted the requirements related to good working conditions and production as under:

1. Location on ground floor or near services elevator.
2. Convenient access to loading and shipping area.
3. Parking facilities.
4. Adequate floor space to assure continuous work flow on an assembly line basis; space for equipment, files, and storage of supplies; and space for receipt of peak load shipment.
5. Adequate lighting and provision for proper electrical circuits and outlets for mechanical and automated equipment anticipated.
6. Telephones located at points of highest use.
7. Proper heating and ventilation, including air-conditioning.
8. Acoustical treatment of working areas, including isolations of noisy machines in sound-proof areas.
9. Provision for housing and use of extensive and bulky bibliographical tools, Library of Congress proof slip, order slips, and the like.
10. Provision of private office or work area for the administrator.
11. Provision for rest rooms and staff lounge.
12. Provision for sinks in the work area, adjacent to machines and near section devoted to physical processes.

"A building programme is a detailed explicit statement of the requirement of a library. It describes the primary elements of design, the inter-relationship between various areas, the estimated size of areas, the most helpful location of each area and states of important building details."

Programming is an important work. A written programme is prepared and tested to its practicality. Testing is made on the basis of:

1. Readers,
2. Type of service needed,
3. How the service rendered.

Programming is never uptodate. It is reviewed time to time. Whatever is planned is never finally programmed and that constant updating may be necessary. Planner plays an important role and need a flexible attitude which encourages the 'give and take' policy among on this part.

Programming need the following considerations:

1. Plan should be specialized and every stage of planning should be reviewed.
2. Other's programmes should not be superimposed on your own building. No doubt that other's programmes should be studied but they in full or partly, should be considered or discussed in light of your needs.
3. Formulas should be planned in detail and considered at the time of programming. It is not always that formulas are necessarily fit in. This suitability is the key point.

3.4.3 *Site*

Site is the first step for library building. It is an important function of the library building committee to choose the best site for the library building. While making any consideration for a site, the following points should be taken in mind:

1. **Easy accessibility**: The site should be chosen on the location point which is an easy approach to all readers. Library is a centre of learning and maximum learning facilities can be exploited by the reader if the site of a library is near to the institution to which it belongs, heart of the city or the population area for which it is established, and in-contact situation to its community, society, and the special class of readers to be served by the library. If site is at the each approach to the reader, it will attract the readers for maximum use of the library.

The suitability of a site differs from the type of library to library. It is —

1. In the heart of the city	- for public library
2. In the campus	- for institutional libraries
3. Near the teaching departments	- for University and College libraries
4. Near the staff room	- for school libraries
5. Near the laboratory or workshop	- for scientific technology or medical libraries

2. **Sufficient size**: The site selected should have sufficient size. It should satisfy the present need of space and the future expansion if needed. Library is a growing organism. It grows in all its wings — material, staff and the readers. A library building is planned for further 20 years. But even after 20 years, the building will need an expansion to meet the growth. Hence, there should be a sufficient space for the site of building. The site should independent and non-effective by other surrounding buildings.

3. **Quiet surroundings**: Reading can be concentratively done at quiet place. There should be peaceful atmosphere around the library building. The site should though directly connected with the main road of the campus, but should not have traffic flow of the vehicle other than the vehicles used to reach the library. The other related buildings should be adjacent to the library building in order to maintain easy communication.

4. **Surface**: The unusual subsoil is also a problem for library building. The surface of land should be hard but not rocky. The soil should have the capacity to wear the load of heavy construction and should maintain its place permanently as any shrink or the shifting of soil can put the building to a great damage.

5. **Shape of the plot**: There are two factors: shop and site. Both are inter-related. The plot should be selected according to the site. On the other hand site should be chosen in view of the plot. For example, if a site is chosen for a university library, it should be between the administrative office and the teaching department. The plot should be designed in a way that it may not

overlook both the adjacent buildings. The shape of the plot should be based on the site.

6. **Orientation of site**: Site should be centrally located facing to north or east rather than west or south. It should be in an elevated position so as to catch cooling breezes and avoid stagnation of water in heavy rains.
7. **Cost of site**: Money makes a man perfect. Money is the main consideration for a site. A good site can be rejected due to non-availability of proper funds. A best and a large site is always expensive. Many a ... library has been sited in a poor strategic position for reasons of 'economy', to the department of the ratepayers. "Cut your coat according to your cloth" applies to the cost of the building. Site should be selected as per the funds.
8. **Size of the site**: Size of the site depends on the shape of the building. If the shape of the building is T type. The size of the flat will be more big in size on one side and short on the other side.

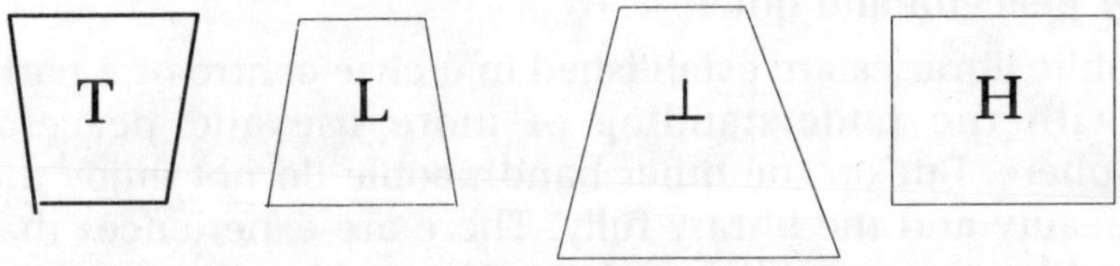

The measurement of the size will be determined by the T, L, ⊥ and H portions. American writers recommend the floor area as the basis of the size of a site. But it is not acceptable to all as there are other things other than floor area, which need space, *i.e.* space for corridors, space for loans, cycle stand etc. Site should be large enough to allow for a garden and also have sufficient provision for future additions to the building.

3.4.3.1 *Site of Public Libraries*

The public library serve the community and provides reading material on citizenship, current affairs, popular subjects, reference books, hobbies, culture and civilization and social problems. They also deal with mostly fictions. Public library is a centre of knowledge for public. It disseminates knowledge to the public reader. Its main object is to serve the maximum service economically.

In view of the objectives, the public library is established in the heart of the city, shopping centre, dense population area, among the community to be served, trading and employment area. It should be necessarily a geographical area in a city, town or a village. Location is an important factor of vast use of library resources. Best location makes the public library known to the public. A public library should have its site in the location where the building is —

(i) easily accessible to the public;

(ii) uncrowded;

(iii) spacious;

(iv) park-like;

(v) permanent;

(vi) clean;

(vii) impressive;

(viii) peaceful and quiet.

Public libraries are established in a civic centre or a park. It is with the understanding of more use and peaceful atmosphere. But on the other hand people do not enjoy the park beauty and the library fully. There are experiences that public libraries established in park could not serve the community of expectations.

The main problems public libraries face are the car parking, sufficient space, and the economical. The city centred library often lack these three factors. The results has made the mind of modern librarians to establish the public library, though in the heart of the city but at some distance of shopping or civic centres. Such site will be economical and spacious.

The building should be well set on the site. A site with forecourt and lawn provisions reduces external noise. It is also advantageous to provide the facilities for cycle stand, and car sheds. It also presents a good view to passers by. Such forecourt avoids congestion and provides free access to the readers.

Determination of site: A site may be determined by both the ways —

1. Inside outward
2. Outside inward

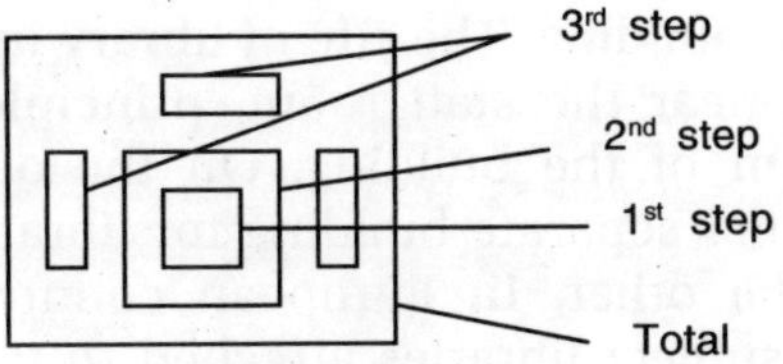

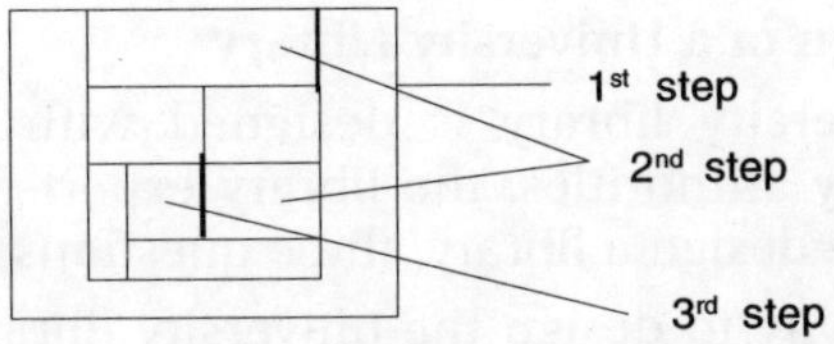

The awkward site may put difficulty in planning the interior accommodation. It is not always to find a suitable site. Ideal sites are available especially in outer area of the city. In the city area or centre of the city, ideal sites are rarely available. Awkward site create problem of adjustment of library departments in accordance to library functioning. Such sites determine the type of plan. The plan is drawn according to the sites.

Type of plan → suitable site
Suitable site → type of plan

However, sites are of many kinds:

1. Crowded sites;
2. Congested sites; (which are not crowded)
3. Noisy sites; (which are not crowded)
4. Sloping site;
5. Triangular site;
6. Plain site;
7. Ideal site.

3.4.3.2 *Site for Educational Institutions*

Normally educational institutions have their libraries has naturally been considered as integral part of the school building.

It is housed in one of the classrooms or the room separately constructed for the purpose. School buildings are found normally in single storeyed building and library find its place in the same building. The site of library in schools is selected in a room near the staff room, principle's room or in the corner room of the building. On the other hand, modern schools prefer separate building for libraries though a single room or the other. In European countries, there are unit branch or subject libraries attached to the subject teachers, boarding house or the subject departments.

3.5 Design of a University Library

University library is designed with the choice of the university authorities, the library experts and the architects. Prefer we design a library, three questions attract our mind —

1. Why to design the university library?
2. What are the famous and popular designs of university libraries?
3. How to start with a preliminary design?

These questions can be sorted out by taking the following three points into consideration:

1. **Broad objectives**: When the word 'why' strikes our mind, another question enters what are you really constructing this building for? The answer will be the thoughts about the general architectural characteristics of the building. Style may be same as it is based on objectives of the institution for which the building is to be constructed.
2. **Facilities required:** Design should include the facilities needed for readers, staff and material. Building is not a matter of today. It lasts long. All provisions for present and future facilities are taken into account. A detailed requirement should be prepared and put before the architecture for planning a design.
3. **Cost of building:** Finance is the final consideration. Big design cannot be planned for low financing. Cut your coat according to your cloth should be the principle of building planners.

There are two types of designs to be prepared:

1. **Modular Design**

Modular design is more appropriate to university library building. There are standard module followed by planners. 'Metcalf Module' is one of the important design followed in U.S.A. Mr. Metcalf was instrumental in the development of planning increments. If the module is square and the ceiling relates to the building module in both directions, the lighting and air-conditioning ceiling systems are also modular. It provides flexibility in all directions. The Metcalf system also includes various Modular combinations of reading tables, individual desk and carrels. With this system it is possible to interchange book stacks with reading facilities as need arises.

Library should be designed with a degree of transparency. The building design should be objective to expansion and adaptable to varying uses as the nature of library service changes. The scheme should be developed to be sufficiently flexible to allow for the possibility of using any area of the building interchangeably for book storage, readers, carrels, or staff work space. Prof. Karla has explained three characteristics of modular design:

1. Maximum utilization of floor space;
2. Economical ceiling weight; and
3. Low construction cost.

We can strongly advocate for modular as the modern way to build better and faster, and for less money. There are six basic reasons for the evidence:

1. Easier estimation as its drawing is faster, easier and more accurate;
2. Easier for workmen, as actual building on the job site is greatly facilitated;
3. Economy is supervision as the number of supervisors can be reduced;
4. Economy, as reduces building cost by reducing

wastage of material, costs of supervision, and engineering.

5. Fine furnishing, as workmanship improves and corrective work is held to a minimum.
6. Standardize the job as it is fruitful to production method and cost analysis the process to an assembly-line procedure.

2. **Architectural or Fixed Design**

There are libraries which have adopted fixed or permanent design for a particular purpose: service, staff or technical work. This system is rigid as the space or accommodation provided for a particular purpose cannot be used for other work and also unchangeable at the time of changes in library methods or techniques under this design. Each area has clear demarcation and fixed partition for each interior area of library.

In India, university library buildings built before 19th century were designed on architectural design. Since 20th century some library buildings have been constructed on modular design. University library buildings of Panjab University, J.N.U., New Delhi, Bangalore University, Agra University, Ravi Shankar University, Raipur and few others are better examples of modular design. In European countries, most of the library buildings have been constructed on modular design. The best library buildings counted as model buildings belongs to universities.

In M.P. there are library buildings constructed during the last two decades, designed not only on modular design but also on architectural design. Saugar and Jabalpur University library buildings are constructed on architectural design whereas the building of Ravi Shankar University library has been constructed on modular design.

3.5.1 *Various Shapes of Library Buildings*

The shape of a library building should be decided by the following shapes:

1. Shape of site
2. Finance

3. Facilities to be provided
4. Open shelf or closed shelf
5. Type of library
6. Nature of library

The shape is effected from —

1. Aesthetic reasons;
2. Idealistic reasons.

Library building differ from library to library. Some libraries are built in various unusual shapes. We can group library buildings in following types:

1. **Rectangular shape**: This shape is usually followed for open access plans of one-room open for small libraries. It is always in equal proportion of 1 × 1 for small libraries. But the proportion for large libraries has been 2 × 1.

   Rectangular shape is generally followed in U.S.A. as it is proposed to be economical.

2. **Square shape:** It is not popular and adopted by few of the libraries. The main reasons of its unpopularity or uncommonness is its unsuitability and unliking from the service point of view.

   On the other hand it is economical as it has less outside walling in proportion to its volume.

3. **Triangular or 'V' shape:** There are library buildings which are built in triangular shape or a plot of land involving 3 angles or corners, *i.e.*

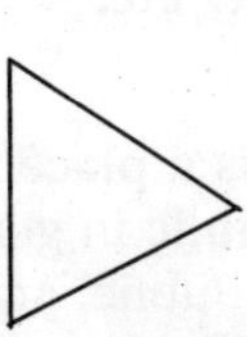

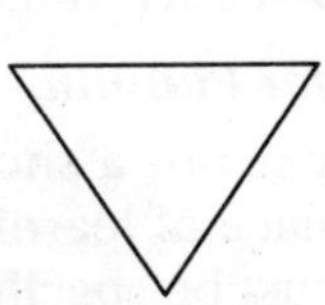

   This shape is more suitable for public libraries because of its outer surface an easy public approach. But this shape is not economical as it has more outside walling in proportion to its volume. It is also called as 'V' shape.

4. **Circular shape:** Circular shape is not a common practice. It is generally applied by public libraries and rarely as it has been proved to be inconvenient to the library function. There are buildings which have circular reading rooms like British Museum. It causes so many difficulties in planning to other departments.

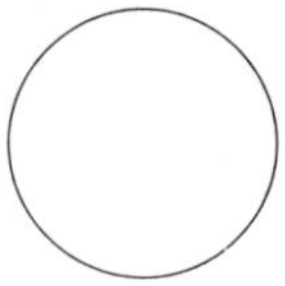

It is more architectural shape but less flexible and economical. For example: Library Congress, Boston Public Library, British Museum reading room and B.H.U. reading room.

5. **Ring shape**: This shape is also called central courtyard shape. It is convenient for open reading room facilities, inner parking facilities, inner garden facilities and indoor games facilities. But Ring shape is not appreciated because it keeps the library departments disconnected and effect reversely the cooperation and coordination among the departments. Readers has to run to the departments and thus time consuming and disturbing. Examples: Cambridge University, John Hopkins University etc.

6. **T shape:** It is a practical shape which may incorporate any extension in the building at every side. In other words, future additions can be made conveniently. It is a common shape followed by most of the libraries. Examples: Birmingham University, Sri Venkateswara University, Aligarh University etc.

3.5.2 *Interior Planning*

Library is not a show-piece. It is a place of service to the staff and place of learning to the public in general or specific. A library must be specific in nature (Public, Academic, Special), usable by all (general public, specific community or special class of public). Interior planning is an important as the external planning. External planning is a body of a man, while internal planning is a physical system of nerves and other parts of the body.

Interior planning is based on following factors:

1. Population of the area to be covered by the library and the rate of increase.
2. Transitive increase in the life span.
3. Rate of growth of knowledge, or increase in book production.
4. Rate of growth in readers.
5. Educational pattern (in case of academic libraries).
6. Objectives of the institute.
7. Development rate of mass media of communication.
8. Social and cultural activities.
9. Book capacity.
10. Type of service.
11. Type of reading material.
12. Library facilities.
13. Number of staff and their nature of work.

Library building is not an exact science for it has to be designed scientifically through:

1. Imagination
2. Experience
3. Conviction

based on the accepted principles and volumes.

3.5.3 *Policy Matter*

Interior planning of a library building is not possible by scattered ideas of library experts. When the library building programme is taken at hand, some policies are laid down. These policies are followed at every step of interior planning. The policies for the purpose are determined on the main objects of a institution and the nature of the library. The policies are framed keeping in mind the following major points:

1. Aims and objects of the institution.
2. Nature of work to be done.
3. Nature of service to be rendered.
4. Nature of personnel to be engaged.

Every institution is established with some aims and objects. It may be expansion of knowledge, eradication of illiteracy, consciousness in public (in case of public library), subject knowledge covering the syllabus, and educational programmes (in case of academic libraries), and micro-knowledge (in case of special or research libraries). In addition to general objectives, there are specific objectives limited to specific aspect of a subject, specific community, specific knowledge seekers, specific degree holders or level of educational standard, specific reading material etc.

Library work is done in many ways, by many methods and in different manner. It differs from library to library. But the nature of work is always the same. There is classification work, cataloguing work, binding work, reproduction work, circulation work etc. Each and every library performs all or any of these works to its clientele. Special libraries have different nature of work than other libraries of general nature. There are reference libraries, documentation centres.

Library service is another important point which effect the objectives of a library. There are libraries rendering special type of services, general type of library such as photographic services, mobile services, reference services, in-library loan services, and lending services etc.

Library staff also effect the policy while programming for library building. Library staff may be professional, semi-professional and non-professional. They may be classifier, cataloguer, documentalists, acquisitioners, supervisors, technicians, photographers, administrators, clerically menials etc. They are accommodated in a library building according to their nature of work, service, and over all their number. They have separate place of work with their instruments.

3.6 Organizational Pattern

Library functions on sound footing based on proper and systematic organizational pattern. Organizational pattern of interior planning of a library building depends on many points to be considered.

3.6.1 *Formal and Informal*

Formal organization is represented by the lines of the

establishment authority, such as various supervisors, bosses and staff members.

Formal organization is typified by the various contents, social and business that do not follow the established formal structure. The library is a growing organism and thus it expands, and its administration will be conducted by specially entrusted persons so as to achieve a high degree of efficiency. It resulted to expansion of library building. Mostly organizational pattern of a library is divided in two ways:

1. Line and staff organization
2. Functional organization

It is very essential to engage library staff with specialization or ability in a job of a particular pursuit. A well organized library has several jobs such as acquisition, maintenance, classification, cataloguing, reference, circulation, and administration. One officer — one responsibility is the principle. Under this system Departmental line organization functions with the help of the staff, and so-called specialists or experts who are in-charge of specific functions that are not similar to each other. Line and staff performs different kinds of functions:

1.	Staff units (Advisory Staff)	-	Committee Room
2.	Line units (working staff) Divisions, Branches, sections and individuals	-	Separate space or accommodation for performing their work.

Functional organization consists in dividing the work of management such that each man from the assistant superintendent to his junior colleagues would perform their allocated functions. The work of one man is confined to single leading function. It implies principles of specialization, facilities of machines of capacities. In such organizational pattern interior planning of a library building is made as to make separate space arrangement to each department or function as each function is of special nature.

3.6.2 *Centralization and Decentralization*

These terms are used as the process of transfer of administrative authority from a lower to higher level. Both processes are nearly related to the building planning. Centralization has the following aspects:

Collection of reading material: Reading material may be collected in a central library and in one stack room and may be transferred to departmental libraries or various sections of the central library. In case of departmental library system, the process of cataloguing, classification, reference work and the acquisition work may be centralized or decentralized. If it is centralized process necessary provision for more accommodation such section is made. The centralized process section will naturally need more space for increased collection, staff and the equipments. On the other hand, if it is centralized process the planning of section accommodation is made according to the necessity.

University libraries are generally faced this problem. Universities have departmental libraries and their separate collection of their need. It is also a general tendency in universities that the central library centralize all the material and give less importance and the facilities to the departmental libraries. This prevent the expansion of these libraries. But by the lapse of line and heavy rush of work in central libraries, the centralization tendency is leaving place to decentralization. The other reason of discarding the centralized process is the continuous and day and night research programmes in departments. The big distance between the central and departmental libraries has also been the reason behind the flourishing of departmental libraries. Thus decentralization has given a chance of expansion to departmental libraries and a check on speedy expansion of central library. Central library if adopts decentralized system, needs less collection, equipment and the staff, that is of its own requirements.

University Grant Commission has set up library committees, library review committees, Library Advisory Committees and sub-committees like building committee etc. which review the developments and discuss the problems including library buildings. The main committees in this regards were referred with the name of Library Committee, 1957 (Chairman — Dr. Ranganathan), College and University Library Committee, 1964 (Chairman — Dr. Ranganathan), Indian Standard Institute also constituted a 'library building committee' under the Chairmanship of Dr. Ranganathan to fix some standards for library building. IFLA set up a sub-section of university libraries in 1964 to discuss the problem of decentralization. The main problem, discussed by these committees, was the design of library building including university library in context of departmental faculty libraries. It was reviewed that there has been a lack of cooperation between the central library and departmental libraries.

It is further experienced that central library has unit library in the same building and follow policy of centralization. Such library buildings are congested and need timely expansion. In case of decentralization, faculty libraries are setup in separate departmental buildings and managed by heads of departments.

However, the interior planning should be based on the policy framed on the basis of centralization or decentralization and reviewed after a period of 10 years.

3.6.3 *Departmentalization*

Departmentalization is directly related to the interior planning: (1) what are the departments to be organized; (2) what are their communication channels; and (3) how far they are coordinate each other. In total what are the functions and the character of the departments?

There are departments dealing with general readers and they are within the first reach of the readers, *i.e.* catalogue cabinet and display section, circulation section. We can call them noisy area. Such departments are accommodated near the entrance. Their functions in this regard are enumerated as under:

1. **Entrance area:** It is near the main gate:

1. Clock rooms,	Example:
2. Display rooms,	Page 173 of Library
3. Exhibition rooms,	Buildings of Britain
4. Catalogue rooms,	and Europe
5. Toilets	(for departmentalization)

Readers enter the library and approach to the above departments/sections on way to proceed to public service area. In large libraries these departments are accommodated with adequate capacities, while in small libraries there are multi-purpose rooms/halls for displays, catalogues and exhibitions jointly.

2. **Public service departments**: It is also an area to deal with the majority of the readers. It is the second round area in interior planning. It includes the following departments: counter or loan service, reference desk, enrolment counter, etc. and lecture or seminar hall. In many libraries, information desk and the enrolment work is done on the circulation counter. In big libraries, counter is better separated from the entrance hall.
3. **Study departments**: Study area includes reading rooms, reference department, reserve department, administrative departments, carrels, and reading terraces. These departments are grouped in area of silence. Traffic is avoided in this area. University libraries provide big reading rooms and in some cases, reference books are also provided in the wall area of reading rooms.

   Modern developments are subject departments. Separate departments for subjects are organized with reading facilities. This system is followed in big libraries. Birmingham University has organized subject departments.

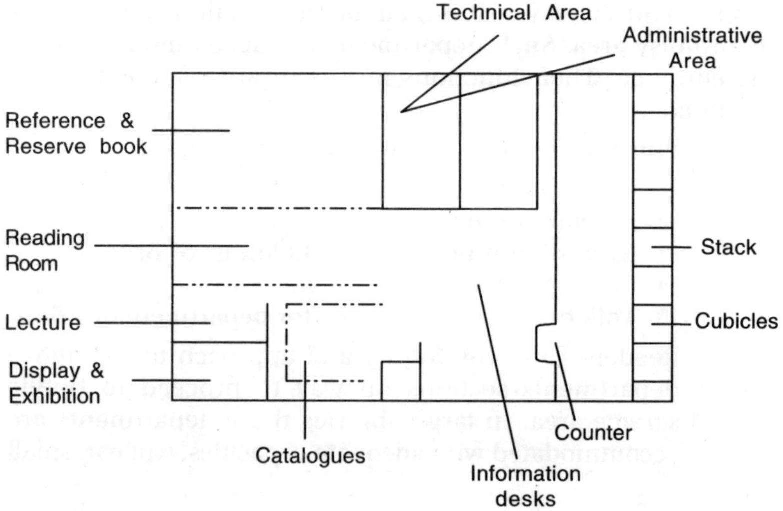

Ground Floor

University library provides separate accommodation to special collection like periodicals. Modern researches much more depend on non-book material, particularly periodicals. The best provision is to separate department to the periodicals where —

(1) Current periodicals are displayed,

(2) Reading facilities are provided,

(3) Prompt acquisition is done,

(4) Qualified staff is available for consultation.

3.6.4 *Stack Area*

The last round of a library building is stack area which is silent in nature, concentrate in atmosphere, secure in safety and weather proof. It is generally beyond the reach of general public. Teachers, library staff and research scholars are allowed to enter and consult. If it is open shelf, the needy or sincere readers approach the stack area.

"Stack area should be compact and orderly in order to save space and staff time. Scattered wings should be avoided, as they cheats long communications and space-wasting." Best stack room involves compactness and the best communications.

3.6.5 *Staff Area*

Staff room is separately accommodated in library building. In ancient period there was separate room for staff. Librarian was no so much recognized and all staff members used the same room. The actual need of a separate room for library staff was recognized in nineteenth century. There were few public and academic libraries, large library where separate provision for staff room was provisioned in library building. Library of Congress, National Library Calcutta, Calcutta, Delhi and Madras Universities had separate staff or administrative room and also for librarian.

There are two types of library work:

1. **Work behind the screen**: Acquisition, technical, binding and maintaining etc.
2. **Work outside the screen**: All services to the readers

including reference work, circulation work, photographic work, reading room, etc.

The first work, behind the screen is performed by the library staff. The staff engaged in this work can be enumerated:

1. Staff of acquisition section including in-charge of the section;
2. Staff technical section including in-charge of the section;
3. Staff of administration section including in-charge, Librarian or Dy. Librarian.
4. Staff of maintenance section including binding staff, building maintenance staff and transcribing staff.
5. Library Officers: Librarian, Dy. Librarian, and Asstt. Librarian.

Thompson has described the staff accommodation through work processing:

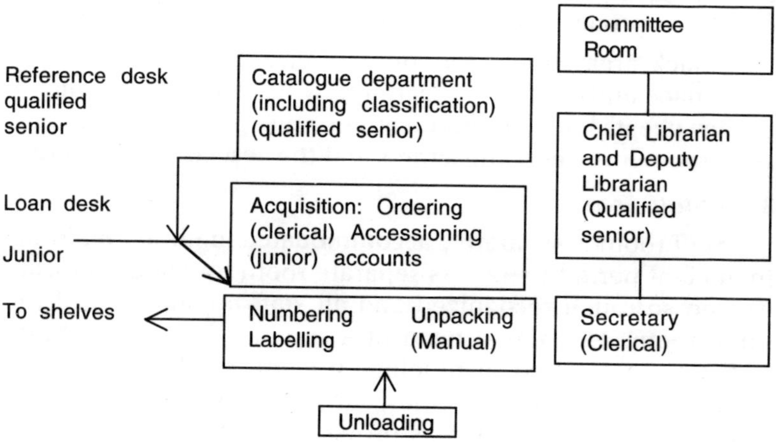

Pre-planning diagram of the book processes, showing the grades of staff and staff links with public service points and administration

Apart from the above classification of staff, the staff have varied of work and their job require accommodation of different space. There are also difference in nature of work. One work need proper silence and concentration while other work may be done jointly or on joint tables.

Staff need more space:

(i) Cataloguer and classifier
(ii) Accessioning staff
(iii) Photographer
(iv) Binder
(v) Staff for public service

Staff need less space:

(i) Ordering staff
(ii) Administrative staff
(iii) Typist

While planning the accommodation provision in library building, the following reasons may be considered:

1. **Work point area**: Staff engaged in work-technical official or semi-official need accommodation for his efficient working. Technical staff needs separate accommodation.
2. Some university separate exit for staff members. European libraries have such provision on the back side of library building. Sometimes goods entrance is also kept separate. From the experiences, it has been noticed that even after the provision of separate entrance, staff members use the public entrance. More entrances should be discouraged. If staff entrance is separately required it should be planned between the administrative and technical departments.
3. Reproduction work require separate accommodation *i.e.* typing of catalogue cards, office typing, cyclostyle work. This work is noisy and needs an accommodation at such a separate place which could be communicated from the concerned department. Cyclostyle work should be done in a separate room near the administrative section or the interior of the building.
4. **Maintenance staff**: Caretaker, workshop, garage, Chowkidar, Gardener and their offices need separate rooms for their smooth-working. This accommodation is generally allotted near the entrance or the stairs.

5. **Service point area**: Staff at service points may need some seclusion, especially the head of a large loans or reference department, who will need a special office near to but secluded from readers.
6. Separate provision of space should be made for typing work as it caused noise.
7. There should be a separate accommodation for staff club, recreation-room or receptionists as employees and persons exchange their view freely on this place. Similarly caretaker, stand to librarian should be given proper but separate accommodation to perform their duties efficiently and confidentially.

SEATING SPACE

Seating space is decided on the basis of several factors taken into consideration while training a policy of library building, he need seating space for many purposes. Mainly three factors effect seating space:

1. Collection; and
2. Reading points.

Library house various types of collection of reading material: Books, periodicals, non-book material including microfilms, maps, manuscripts and audio-visual aids. They have different varieties and attract different types of reading committee, which requires separate space for their housing in order to put them on maximum use. But collection is not the only governing factor to determine the number of seats in the reading area of library. The other factor is reading points. Nature of collection determine the reading points. It will not be proper to put books with manuscripts at one place, because it may cause rough handling of manuscripts which are rare and sophisticated. They require special preservation in waterproof, weather proof place and need special care and security. On the other hand periodicals are put separately with books as it requires continuous operation and dealing with publishers. Books are of many types: Rare books, Textbooks, reference books and require separate treatment. "The reserve book reading area and the textbook reading area which may not be near the public catalogue should have sufficient seating space in addition to subject reading areas." Reading space is also determined by individual's demand *i.e.* Research cubicles etc.

REFERENCES

Air Conditioning for Books. *Lib. Jrl.* 62, 1937.

ALA Committee on Library Equipment and Appliances. *ALA Bull.* 28, 1934.

Burchard, J.E. *Planning the University Library Building.* Princeton Univ. Press, 1949.

Hanley, E.R. "College and University Lib. Building". *Lib. Jrl.* 70, 1945.

Krachenbuehl, John O. "Lighting the Library". *Coll. & Res. Lib.* 2, 1941.

Lawami, S.M. "Storage and Preservation of Microfilm". *Libri.* XVIII. 1968.

Mc Grum, D.Q. *Public Library Building.* Los Angels, M.O., 1935.

Parker, W.W. "Few Barriers in Buildings". *Lib. Jrl.* 73, 1948.

Scribner, B.W. "The Preservation of Records in Libraries". *Lib. Qrly.* 4, 1934.

Sharma, C.K. *Modern Library System.* Agra, Y.K. Pub., 1990.

Sharma, C.K. *University Library: Management & Organisation.* Delhi, Metropolitan, 1977.

Srivastava, S.N. *University Libraries in India.* Delhi, Sterling, 1980.

Walter, F.K. *University Library Building.* New York, Scribner, 1941.

Wilfred, J.P. *The Preservation of Books in Tropical and Subtropical Countries.* Oxford Univ. Press, 1967.

4

Library Equipments and Furniture

Library equipments are as important as good library building. They are personality traits for a library building. No library can achieve its goal unless it is well equipped. A functional library must equipped with the following equipments:

1. Card Catalogue Cabinets
2. Display Board
3. Glass Board
4. Wall Penal
5. Inter-connected Board
6. Periodical Display Rack/Stand
7. Revolving General Book Stand
8. Newspaper Rack
9. Study Tables
10. Library Counters
11. Revolving Reference stand
12. Lecture Stand
13. Exhibition Stand
14. Dictionary Stand
15. Atlas Stand
16. Charging Tray
17. Charging Tray Cabinet
18. Book Display Rack
19. Card Sorting Tray

20. Book Trolley/Truck
21. Island Book Rack
22. Cardex Cabinet
23. Library Almirahs with Glass Doors
24. Book Stacks (Wooden)
25. Book Stacks (Steel)
26. Reading Tables
27. Publication Stand

4.1 Card Catalogue Cabinets

Catalogue cards are arranged and displayed in these cabinets. They vary in size and shape. Cabinets are prepared according to the size of catalogue cards. Generally catalogue cards are used in two sizes 5″ × 3″ or 8″ × 4″. The standard size is 12.5 cm × 7.5 cm.

Card catalogue cabinets are made of teak wood, preferably seasoned C.P. Teak wood and ISI marked. These are also made of Blackboard and plywood. Cabinets are skilfully prepared in a accurate size of catalogue cards. These are duly fitted with highly nickeled shape rod and Ring-pull level holders on the forefront of each drawer. It has inter-locking construction. It may be simple of wood or laminated with sunmica on two sides and top.

Catalogue cards are also made of steel.

Dimensions — Inside dimensions of drawers are $5^1/_3$″ wide by $3^5/_8$″ high and 13¾″ deep. The inside 13″ filling space will accommodate approx. 1200 medium weight catalogue cards of size 5 × 3 inches.

Different sizes of catalogue cards

(a) Height 7¾ width 14¾ depth 16″ — 2 drawers
(b) Height 12¾ width 14¾ depth 16″ — 4 drawers
(c) Height 43¼ width 21¾ depth 16″ — 9 drawers
(d) Height 47¼ width 21¾ depth 16″ — 12 drawers
(e) Height 41¼ width $36^1/_8$ depth 16″ — 20 drawers
(f) Height 47½ width 42¼ depth 16″ — 24 drawers

(g) Height 47½" width 111½" depth 16"— 32 drawers (2 units)

(h) Height 45½" width 37¾" depth 16" — 30 drawers (in upper lower two units combined)

Card Catalogue Cabinet and Information File

This is convenient and space saving unit of card catalogue cabinet. It combines a 15 drawers cabinet and two legal file drawers with low leg base for file unit. This cabinet has a capacity of filing approx. 18000 medium weight catalogue cards of size 5" × 3".

4.2 Display Board/Stand

It is used to display the jackets or any other papers, drawings. It has mitered corner and locked in to position so that they are not separated. Two plated hangers can be attached to the top. These may be fitted with soft cork board panels.

These display boards may be of many dimensions —

(a) Wide 24" high 18"

(b) Wide 48" high 36"

(c) Wide 72" high 48"

These boards are also perforated. It may be double sided with stands. Heights and angles adjustable. Exhibits can be displayed with various accessories.

4.3 Glass Board

It varies in sizes 5 mm thick ground glass duly painted on the back in green black colour. It is made of teak wood frame. Ordinary chalk is used for writing.

4.4 Wall Panel

It is prepared in two systems — Clip system which is perforated and the other pin system, which is soft covered with Jute/Tapestry.

Size: 3' × 4' single sided with aluminium beading.

4.5 Inter-connected Board

It is in many sizes. It is made of perforated or soft board. It is double sided with stands. Heights and angle adjustable. Exhibits can be pinned on the board.

Popular size — 3′ × 4′ × 4′ or 4′ × 4′ × 6′

Stand legs — Size 4½′ high × 1′ DD Chromium plated or painted.

Types — Thin type, thick type, Z type

Plastic letters — Size 1½″ and ¾″

4.6 Periodical Display Rack/Stand

Current periodicals are displayed in a library. It is a media of communication to aware the readers with current available issues of periodicals. Periodical of current day/week/fortnight/monthly/quarterly/half-yearly/annual are displayed on the upper/open side of periodical display rack and the back issues of the same year or volumes are kept inside the drawer of display rack. Specifications — Periodicals displayment is in a unit type, using a connected method of construction. It is made of teak wood/board with intermediate upright pigeon holes and exposed surfaces of base and canopy. Each pigeon hole consists of a sloped display shelf, hinged to lift up and expose a flat storage space for the periodical, storage space is concealed, while shelf is in the natural position. All drawers are 16″ deep. Sizes of drawers may vary according to the size of periodical.

Sizes of pigeon holes in sloping Periodicals display rack

High	10″	Wide	12″
High	11″	Wide	12″
High	13″	Wide	12″
High	15″	Wide	12″

Dimensions —

6 compartment High 51″ Wide 27″ Depth 14″
10 compartment High 75″ Wide 27″ Depth 14″
18 compartment High 51″ Wide 78″ Depth 14″
24 compartment High 63″ Wide 78″ Depth 14″
30 compartment High 75″ Wide 78″ Depth 14″

4.7 Revolving General Book Stand

It is a book stand to be kept with the Section In-charge or librarian. All such books which are demanded or needed for ready consultation, are kept in this stand like office handbooks, popular dictionary, yearbooks and other official publications.

It may have 20 pockets in all. 10 pockets 12" long and 10 pockets 18" long for display of 50 books.

4.8 Newspaper Rack

It is used to display newspapers. The newspaper sticks to hold as many newspapers are supplied with this table type rack. It takes minimum floor space. It has tapered legs.

Size — 1¾" square and 38" long with nickled screw bolts.

4.9 Study Tables

Study tables are found in three types — wooden study table, steel study table and fiber study table. Wooden furniture (table) is always prefered as it proves more convenient in maintenance and can be repaired easily. There is less noise if wooden furniture is preferred. Table features a hardwood blinder and carrel has a handy bookself. Each unit has a generous 32" width and 24" depth.

Specifications

(a) Single carrel : Height 48" × 32" × 32"

(b) Double carrel : Height 48" × 32" × 64"

Face to face configuration and side by side configuration.

(c) Four unit carrel: 48" H × 64" × 64" D

4.10 Library Counters

Library counters are used for issue and return of the books. These are also called charging desk. There may be one big library counter for enquiry and charging work. But separate counter is more convenient for smooth working. Library counter usually keynotes the entire mood and motif of the room. A particular shape and atmosphere is installed in keeping with the particular audience served. It is fitted with charging tray cabinets, open shelves, cupboards and regular use drawers and showcases.

4.11 Revolving Reference Stand

It is used by reference librarian and kept near his desk.

Specifications — 5 laminated planks making 4 compartments. There will be space between them adjustable for spire display or approx. 180 books. It is heavy cast iron based and made of Aluminium angles and pipes.

Size (Planks): 1½′ × 1½′ × ¾″.

4.12 Lecture Stand

Big public and university libraries have separate seminar or meeting hall where meetings, lectures, seminars and conferences are generally organized. Moreover, book exhibitions are also organized in this hall. It needs a lecture stand. Lecture stand is made of wood or steel. Wooden lecture stand is preferred. Its height is adjustable as per demand. Mostly it is based on a steel pipe or round wooden pillar.

Lecture stand is kept in lecture hall to deliver lectures. It has a shelf and foot rest with panel of teakwood or sunmica on the front. It has lockable wheels at the base with an adjustable lighting (Bull type).

Rectangular Shape — duly provided with a shelf and a foot rest with indirect lighting arrangement (without wheel).

4.13 Exhibition Stand

It is a four-wheeled stand. It is double sided with 8 pockets, 4 on each side of 30″ × 5″ with 2 standing shelves for display of books.

Size — 30″ × 5″

Size — 14″ × 3″

It is also made in minimize. Double sided with 8 pockets, 4 on each side of 14″ × 3″ with 2 standing shelves for display of books.

4.14 Dictionary Stand

There are standard International dictionaries like Oxford large dictionary, Webster's International dictionaries, which are heavy and bulky and also large in size. It is troublesome to lift these dictionaries by everyone. Such dictionaries are also not generally taken by every reader. However, such dictionaries are kept on dictionary-stand once a day and readers consult it at their convenience.

Specification — A sloped top at comfortable reading angle and two shelves hold large dictionaries and reference volumes. It is generally made of Teak wood. The stand is adjustable.

4.15 Atlas Stand

Atlas are big in size even sometimes of 2′ × 3′ and need separate display in big libraries. Atlas case is designed with safety features to secure large and valuable volumes. Atlas stands are prepared in various sizes according to the size of atlas, where it can securely displayed open volumes on spacious booking top designed with a safety 2″ lip containers.

Size: Height 39½″ at the front
Back 432″
Wide 292″
Deep 262″

having clear 3 inches space in the shelves. It has a sloping top.

4.16 Charging Tray

It is important furniture unit of a library charging/issue counter or desk. All borrower cards or books cards are kept and arranged in charging trays. These are made of wood and in a suitable size similar to book card or borrower card. It has adjustable drawers/blocks and felo base. These are in handy sizes.

Specifications — Each compartment of the tray is of different size and accommodates 500 to 2000 cards with necessary guides and tickets. Depth of each tray is 18″

Size: 2 compartments for 5″ × 3″ cards.
4 compartments for 5″ × 3″ cards.
6 compartments for 5″ × 3″ cards.

4.17 Charging Tray Cabinet

In big libraries charging tray cabinet is fitted instead of handy charging trays. It proves more efficient in charging and discharging operations. Charging tray cabinet is kept attached with charging desk. It may be on revolving wheels and adjusted at any corner of the charging counter. In this cabinet charging trays are turned a shape of drawers and in 3-4 drawers which are inserted in a cabinet. In this way we can put out the required tray on arranging the cards. The cabinet has a automatic locking device as a whole or separate drawers. All trays and the cabinet is laminated with sunmica on two sides and top. Drawers have engraved wooden handles-cum-level holders. These are fitted with chair height stand so that person sitting on the counter can operate it.

Size: 4 drawers and each drawer with 6 compartments for 5″ × 3″ cards.

4 drawers and each drawer with 6 compartments for 2″ × 3″ cards.

4 drawers and each drawer having 8 compartments for 5″ × 3″ cards.

4 drawers and each drawer having 8 compartments for 2″ × 3″ cards.

4.18 Book Display Rack

Library display books from time to time on their purchase to know the readers about their new arrivals. Special interest books on special days or occasions are also displayed.

Specifications — Book display rack is made of double sided cork bulletin board of 36″ wide 20″ deep and 35″ high without bulletin. It may be wooden or steel made. Inside area 9″ high and 36″ wide. Stopping book troughs are 3¾″ deep.

4.19 Card Sorting Tray

Sometimes cards are sort out where they are in large number. For convenience first cards are sort out according to author, title and subject and sometimes according to class numbers. Card sorting trays help sort out the catalogue cards or temporary cards. These trays have three or four equal compartments suitable for use with 5″ × 3″ catalogue cards.

4.20 Book Trolley/Truck

Library building has many sections which deals with transaction of book service to readers, staff for lending and technical process. It is also demanded the transfer of books from one section to other section *i.e.* circulation section to stack room, acquisition section to technical section and technical section to circulation section. All this book carrying work is done with the help of book trolley and book truck. Stack room is made multistoried where book transaction is made throughout the day. Such stacks are connected with book lift or sloping stairs, which help in carrying books kept in book trolleys or book trucks.

These trucks are easy to handle, practical, sturdy and holds 120 to 135 books for easy selection on four shelves.

Specifications — Two 6" ball-bearing casters give manoeuvrability; two 6" ball-bearing stationary wheels bridge elevator gaps which give free wheeling. Swivel casters may be mounted either in front or at rear.

Size: Wide 20", long 32" height 48½".

It has big storage space at bottom takes care of extra books taken or picked up. Sliding self-locking supports on six upper shelves keeps book upright at all time. Front edges of magazine rack are equipped with rubber bumpers. The card tray and storage space between the top shelves which can also be used for the ever popular "pocket-books".

Size of Book trolley —

Long 49½" Wide 16¼" High 42".

(From tilted shelves and a bottom flat shelf will good accommodation).

4.21 Island Book Rack

Such book racks are used to keep reference books or other acceptable books at counter, circulation section or on Asstt. Librarian's desk/table.

Size: High 39" Wide 30" Deep $10^5/_8$".

4.22 Cardex Cabinet

There are libraries maintaining Index cards for recording the details of periodicals. Every periodical, while received in library is entered in index card. These cards are arranged in cardex cabinet.

Size: Index card size 8" × 5".
Cabinet 8 trays, 12 trays and 16 trays.

4.23 Library Almirahs with Glass Doors

Library almirahs are used to house books in a library. These almirahs have glass doors. It has 6 shelves. All the shelves and both the sides laminated with sunmica.

Dimensions — Height 84" Wide 43" Deep 12".

4.24 Book Stacks (Wooden)

Library has separate stack room/stack rooms in its multistoried stack area. These stack rooms are equipped with stacks. Stacks may double faced or single faced. These are made of wooden or steel.

Double faced — 6 shelves on each side.

Size: Height 7' Width 3' Deep 19'-½"

Both the sides laminated with sunmica.

Single faced — 5 shelves on each side.

Size: Height 6'-½" Width 3' Deep 19'-½"

All the shelves and sides laminated with sunmica.

4.25 Book Stacks (Steel)

It have 28 adjustable shelves on both the sides. Shelves made up of 20 gauge heavy CRC steel with in-built sliding book stopper of 16 gauge side penals. Centre column of 2 gauge steel foot shoes of 14 gauge steel.

4.26 Reading Tables

These are manufactured with teakwood frame or steel frame. Wooden almirahs are laminated with sunmica on top and foot rest at the base.

Size: Length 8' Width 2½' Height 30"
Length 8' Width 3' Height 30" (Popular Size)
Length 6' Width 3' Height 30"
Length 5' Width 3' Height 30"

Reading tables may be in oval shape.

4.27 Publication Stand

University libraries have their own publications of rules, bibliographies, handbook, catalogues and books. These are displayed on publication stand.

Specification — Publication stand consists of 6 laminated shelves in size 15″ × 18″ fitted on a stand with heavy base. 5.5′ high, height and angle of shelves are adjustable.